HOW TO STUDY LI
General Editors: John Peck a

HOW TO STUDY A JOSEPH CONRAD NOVEL

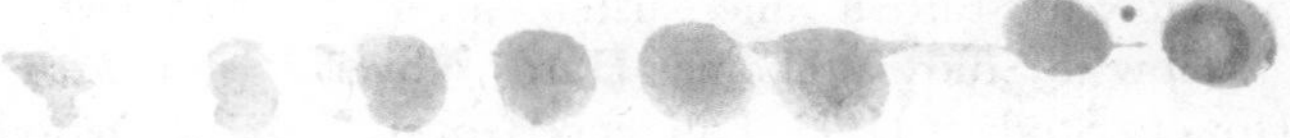

IN THE SAME SERIES

How to Study a Novel *John Peck*
Literary Terms and Criticism *John Peck and Martin Coyle*
How to Study a Shakespeare Play *John Peck and Martin Coyle*
How to Begin Studying Literature *Nicholas Marsh*
How to Study a Jane Austen Novel *Vivien Jones*
How to Study a Thomas Hardy Novel *John Peck*
How to Study a D. H. Lawrence Novel *Nigel Messenger*
How to Study a Charles Dickens Novel *Keith Selby*
How to Study a Renaissance Play *Chris Coles*
How to Study Modern Drama *Kenneth Pickering*
How to Study a Poet *John Peck*
How to Study Chaucer *Rob Pope*
How to Study Romantic Poetry *Paul O'Flinn*
How to Study Modern Poetry *Tony Curtis*

IN PREPARATION

How to Study a James Joyce Novel *Chris Coles*
How to Study an E. M. Forster Novel *Nigel Messenger*

HOW TO STUDY A JOSEPH CONRAD NOVEL

Brian Spittles

MACMILLAN

First published 1990

Published by
MACMILLAN EDUCATION LTD
Houndmills, Basingstoke, Hampshire RG21 2XS
and London
Companies and representatives
throughout the world

Typeset by J&L Composition Ltd, Filey, North Yorkshire
Printed in Hong Kong

British Library Cataloguing in Publication Data
Spittles, Brian
How to study a Joseph Conrad novel.—(How to study literature)
1. Fiction in English. Conrad, Joseph, 1857–1924—critical studies
I. Title II. Series
823′.912
ISBN 0–333–49162–9

For
Ernie and Hilda

Contents

General editors' preface

EVERYBODY who studies literature, either for an examination or simply for pleasure, experiences the same problem: how to understand and respond to the text. As every student of literature knows, it is perfectly possible to read a book over and over again and yet still feel baffled and at a loss as to what to say about it. One answer to this problem, of course, is to accept someone else's view of the text, but how much more rewarding it would be if you could work out your own critical response to any book you choose or are required to study.

The aim of this series is to help you develop your critical skills by offering practical advice about how to read, understand and analyse literature. Each volume provides you with a clear method of study so that you can see how to set about tackling texts on your own. While the authors of each volume approach the problem in a different way, every book in the series attempts to provide you with some broad ideas about the kind of texts you are likely to be studying and some broad ideas about how to think about literature; each volume then shows you how to apply these ideas in a way which should help you construct your own analysis and interpretation. Unlike most critical books, therefore, the books in this series do not simply convey someone else's thinking about a text, but encourage you and show you how to think about a text for yourself.

Each book is written with an awareness that you are likely to be preparing for an examination, and therefore practical advice is given not only on how to understand and analyse literature, but also on how to organise a written response. Our hope is that, although these books are intended to serve a practical purpose, they may also enrich your enjoyment of literature by making you a more confident reader, alert to the interest and pleasure to be derived from literary texts.

John Peck
Martin Coyle

Acknowledgements

I AM extremely grateful to my editors for their enormous help, and in particular to Martin Coyle for his enthusiasm, patience and absolutely invaluable practical assistance. I wish also to acknowledge the value of the encouragement of those students with whom I discussed this book. My thanks to Dr Ruth Whittaker, who sent me off on this journey with a blithe faith in my ability to arrive at the terminus. Ultimately, I wish to record my profound appreciation for the help of Margaret Wickett, who selflessly contributed the best ideas in this book, and was always ready to help me out of any intellectual slough into which I stumbled.

B.S.

1

Reading a Conrad novel

Introduction

YOU may be reading a Conrad novel because you are studying English at school, college or university; or simply for enjoyment, and perhaps escapism, as I found myself doing when working in a dull warehouse job immediately after leaving school. In any case, most readers are likely to face the same problem after the initial pleasure they gain from the story: how can we make sense of a novel? You may just want to think about its meaning, to discuss it – formally or informally – with other people, or you may have to write an essay on it. Reading is generally an enjoyable exercise; however, writing a critical response can sometimes be a chore. It seems to be a feature of most novels we study, or read seriously, that they resist our attempts to analyse them. Conrad's novels are no exception to this general rule. The plots are often extremely complex, the ways of telling the story complicated, the language sometimes dense, the characters and characterisation unusual, and the meanings elusive. If we come to Conrad after the great nineteenth-century novelists – Jane Austen, Charles Dickens, George Eliot, Thomas Hardy, for example – we may find our expectations of what a novel should be disturbed. Victorian novels are complex, but we usually gain a clear impression of a society and the characters in it, and the story always unfolds in a clear and comprehensible way. With Conrad, by contrast, it is difficult to know what we are meant to be looking for, or how we are supposed to see it. At this point some students – in which category I include anyone who wants a better understanding of literature, for whatever reason – may turn to critical books for assistance. Far from being helpful, these can be an added source of confusion. For example, some critics castigate Conrad for being a right-wing reactionary because he appears to present anarchists in a bad light, while others complain that he is biased in favour of left-wing views because he condemns the excesses of Victorian imperialism; some think that he has no sense of humour, while others say that he treats serious subjects such as religion, politics and morality with comic irreverence; and some commentators consider the novels superficial masculine adventure stories, while others find Conrad too abstractly philosophical. Such views can be more than confusing, for if you did not notice these possibilities in the novel you are reading you may feel rather demoralised. At this stage it is easy to opt for one critic's view, ignoring other interpretations and forgetting your own responses and enjoyment.

This is the point at which many students give up trying to understand the novel for themselves, because there appears to be too great a gap between their own responses and the criticism they have read. Most students, even so, realise that studying English, or reading literature more than superficially, will only be worthwhile if they are able to shape and express their own views of a text. The major aim of this book is to illustrate how you can move from your reading of a Conrad novel to organising and articulating your responses to it. A central point, which will be stressed repeatedly, is that the best way to construct a critical response to a text is by starting with a few clear, simple ideas about the novel as a whole and then using those as a base on which to build your thinking. To achieve this, however, it is first necessary to learn how to read a novel analytically, and to identify what the text is about.

Identifying what a novel is about

Your first impression of a novel is likely to be swamped by the story's details, so that you may have little sense of any larger pattern in the text. This is natural, but it is precisely the grasp of a greater pattern controlling the novel that you need to establish when you begin to think critically about a text. This book is concerned with ways of moving beyond the initial confusion to a more organised response.

There are two points that may be immediately helpful. The first is that novelists in general tend to return to the same, or very similar, ideas and issues throughout their works. A strong grasp of the sense of a story line, and the ability to reduce its complexity to a few basic points, is a fundamental first step in recognising the recurrent ideas and issues. Secondly, remember that virtually all literature is concerned with some form of **conflict or opposition**.

You may have noticed in studying poetry, or a Shakespeare play, for example, that the work is commonly structured around basic oppositions in order to express the ideas and meaning of the text. The oppositions or conflicts can be of any kind: storms and sunshine, summer and winter, day and night, mankind and nature, good and evil, old and new, innocence and experience, love and hate, and so on. These are all features of the world in which we live, and some observers believe that as we grow up we make sense of our experiences and impressions of life through such binary opposites. In any novel we are likely to find that the novelist organises patterns of events, characters, situations, settings in terms of oppositions – dramatising and illustrating the conflicts and ideas at the centre of the novel.

The most generalised pattern we might expect in a novel is a form of conflict between society and one or more individuals within that society. What we call society may be a large amorphous mass of people, as in a concept such as 'British society', or a very small and closely defined group thrown together by a common interest or purpose, such as the crew of a ship who have to live together at close quarters for months on end. The conflict may be over conventions of behaviour, political attitudes, differences of wealth or other factors. In Conrad's novels the tension often appears as a **conflict between an individual's ideals and the harsher aspects of reality**: the oppressive facets of society, the destructive elements of Nature and the darker psychological forces of human nature all bear down on an idealistic, often fairly young or inexperienced, character. We shall look at this tension in Conrad's works in greater detail later. At present it is important to appreciate that in general some kind of conflict resides at the centre of all novels. If we can understand the nature of this conflict it will assist us in seeing how all the details of the novel fit together to produce an overall pattern. Then we can begin to work on our own coherent critical response to the novel as a whole.

This will be – to summarise very briefly – based on a strong, clear sense of the story being told, and the ability to express it concisely; and the recognition of the fundamental conflict, or tension between opposite forces, that forms the core of the novel. This approach will provide my framework for this book, but it is also a useful process for the critical analysis of almost any novel. It is a process that starts from simple ideas of what a novel is about, moves to an analysis of the details on the page, and then allows us to consider again the greater pattern, issues and ideas of the text as a whole. The strength of this approach is that it requires you to work from the text, drawing your evidence from a close reading of the details contained in the words on the page. The process will be demonstrated in relation to specific texts in subsequent chapters. As we discuss the texts you will find it helpful to remember the points summarised here, and especially the notion of a core conflict or tension around which a novel may be constructed. Now, however, I should like to consider further the nature of the central opposition as it is often found in Conrad's novels.

The nature of the conflict in Conrad's novels

You may remember my earlier observation that the most generalised pattern we might expect in a novel is a form of conflict between society and one or more individuals who belong to that social group. In Conrad's novels the tension is often expressed as an opposition between two sets of ideas: on the one hand there is desire for love, trust, equality, a need for life to have meaning and purpose; on the other there is cruelty, selfishness, greed, deceit, injustice and hardship produced by social, psychological and natural factors. The opposition can be further simplified to a conflict between ideals and reality.

Part of the reason for Conrad's recurrent concern with this conflict can be seen in his own background, part in the period in which he was writing. Conrad was born in 1857 in a region of Poland controlled by Tsarist Russia. Virtually all Poles of that time and place had a nationalist ideal of revolution and liberation, which was brutally repressed by the Russian militia. Conrad fled first to France and ultimately to England as a sailor in days when life at sea was exceptionally tough and dangerous. Naturally he had idealistic thoughts about Western Europe, which had provided him with a new home and identity – but he also saw that society with an outsider's vision. Aspects of life that seemed part of the natural order of things to Western Europeans appeared as supremely unnatural to Conrad. For example, many Europeans saw the colonisation of Africa, which was at its height when Conrad began writing, as inevitable, and as ultimately bringing good to the natives whose land was occupied by foreign forces alien to their culture. As a Pole who had been on the receiving end of territorial imperialism Conrad was sceptical of the benefits it brought. He saw that behind the rhetoric of the ideals of spreading Christianity and European civilisation there could lie a reality of basic, cunning, power-hungry materialism. Conrad realised that there were three types of people professing ideals: those who were sincere; the hypocrites who deliberately used the language to hide their motives; and the self-deluded who somehow convinced themselves that they meant well while doing evil. These ideas were related by Conrad not only to imperialism, but also to many other aspects of late nineteenth- and early twentieth-century life and society. When reading the novels it is also worth remembering that Conrad is the only major English-language novelist who chose to write in his *third* tongue. Just as his Eastern European upbringing, and his seaman's experience in many diverse parts of the world, gave him a special perception of Western behaviour and attitudes, the fact that he came to English after Polish and French gave him a peculiar sensitivity to English, and to language in general. Conrad is aware that words do not always mean what they say, and that there are things language cannot express. Both these aspects come through in his own use of English in the novels, and can present particular difficulties – although they also produce great delight for the reader.

The period in which Conrad lived saw many examples of how what had been thought of as ideals had degenerated or been destroyed when they came in contact with reality. The expanding materialism that had forced Victorian society on was beginning to founder by the end of Victoria's reign in 1901. The ideal of poverty being ended by an infinitely expanding economy had struck financial reality. Another related factor was that Britain, idealised as the bringer of peace and civilisation to the whole world, was being challenged by the expanding economies of other countries, notably the United States and the recently unified state of Germany. As a result of that economic rivalry Germany was also threatening Britain militarily, not through direct invasion but through the colonies. At the time this dispute was often seen as one between British liberalism and enlightenment and the reality of German power-seeking. It may be seen to have culminated in 1914 in the outbreak of the Great War, portrayed as a combat between the forces of ideal freedom and the forces of tyranny. Around that time, too, Freud was working on his theories of dreams and the unconscious, which would reveal the unpleasant dark forces of the human mind. Even idealistic dreams could be capable of negative interpretations. The ideal of universal free education and literacy which had been incorporated into the Education Act of 1870 had in reality produced a generation of readers not of fine literature, but of cheap popular sensationalist newspapers, several of which were founded in the 1890s and early 1900s to exploit the new readership market. Conrad was not writing just for himself in exploring the dark and destructive side of social realities, economic systems, human nature and natural forces – he touched on many of the central concerns of the times.

In these circumstances it is not surprising that the opposition of ideals and reality should form the core of Conrad's novels, or that he is so fascinated by the process of the testing and loss of ideals. The conflict between ideals and reality usually results, in the novels, in two forms of suffering: that of the innocent victims of other people's misplaced idealism; and that experienced by the idealists themselves as their faith splinters and disintegrates, and they see the consequences of their folly.

Conrad's background as a working seaman – with experience both of other countries and of being in danger of death at sea – and as a multilingual Pole, both outsider and participant in British society, writing in a context of increasing political and cultural uncertainty and insecurity, led him to feel that he could best express his ideas through a kind of novel that diverged somewhat from the conventional Victorian form. It is this aspect of his work that can create difficulties for us as readers. Earlier, nineteenth-century novelists such as Austen and Hardy had generally told their stories in a fairly straightforward way. Their novels have a clear beginning, middle and end; and the characters are normally depicted in a manner that makes them easily recognisable. Most of their novels are written in the style of a third-person narrator, someone who is outside the story and can comment on all the events and characters from a position of knowing and understanding what is happening, and why, and what everyone is thinking about. Occasionally there is a first-person narrative, such as Pip's autobiography in Dickens's *Great Expectations*, but the story still moves logically from one action to the next. These features are not always followed by Conrad. He sometimes starts in the middle of a sequence of events and then works backwards and forwards in time; on other occasions he disappears from the novel as author and has the story told not merely by one narrator but by two, or even three or four. These switches in time and in the voice telling the story can be confusing, and are certainly designed to make reading complex. I think Conrad is often trying to slow us down, to make us read thoughtfully and consider carefully not only what is happening but also why it is happening and how. He once wrote, 'My task ... is, before all, to make you *see*. That ... is everything.' By emphasising the word *see* he drew attention to the fact that he meant more than just seeing with the eyes: he wanted his readers to see in the sense of fully understanding, of comprehending the facets of life and motivations of behaviour that lie beneath the surface. The form of his novels is exactly right for exploring the recurring conflict in his narratives between the ideals of individuals and psychological and social reality. By holding up the action in various ways Conrad returns our attention to, and stresses the importance of, the 'why' and 'how' of events, attitudes and motives. Real understanding lies beneath the surface; as in dreams the actual meaning needs to be interpreted rather than simply read off as though it was a computer print-out of irrevocable facts. These factors make identifying what Conrad's novels are about extremely difficult, but the rewards of discovering and understanding are immense.

We can achieve this if we remember that, beyond the immediate difficulties caused by the shifts of time and narrator, the purpose of the novels is to explore the idealistic side of human nature in conflict with darker psychic forces and with an indifferent, or actually hostile, society. At the centre of a Conrad novel we may expect to discover a character, or several characters, caught between these opposing worlds – perhaps as the innocent victim of someone else's misplaced altruism or optimism or of another character's dark cruelty and egoistic selfishness; or as someone whose ideals are shattered and destroyed when they strike the rock of reality. For ideals are not simply laudable and beautiful aspects of life: they make their own demands and, as Conrad presents them, are harsh taskmasters, deluding characters into foolish, ill-considered and sometimes destructive acts. Although abstractions, they are as capable of determining relationships between people as legal documents or ties of blood. As this conflict between ideals and reality is a recurring feature of Conrad's novels, it provides us with a useful framework for constructing an analysis of his work.

Putting a novel back together

An awareness of the ideals–reality opposition in the novels should give you a good foundation on which to build your reading of any individual Conrad novel. It should help you to make sense of the episodes that make up the story, and assist in the interpretation of specific details and scenes. If you always look for the conflict of ideals and reality you should be able to interpret any scene or detail in any of Conrad's novels. You may think this idea of a recurring central conflict a restricting one, but it should not prove so in practice. While I am suggesting that a fundamental pattern exists in Conrad's fiction, it is the way you build on this foundation that will make your reading of a Conrad novel distinctive. Remember, more than one interpretation of the text may be valid. This is one reason for not accepting the views of any single critic without careful consideration of them.

Sometimes, however, rather than simply building and developing your own discussion of a novel you may be asked to follow up a specific topic. When preparing for an examination, for instance, you might be asked to explore such matters as the way in which Conrad presents political ideas, or his concern with fate in the lives of some of his characters, or his attitudes in a particular novel to wealth. It is a common mistake for students to treat such aspects of Conrad's work as though they were entirely separate themes, writing about them as if they were unrelated topics. It is important to realise that all these issues are connected, related to one another through the pattern of the whole novel. The most effective method of tackling these themes is to explore and analyse them in the light of the ideals–reality conflict. This will help you to focus your ideas, and provide a good framework for relating one element of the novel to all the others.

Think, for instance, of the idea of fate as it appears in the novels. It is not unusual for students, and sometimes critics, to write as if Conrad were a mere pessimist who enjoyed creating characters he could then hunt down and destroy. Some of the published work on Conrad is unhelpful, and even misleading, since it concentrates on a few instances in his personal life that provide evidence of a deep melancholy. While these incidents are not untrue, they are taken out of the context of his whole life and isolated. The writer then ignores all the hopeful essays and letters that Conrad wrote. If, however, we approach the problem of fate through the ideals–reality conflict, we can appreciate its complexity and see its relation to the overall pattern of the novels. A character who has ideals is almost certainly fated to come into conflict with reality at some point; or a character may be caught up in the disintegration of someone else's ideals. In either case the character concerned is pursuing his or her life in the belief that he or she has control over it, but is then overtaken by an unexpected turn of events. This can be seen as fate. It is also the working-out of the central ideals–reality opposition. In the most extreme cases the outcome is the character's death: Decoud in *Nostromo*, Stevie in *The Secret Agent* and Heyst in *Victory*, for example, all die – not because Conrad grows tired of them, but through their involvement with an ideal that inevitably collides with a stronger reality. Conrad would argue this is what happens, although not necessarily so dramatically, in real life. The conflict is inevitable, the outcome is unpredictable; most characters survive, although with their ideals ruined or modified. Sometimes they emerge from the experience actually stronger. Marlow, the main narrator of both 'Youth' and *Heart of Darkness*, certainly becomes more realistic through the shocks he experiences. The complexity arises because fate can be a positive, as well as negative, force. Conrad is not a fatalist but a realist in the way he presents the conflict of ideals and reality.

In the following chapters we shall see how we can tackle other features of the novels by means of a similar method, working from this central idea. At this point, though, my argument might seem to have become a bit abstract. You may not have read any of the novels yet, and I appear to be anticipating ideas that must be discussed in the rest of this book as it develops. So, to return to the central concept: a reiterated pattern exists in Conrad's novels, and this can be expressed as a conflict between ideals and reality. This fundamental tension runs through the novels and can be used, as I shall illustrate in the chapters that follow, as a framework and organising pivot for all your discussion and analysis of the novels.

Analysing a novel

I have been stressing the existence of a basic pattern of tensions in Conrad's works. However, when you consider a novel as a whole you are involved in identifying and expressing your own responses to the features of the work that are specific to it, the particular quality of the novel's style and texture. The following chapters illustrate how to go about this. Conrad wrote a great many novels and no single book on them could do justice to them all, so I have selected some that are generally thought to be among his major achievements. This is reflected in the way these titles recur in the examination papers of schools, colleges and universities. Do not be put off, however, if I do not explore the specific novel in which you are interested. Whichever novel you want to study, the steps of analysis are the same. Each chapter is devoted to one novel. I start the discussion by using the framework of the fundamental pattern of Conrad's fiction, moving on to analyse a particular passage in order to identify the actual nature of the tension working through the chosen novel. Armed with the understanding gained from this passage I then look closely at a number of further extracts from the remainder of the novel. The object is to see how the novel works and expresses its main themes and ideas.

It is extremely important to understand, and hold on to, this basic method for working on the text: that the best way to build a critical response to a Conrad novel is to **approach the novel with a grasp of the opposition that is probably at the core of the story, and then closely examine a number of extracts with that opposition in mind**. The method encourages you to clarify your ideas from the beginning, and makes you subsequently analyse the words on the page. You may raise the objection that the method appears too simple, that concentrating on a few passages from a complex novel cannot lead to a full understanding. In fact detailed analysis of this kind will help you formulate and write very much more penetrating and concise critical appreciation than attempting too much too vaguely.

As you work through this book, remember that my main purpose is to show you how you can study a Conrad novel on your own. Select and consider some extracts yourself and you will find the experience rewarding and enjoyable, enabling you to build up a wonderful independence of judgement. You may be studying only one of the novels I discuss, and in that case may be tempted not to read the chapters on other novels, but you will find it helpful to do so. I am not able to discuss every aspect of Conrad's work in each chapter, so problems and questions that are relevant to the story you are studying may be dealt with in a chapter mainly devoted to another novel.

You may not have time, even so, to read all this book. Nevertheless I strongly recommend you to read the next chapter, on the short story 'Youth', because it is there that I illustrate in most detail the formula for approaching a text that this book uses.

2

'Youth' (1902)

Constructing an overall analysis

'YOUTH' was published in a collection of stories in 1902. It is not a novel, being only forty pages long, but I have chosen to start with it because it is a very fine short story, it frequently appears as a set text, and it provides an excellent introduction to Conrad's ideas and writing methods. Rather than go through a long introduction to the story, however, I would rather get on with the method of approach I shall use throughout this book. The page references given after quotations from the story relate to the 1987 World's Classics edition of *Youth, Heart of Darkness, The End of the Tether.*

1 *After reading the story, think what kind of pattern you can see in the text*

The tale takes place in the days of sailing ships. The main story is told by a forty-two-year-old seaman, Marlow, and concerns a voyage he made when he was twenty. It was important to him at the time for two reasons: it was his first appointment as second mate, which meant it was a promotion for him; and it was his first voyage to the East, to Bankok, an exotic port in South-East Asia. It was also the first time Captain Beard had commanded a ship, though he was around sixty years old and a little late to reach that position of responsibility; as it happened, it was his first journey to the East too. Both the young Marlow and the old skipper are full of idealistic enthusiasm for the journey as they begin this new experience in their lives.

The ship starts by sailing from London to Newcastle. In the North Sea it encounters a ferocious gale and is grounded on a sandbank. This accident causes the ship, the *Judea*, to arrive late in Newcastle. It is eventually loaded with coal, but then further delayed by a collision with another vessel, during which incident young Marlow is full of admiration for the way the old skipper, acting like a younger man, rescues Mrs Beard from danger. The *Judea* at last starts for Bankok over two months late, but in the English Channel encounters another gale and springs a leak. The double effect of the leak and the storm almost destroy the ship, though the efforts of the crew manage to bring it into Falmouth harbour. There follow more weeks of frustration and delay. When the vessel is sea-worthy again two other unusual events occur: the rats that infest the ship desert it, just when it seems unnecessary to do so; and the ship has such a bad reputation that it is impossible to recruit a local crew. Throughout all these misadventures Marlow remains convinced that he will get to Bankok, and looks upon the disasters simply as challenges that make the job, and the voyage, more exciting and worthwhile. Captain Beard, too, responds to the setbacks by becoming more determined and resolute. In the earlier stages of the journey both reinforce their initial ideals about its final outcome.

Ultimately a crew has to be sent from Liverpool, and with it the *Judea* reaches the Indian Ocean, very slowly but without further incident. The cargo of coal then catches fire. Captain Beard decides not to sail for the safety of Australia, but to attempt smothering the fire by closing down all possible ventilation. The result is to fill the whole ship with acrid smoke – but without stifling the smouldering cargo. Pouring water on the coal also fails. Just as the crew prepare to abandon ship the fire appears to go out and the smoke disappears. The crew feel they have overcome all the hazards and are on a safe course for port, but at that point the cargo, which has in fact still been smouldering, explodes. The captain of the disabled *Judea* manages to get his ship towed by one that is passing and responds to his distress signals. Unfortunately the wind created by the speed of towing then fans the smouldering into flames. Captain Beard, apparently deranged by the experience, decides to cut the tow-rope and abandon ship, taking as much of the owner's goods as possible in the open boats. When the *Judea* finally sinks, the crew head across the open seas of the Indian Ocean in three boats, Marlow himself, the narrator, being in charge of the smallest of them – his first naval command. After many days of danger and privation the open boats reach port safely, Marlow's – much to his pride and satisfaction – being first. Marlow has achieved his great ambition, but the deranged old skipper has lost his first command and arrives in the East exhausted and under the shadow of disgrace. The short story ends, significantly, with the forty-two-year-old Marlow commenting sardonically on the difference between his attitudes and elation when a young man as against his present maturity and scepticism.

As you think about this plot outline, bear in mind my comments in the previous chapter on the tension in Conrad's fiction between ideals and reality. Before you continue think about how that conflict can be seen in this summary of the story. You might look at it in terms of the two main characters. Beard and Marlow both start with high hopes about the future and their respective careers. Compare these with the situation at the end of the story. Beard arrives at his destination without the *Judea*, which he has left at the bottom of the Indian Ocean. His first command is likely, because of his age and failure, to be his last. Beard's high aspirations have been destroyed by the reality of the voyage. It is worth thinking about the physical change he has undergone, and how that emphasises the idea of someone who has lost everything. At the beginning Beard is quite sprightly, and Marlow even sees him as heroic when the captain rescues Mrs Beard at the time of the collision in Newcastle docks. By the end Beard has become mentally unstable and is physically exhausted. Marlow says of him at the end, 'he looked as though he would never wake' (p. 41). I think this suggests that in a way Beard resembles a dead man. He is not literally dead, but the high spirits and ideals with which he began the journey have died through their contact with reality. By looking at the development of the character of Captain Beard, then, we can see that it embodies the central conflict between ideals and reality. An individual's ideals are thwarted by the reality they come up against.

You might feel uneasy about applying this to the character of the young Marlow. He ends the journey full of excitement and with a feeling of triumph. But, as you read on, think about how Conrad encourages us to challenge Marlow's idealistic innocent amazement. Marlow feels triumphant because his first command has been successful. We know, however, that he has been in charge not of a large ship, but of a small open boat with a crew of only two other sailors. If Marlow idealises his arrival, we can see the rather pathetic reality. There is another way in which the young Marlow's reactions are challenged. To appreciate this we must remember that the story is narrated by the same man, but when he is twenty-two years older. The older character's sceptical comments on his own youthful innocent idealism are the remarks of a man who has experienced the full responsibility of command, who has a different notion of reality.

No matter how difficult the text appears to be at first glance, we can always begin to make sense of it by looking for the central tension around which it is organised – the conflict between ideals and reality. This is what I have tried to do so far. I have attempted to get at the issues at the heart of the story by considering the overall pattern in terms of the conflict between ideals and reality. You do not have to accept my impression of the text uncritically: try to apply the idea of an opposition to your own summary of 'Youth', and think about your own understanding of the issues involved. You should find that in your first look at the text you can see an overall opposition, and that will provide your analysis with a firm foundation on which to build.

2 *Select a short passage for discussion and try to build on the ideas you have established so far*

Once you have established some sense of an overall pattern, you can move on to working out a more detailed view of the story or novel. The best way to achieve this is to focus on small areas of the text: you will not only be illuminating these particular passages but also be gaining a more confident understanding of the work as a whole. But how do you choose appropriate passages for discussion? It makes sense to start with one of the main characters. As Marlow is the central figure, he seems a suitable choice. In this case, since it is a story told by the older man about his own youth, we might begin with the way that relationship is set up by the author.

This occurs early in the story when Marlow also introduces the other main character, Captain Beard. Marlow commences his narration by addressing the other four travellers to whom the story of his youth is told:

> Yes, I have seen a little of the Eastern seas; but what I remember best is my first voyage there. You fellows know there are those voyages that seem ordered for the illustration of life, that might stand for a symbol of existence. You fight, work, sweat, nearly kill yourself, sometimes do kill yourself, trying to accomplish something – and you can't. Not from any fault of yours. You simply can do nothing, neither great nor little – not a thing in the world – not even marry an old maid, or get a wretched 600-ton cargo of coal to its port of destination.
>
> It was altogether a memorable affair. It was my first voyage to the East, and my first voyage as second mate; it was also my skipper's first

> command. You'll admit it was time. He was sixty if a day; a little man, with a broad, not very straight back, with bowed shoulders and one leg more bandy than the other, he had that queer twisted-about appearance you see so often about men who work in the fields. He had a nut-cracker face – chin and nose trying to come together over a sunken mouth – and it was framed in iron-gray fluffy hair, that looked like a chin-strap of cotton-wool sprinkled with coal-dust. And he had blue eyes in that old face of his, which were amazingly like a boy's, with that candid expression some quite common men preserve to the end of their days by a rare internal gift of simplicity of heart and rectitude of soul. (pp. 3–4)

You have selected a passage, but what do you say about it? Sometimes you might know precisely what you want to say about a passage like this, but if you are unsure it is always a good idea to tackle the extract systematically. Try following this sequence of steps.

(a) State briefly what the passage is about.
(b) Search for an opposition or tension within the passage.
(c) Analyse the details of the passage, relating them to the opposition already noted.
(d) Try to say how the passage relates to the story or novel as a whole.
(e) Search for anything distinctive about the passage, particularly in the area of style, which you have not already noted.

This set of steps underlies the analysis of all the extracts discussed in this book, but it is only in this chapter that I label each step. Undertaking this set of tasks, even when you are working on a piece of text you think you know well, or even if you do not always want to work through every step, will help you to organize and express your response with the greatest efficiency. It will help you direct your thinking purposefully, and use your time effectively.

If we look at the passage above, it is clear that it is about (**step a**) Marlow's memory of an extremely important and formative episode in his life, and of a man with whom he shared it. The opposition (**step b**), especially in the first paragraph, is between an ideal state – success at achieving what one has set out to do – and the conditions that prevent it from being realised. At this stage, the beginning of Marlow's narration, the opposition is stated in generalised, abstract terms. The details in the passage (**step c**) help to convey the sense of the opposition between ideals and reality in more human terms. The repetition of 'first' – it is Marlow's first voyage to the East, his first with the rank of second mate, and the skipper's first as captain – emphasises the inexperience of the two main characters. Naturally they have high hopes, but they do not really know what reality to expect. There is also a tension between youth and age. We are reminded that Marlow is remembering an episode, something that happened in the past. The narrator stresses the skipper's age, particularly in relation to his inexperience as a captain. This is underlined by the paradox in the captain's appearance: in some ways he looks very old, with bowed shoulders, bandy legs, a Punch-like face and 'iron-gray' hair. But these are offset by unexpected youthful aspects: his eyes, which are 'amazingly like a boy's'; and his 'candid expression' that shows a 'simplicity of heart' – he is a man with the ideals of youth about to come into conflict with the reality of his age and the responsibility of command. A final detail we might note as contributing to the central tension is the odd observation that although the skipper is a seaman he has the appearance of 'men who work in the fields', an agricultural labourer. Our impression of seamen and farm workers is likely to be that they are completely different, that the skills and experience of the one group have no relevance to the other. The tension created by the description of the captain contributes to the sense of an overall opposition. He does not measure up in reality to any notion we may have of an ideal ship's captain.

The assumption you have to make in looking at a passage is that it will reflect the larger concerns of the story or novel. When you look at an extract, therefore, you must step back and relate it to the text as a whole, trying to sum up what the passage has added to your overall impression (**step d**). What you might conclude from this passage, for example, is that the main characters are entering on an experience for which they are not fully prepared, that they have expectations that may, and do, prove false when measured against reality. No one, for instance, is prepared for the various disasters that occur, or for the way the crew ultimately enter the Eastern harbour. The passage gives a sense of the characters' underlying naïveté that is tested as the story progresses. As a final point we might note Marlow's comment that his narration is to be of a voyage that is 'ordered for the illustration of life, that might stand for a symbol of existence'. This seems a clear indication that we are about to read a story that goes beyond simple adventure, requiring us to interpret it as an illustration of life in a wider, symbolic or metaphorical sense. We must look for the author's purpose beneath the surface of events.

The final step in looking at a passage is a close look at its style (**step e**), but I am going to ignore this at the moment as I want to conclude this section by summing up what you should be trying to do as you turn to the text. That is quite straightforward: you should be trying to flesh out and develop your initial ideas to build a fuller sense of the story or novel. I began, for example, with an overall sense of the opposition between ideals and reality; but I have already started to refine this and expand it by seeing how it is linked to, and expressed through, other conflicts: youth – the title of the story – and age; inexperience and experience; expectations and reality. These additional tensions help me to clarify my ideas about the text as a whole.

3 *Select a second passage for discussion*

Each additional passage you consider should add to your overall impression: keep on asking yourself, 'What can I now say about this text that I did not know before?' The best way to select passages for discussion is to look again at those scenes or incidents that have stayed most vividly in your memory. In a story full of disasters, one of the sections that stays in my mind, because of its unusual contrast to all the action, is the period of calm between the early storms, collision and leak, and the later fire and sinking. It is in fact immediately before Marlow discovers the fire in the cargo hold, a period of boredom and waiting:

> And for me there was also my youth to make me patient. There was all the East before me, and all life, and the thought that I had been tried in that ship and had come out pretty well. And I thought of men of old who, centuries ago, went that road in ships that sailed no better, to the land of palms, and spices, and yellow sands, and of brown nations ruled by kings more cruel than Nero the Roman, and more splendid than Solomon the Jew. The old bark lumbered on, heavy with her age and the burden of her cargo, while I lived the life of youth in ignorance and hope. She lumbered on through an interminable procession of days; and the fresh gilding flashed back at the setting sun, seemed to cry out over the darkening sea the words painted on her stern, '*Judea*, London. Do or Die.'
>
> Then we entered the Indian Ocean and steered northerly for Java Head. The winds were light. Weeks slipped by. She crawled on, do or die, and people at home began to think of posting us as overdue. (p. 18)

(a) This extract is about Marlow's thoughts as the ship very slowly pursues its course towards its exotic, romantic destination. It emphasises the boredom of the process.

(b) There is an oppostion between the ideal of excitement and the reality of frustration, of having to wait patiently for weeks while the ship only crawls towards Bankok. Linked to this is the tension between the youth of Marlow, with all his life before him, and the ship which is heavy and slow with age.

(c) We can see this also in the references to the old civilisations. Marlow is young, ignorant and hopeful; but many sailors had passed that way before – his youth and inexperience is presented against the fact that it has all happened before, that he is simply going to learn what others have learnt. Those ancient people also idealised their voyages to exotic, splendid and unknown lands. They had their realities too: ships that sailed slowly and gave their crews problems, and meetings with cruel kings.

(d) I now need to pull back and relate these impressions to my ideas about the story as whole. I have already mentioned that the central opposition is partly expressed through the tension between youth and age, and I think we can see this here too. Aging is a temporal process and this extract is partly concerned with the passing of time, past centuries and the slow procession of days that run into weeks until the ship is overdue. The action, hope and idealism of youth are also reflected in the old ship's motto 'Do or Die'. The ship does die, and, as we have seen, its captain dies metaphorically, while the young Marlow goes on to 'Do', to involve himself in actions. One feature of idealism is an obsession with a particular idea, a desire to 'Do' a particular thing, to achieve a specific aspiration, regardless of practical realities. Here I think it is related to the desire of sailors to go to exotic destinations, despite the possible consequences.

(e) One of the features of the style of the passage is the repetition. This is not merely a matter of saying the same thing over and over again, but serves to emphasise and qualify some of the main ideas. The word 'youth', for instance, occurs twice in the first paragraph. On the first occasion it is associated with 'patience', but later with 'ignorance and hope'. It is not that one association is wrong and the other right, but rather that Conrad is getting at the idea of the different facets of youth. By contrast, the repetition of 'lumbered on' stresses the age of the ship and the sense of effort involved in the journey.

4 *Select a third passage for discussion*

I hope it is clear how simple this method of analysis is: all it involves is having a few controlling ideas and then interpreting passages in their light. It is a simple method, but it should enable you to produce your own distinctive reading of the text as you respond to what you think is central in a passage and then relate it to your developing sense of the work as a whole. One of my controlling ideas is the notion that an obsessive idea can become an ideal, something someone believes in against all odds and reality. Or, putting it the other way round, one kind of ideal is an obsessive idea, an objective that drives all other rational considerations to one side. This can be seen in the character of Captain Beard, especially at moments of crisis. For example, just after the explosion caused by the burning cargo of coal Marlow describes Beard as mad:

> The old chap, it seems, was in his own berth winding up the chronometers, when the shock sent him spinning. Immediately it occurred to him – as he said afterwards – that the ship had struck something, and ran out into the cabin. There, he saw, the cabin-table had vanished somewhere. The deck being blown up, it had fallen down into the lazarette of course. Where we had our breakfast that morning he saw only a great hole in the floor. This appeared to him so awfully mysterious, and impressed him so immensely, that what he saw and heard after he got on deck were mere trifles in comparison. And, mark, he noticed directly the wheel deserted and his barque off her course – and his only thought was to get that miserable, stripped, undecked, smouldering shell of a ship back again with her head pointing at her port of destination. Bankok! That's what he was after. I tell you this quiet, bowed, bandy-legged, almost deformed little man was immense in the singleness of his idea and in his placid ignorance of our agitation. He motioned us forward with a commanding gesture, and went to take the wheel himself. (pp. 24–5)

(a) The extract is about Captain Beard's reaction to the unexpected explosion.

(b) The central tension is between the enormity of the catastrophe and the placid response of Beard, who has failed to register the effect of the event on his crew. Marlow speaks of his captain having a placid ignorance of the sailors' quite natural agitation. We can say that the passage reflects the opposition we identified at the beginning of this book: the conflict between an individual with an ideal, and reality.

(c) The text's details illustrate the point precisely. The reality of the ship is that the deck has fallen into the stores room, 'the lazarette', the cabin table has disintegrated and apparently vanished, and the whole is described as a 'miserable, stripped, undecked, smouldering shell'. Even in a single paragraph the picture of real desolation is built up and emphasised. So too is Beard's idealist obsession. This is brought out through the contrast between his unimpressive stature, which again is stressed in the details – 'bowed, bandy-legged, almost deformed little man' – and 'the singleness of his idea' that makes him 'immense'. He seems actually to grow bigger, and becomes 'commanding' under the influence of the ideal, the obsessive idea, of reaching Bankok.

(d) The force of this passage is that it shows just how powerful the effect of an ideal can be. It illustrates how narrowing and blinding such an influence is in this case: the captain doesn't even notice the alarm of his crew. But the passage also depicts how the ideal raises Beard above the panic – even in what Marlow calls his insanity he notices the practical things, the wheel deserted, the ship drifting off course, and he takes command. Conrad is clear about the attractiveness of an ideal as well as its limitations and dangers for the individual holding it, or being held by it.

(e) The style of the passage reveals that all the ideas are presented in terms of contrasts. The duality of Beard's condition is expressed through the contrast between something 'awfully mysterious' and his practical seaman's sense that someone must take the ship's wheel to stop the vessel drifting. The adjectives often work in similar pairs: 'little' and 'immense', 'placid' and 'agitation'. We are constantly being shown two different aspects of the characters and situations.

5 *Select a fourth passage for discussion*

My analysis of the story so far has centred on the opposition between an ideal and the reality in which someone attempts to achieve it.

Marlow has so far been somewhat protected from the worst features of reality, because Beard has borne the main responsibility. I now want to see how Marlow fits in with this scheme of things when he has to take responsibility. After the *Judea* has sunk, the three open boats head for the nearest, although still very distant, port:

> Before sunset a thick rain-squall passed over the two boats, which were far astern, and that was the last I saw of them for a time. Next day I sat steering my cockle-shell – my first command – with nothing but water and sky around me. I did sight in the afternoon the upper sails of a ship far away, but said nothing, and my men did not notice her. You see I was afraid she might be homeward bound, and I had no mind to turn back from the portals of the East. I was steering for Java – another blessed name – like Bankok, you know. I steered many days.
>
> I need not tell you what it is to be knocking about in an open boat. I remember nights and days of calm, when we pulled, we pulled, and the boat seemed to stand still, as if bewitched within the circle of the sea horizon. I remember the heat, the deluge of rain-squalls that kept us baling for dear life (but filled our water-cask), and I remember sixteen hours on end with a mouth dry as a cinder and a steering-oar over the stern to keep my first command head on to a breaking sea. I did not know how good a man I was till then. I remember the drawn faces, the dejected figures of my two men, and I remember my youth and the feeling that will never come back any more – the feeling that I could last for ever, outlast the sea, the earth, and all men; the deceitful feeling that lures us on to joys, to perils, to love, to vain effort – to death; the triumphant conviction of strength, the heat of life in the handful of dust, the glow in the heart that with every year grows dim, grows cold, grows small, and expires – and expires, too soon, too soon – before life itself. (pp. 36–7)

(a) The passage is about Marlow's experience as commander of an open boat with two other sailors.

(b) There is an opposition between Marlow's youthful ideal, his desire to reach the blessed East, and the reality of the journey with its hardships and dangers. You might see a further tension between youth in general, a feeling of dominance, the ability to overcome all difficulties, and the natural processes of aging, which gradually wear away a person's strength and vitality.

(c) The details of the passage make this clear: Marlow's fear, in the first paragraph, of being taken home before he has seen the East leads to the specific instances of suffering in the second paragraph – the difficulties of making progress, the threat of death through thirst because of the heat, and the danger of dying by drowning when it rains. Marlow's optimism in steering heedlessly for Java is countered by the detail of the 'drawn faces' and 'dejected figures' of his crew. This optimism is partly related to Marlow's youth, 'the feeling that I could last for ever'; but that is opposed by the details of aging, the glow of youth growing dim, cold, small and finally expiring.

(d) This relates to the central conflict between ideals and reality by showing how the young Marlow becomes obsessed by the overriding idea of reaching a harbour in the East, regardless of the real suffering it causes the sailors whose lives are his responsibility. His youth gives him the strength and determination to accomplish what is almost impossible, but we are reminded that the reality of his youth – and all youth – is that it will ultimately be lost.

(e) The main point I would like to stress about the style is the way in which the text emphasises that Marlow is narrating an adventure that happened to him a long time ago – twenty-two years ago, to be precise. In the second paragraph of the extract 'I remember' occurs five times, and repetition – as we have seen earlier – is always significant. The repetition here, towards the end of the story, is emphasising the difference between the young man who experienced the adventure and the older, maturer one who is able to comment on his younger self. The processes of aging also involve changing, and seeing things differently. You may remember that in Chapter 1 I pointed out how important seeing, in the sense of understanding, was to Conrad. At the age of twenty Marlow was able to see only the ideal, the goal of reaching an exotic land; twenty-two years later, when telling the story, he is able to see both the ideal and the reality: the strength of youth and the fact that it is limited by time.

6 *Have I achieved a sufficiently complex sense of the story?*

By this stage, having looked at four passages, you should have pieced together a view of the story. If you are still puzzled, look at more passages until you feel that you have worked out a coherent reading. Your ideas might well develop in a very different direction from mine, but this is the whole point about this method of looking at a text, that it allows you, as you move from passage to passage, systematically to develop your own interpretation of the story or novel. At this stage, however, stop and ask yourself whether you feel you have got to grips with the work. Try to be precise: what still puzzles you about the text?

One gap that I am aware of in my analysis of 'Youth' is that, since I have concentrated on characters and events, I have not looked very closely at the narrative organisation of the story. I have commented that Marlow is both participant in, and teller of, his own tale – but he is not the overall narrator of the text. That person is anonymous, but we are reminded from time to time that Marlow is talking to an audience. One member of that audience is the writer of the full story. The sensible thing to do now, therefore, is to look at a relevant passage. I have chosen the final paragraph, after Marlow has finished speaking:

> And we all nodded at him: the man of finance, the man of accounts, the man of law, we all nodded at him over the polished table that like a still sheet of brown water reflected our faces, lined, wrinkled; our faces marked by toil, by deceptions, by success, by love; our weary eyes looking still, looking always, looking anxiously for something out of life, that while it is expected is already gone – has passed unseen, in a sigh, in a flash – together with the youth, with the strength, with the romance of illusions. (p. 42)

I must admit that as a student I would have found it extremely difficult to know what to say about a passage such as this, because it seems to be tacked on, without any real reason, to the end of Marlow's tale. But any passage can be coped with if you approach it in a systematic way. Part of the secret is telling yourself that the passage must be dealing with issues which you have already registered as central to the text as a whole.

Let us see, then, what can be made of this passage.

(a) It is about the listeners' response to the main story, Marlow's tale.

(b) Because it is meditative you might find it difficult to spot an opposition here, but bear in mind the idea we have already developed of a tension between an ideal and the reality in which it has to survive. What strikes me in this passage is the contrast between the reality of the listeners – their gnarled weariness – and the fact that even in that condition they are still looking for some ideal state of life, for some experience in life that would give it meaning.

(c) The details in the passage convey the aging-experience of the silent characters: 'lined', 'wrinkled', 'marked', 'weary'; while the repetition is again significant, suggesting the continued search for an ideal even in these conditions – 'looking still, looking always, looking anxiously'.

(d) How all this seems to relate to the story as a whole is that it illustrates how ideals, although often leading to illusions, to a false perception of the world and of experience – which is the lesson Marlow draws from his own tale – nevertheless remain attractive. The reality for the listeners is that youth has passed, 'is already gone', but they still seek its strength and romance.

(e) The centrally important feature of the style is that we are reminded that Marlow has been telling a tale of his youth, which has passed. Marlow finishes his story by commenting on it; this passage comments on both Marlow's tale and his thoughts on it.

Having looked at this passage in some detail I feel I can now sum up the impression that the story as a whole makes on me. Different readers will interpret the evidence differently, but it seems to me that Conrad is writing about the fact that ideals lead people into illusions, difficulties, even danger, dominate them by making them slaves to obsessive ideas, which are ultimately futile because they will be destroyed by reality. Despite all this, however, people continue to search for, and even need, ideals in order to live their lives. There is nothing particularly original in this reading of the story, but criticism does not have to strain after wildly new interpretations. What matters is that, as in this analysis of 'Youth', you work closely from the evidence of the text to build a coherent reading of the story, or novel, which does honestly reflect your own response to it.

Aspects of the story

When you have constructed your overall analysis you might want to look more closely at certain aspects of the story or novel, at the kind of topics that often feature in examination questions. This is something I take up in the following chapters. In this chapter I want to deal with the smaller, but perhaps equally important, issue of how to respond critically to each and every scene, character and detail in a text. The first part of this chapter has already shown you how to do this – it is a matter of interpreting every detail in the light of the ideas you have previously established – but so many students find it difficult to make these connections that it might help if I offer some additional guidance here. The examples are all from 'Youth', but similar details and features will be encountered in all Conrad's stories and novels.

We can start with the way in which Conrad uses **objects** – and, although I shall not use specific examples here, also places – as **extended metaphors or symbols**. By this I mean the way in which they almost become lifelike and contribute to the development of the central tension, which, as we have seen, is the conflict between ideals and reality. To illustrate my point I am going to look at the ship, and Marlow's first impressions of it. He has just commented on his own youth, and age of twenty, in comparison to the greater age of his two superiors, the captain and mate:

> The ship also was old. Her name was the *Judea*. Queer name isn't it? She belonged to a man Wilmer, Wilcox – some name like that; but he has been bankrupt and dead these twenty years or more, and his name don't matter. She had been laid up in Shadwell basin for ever so long. You may imagine her state. She was all rust, dust, grime – soot aloft, dirt on deck. To me it was like coming out of a palace into a ruined cottage. She was about 400 tons, had a primitive windlass, wooden latches to the doors, not a bit of brass about her, and a big square stern. There was on it, below her name in big letters, a lot of scrollwork, with the gilt off, and some sort of coat of arms, with the motto 'Do or Die' underneath. I remember it took my fancy immensely. There was a touch of romance in it, something that made me love the old thing – something that appealed to my youth! (p. 5)

(a) The passage is about Marlow's first impressions of the ship in which he has been appointed for the first time in the rank of second mate.

(b) There is a contrast between the great age and tired dilapidation of the ship and Marlow's youth and excited enthusiasm.

(c) We are told that the ship is old, but the details of the description emphasise that she has apparently gone beyond working age: she has been laid up for ever so long; she is covered in rust, dust, grime, soot and dirt; her machinery is not just old but 'primitive'.

(d) The reality of the ship is that she is like 'a ruined cottage', and Marlow is used to palatial vessels. Despite this, she appeals to Marlow's idealistic youth, taking his 'fancy immensely' with a 'touch of romance'. At this stage in our understanding we might recall that the story ends with the phrase 'the romance of illusions'. Marlow's ideals about the ship lead him into illusions, and in reality the ship sinks in the Indian Ocean, overcome by age and disasters.

(e) I think even the name of the ship is important. This may be more difficult for us to appreciate than for Conrad's original readers, many of whom were brought up on the Bible, but Conrad often makes the smallest detail of a text significant in contributing to its main ideas. We might note here that the text itself draws attention to the name: 'Queer name, isn't it?' Marlow asks us, suggesting, maybe, that we should think about it. Judea is the land in which Christianity began, facing very hostile conditions with a 'Do or Die' attitude in its fight for survival. After nearly two thousand years it too has perhaps grown dilapidated, its idealism defeated by its encounter with reality. Conrad often works in this way, broadening ideas so that they extend beyond the individuals of the story and evoke the experience of humanity in other ages, civilisations and cultures. One of his ideas, as we have seen, is that people in all ages of history have similar, although obviously not exactly the same, experiences.

You may find this a little difficult to accept at this stage in your understanding of Conrad's work, and if that is the case don't worry about it. The more practice of reading and analysis you have the clearer it will become. The point to appreciate here is that such details as objects, and places too, do not simply fill out the plot or enhance the atmosphere but can always be seen in terms of the broader thematic concerns that you have detected in the text. Each additional detail will provide a fresh perspective on the ideas and add to the overall complexity of the picture presented. But to get hold of the detail you do need to look at a passage, or passages, as this will enable you to move beyond vague impressions and help you define a precise idea of how and where the detail fits in. Ask yourself simple questions: ask, as I did with this extract, how ideals are expressed and how reality is reflected in the passage.

The **minor characters** in Conrad's works can be looked at in a similar way. It is not enough to say that the minor characters add to the plot and atmosphere, since they also reflect the broader concerns of the text. As before, the best way to crystallise your sense of this is to look closely at a passage, or passages, in which they appear. Because 'Youth' is a short story, there is not a lot of evidence of minor characters, though we can take Mahon as an example:

> The mate looked me over carefully. He was also an old chap, but of another stamp. He had a Roman nose, a snow-white, long beard, and his name was Mahon, but he insisted that it should be pronounced Mann. He was well connected; yet there was something wrong with his luck, and he had never got on. (p. 5)

(a) This is Marlow's first impression of the ship's second-in-command, described in comparison to the old captain.

(b) There is an opposition between Mahon's good connections, which suggest that he should have risen quickly in rank, and his bad luck which has kept him from becoming a captain (Marlow has earlier made the point that Beard, who is roughly the same age as Mahon, has gained his first command at a relatively late age).

(c) Mahon's appearance – his long snow-white beard, setting off his aristocratic Roman nose, giving him a look of authority – and his insistence on a particular non-phonetic pronunciation of his name suggest that he is very conscious of his dignity as a long-serving seaman. This self-conscious dignity is at odds with the fact that, as ship's mate, he is only second-in-command.

(d) Mahon is a man who should have succeeded, for having good connections – by which is meant family influences within the world of shipping – is an ideal start for a potentially glorious, ideal career. None the less, he has foundered on the reality of ill fortune. Once you have begun to grasp the details of the story as a whole you might be able to relate this introduction of Mahon to his final appearance as his open boat drifts into the Eastern port: 'Farther out old

Mahon's face was upturned to the sky, with the long white beard spread out on his breast, as though he had been shot where he sat at the tiller' (p. 41). Mahon, like Captain Beard, has been metaphorically killed by the journey and the misadventures. His ill luck has been with him until the last, and the detail of the conspicuous beard seems to emphasise that he is finished as a seaman. The ideal of his dignity has finally met the reality of his bad fortune. Although only a minor character, Mahon contributes to the development of the main themes.

What should be obvious by now is that, wherever you turn in a Conrad text, you will encounter some sense of a conflict between some kind of ideal and some kind of reality, though both of these are expressed in many ways. This is just as evident in **big dramatic incidents** as in the smallest details of a text. To consider big dramatic scenes first: in all of Conrad's works there are episodes of vivid action, scenes that are extremely visual. Examples here are the attempts to put out the fire on the *Judea*, the explosion and its effects, the long and dangerous journey from the ship in the open boats. Even when these scenes are quite lengthy, it is sufficient to focus on a couple of paragraphs in order to analyse them. As always, try to see how the larger concerns of the text are reflected and expressed in the passage you are analysing. It should be particularly easy to see this in such scenes, as dramatic moments tend to throw the concerns of the text into very sharp focus. If you consider the incident when the crew finally abandon the *Judea*, what you will be likely to conclude is that Captain Beard realises that this is his moment of truth, of reality: after sailing the ship for as long as possible, and salvaging as much from her as he can, he 'lingered disconsolately', despite the danger to his life, 'to commune alone for a while with his first command' (p. 34) and eventually has to be led away. In Conrad's big dramatic scenes, then, you should find the tensions of the text embodied and expressed in an especially striking way.

With **small details**, however, you might have to use a little more ingenuity and imagination to see how they relate to the story or novel as a whole. What you can be sure of is that in some way they will reflect the central ideals–reality opposition of Conrad's fiction. I shall look at just one such detail here. Just before the ship eventually leaves England after a series of infuriating and frustrating delays and accidents, at the moment when all the problems seem to have been overcome, 'Then, on a fine moonlight night, all the rats left the ship' (p.17). This is rather amusing, since rats are supposed to desert only sinking ships, and the incident may seem to be an odd detail with no bearing on the story's themes. It is, however, a portent, for ultimately the ship does sink. In the conversation Marlow and Mahon have about the incident they take the idealistic view 'that the wisdom of rats had been grossly overrated' (p. 17). Under the amusing surface of the episode lies the meaning that the ideal interpretation of the rats' unexpected action is likely to fall foul of the reality of their desertion, which it finally does in the Indian Ocean when the ship actually sinks. The point I am making here is that every small detail in the text will, in some way, be reflecting the work's larger concerns. You may have to niggle away at some details that catch your eye before you can work out their place in the scheme of things, but eventually you should always be able to see how they help create the broader impression that the story or novel conveys of what it is like to live in a world where it is natural, and even necessary, for people to have ideals, but almost certain that their ideals will lead them into difficulties and suffering, and eventually be destroyed by the nature of reality.

3

Heart of Darkness (1902)

Constructing an overall analysis

ALTHOUGH it is Conrad's shortest novel, and an early one, first published in book form in 1902, many readers have found *Heart of Darkness* to be his most complex, profound and difficult work. To some extent the initial problems are caused by the style, and other difficulties may arise from the apparent inconclusiveness of the story. While *Heart of Darkness* may not be an easy read, it is, however, tremendously exciting once you have got to grips with it. Conrad seems to be using new methods of writing in order to challenge a lot of the preconceptions of his original readers. Even now we share some of those expectations and prejudices. They get in our way when we read a novel such as *Heart of Darkness*, expecting, perhaps, a straightforward story with well-delineated and recognisable characters. This is not quite the way in which Conrad chooses to work. If you are at all confused by, or about, this great novel, you will find that it yields to an intelligently systematic approach such as we explored in the previous chapter, and the more you understand it the greater will be your appreciation and eventually admiration and excitement. Even so, after following this approach you may feel that there is still something missing in your appreciation of this curious text. This is likely to be because any initial consideration of the novel will almost certainly concentrate on themes and characters, without coming fully to grips with the novel's difficult form. So, in the second part of this chapter I present some ways of thinking about its form, but we must start with an overall analysis of the text. The page references given after quotations relate to the 1985 Penguin edition of the novel.

1 *After reading the novel, think what kind of pattern you can see in the text*

The story takes place some time in the latter part of the Victorian period, although it was published at the beginning of the twentieth century. A sailor, Marlow, whilst waiting for the tide to turn so that his ship can get under way, recounts to his passengers an experience he had as a young man. His story is about his first command. Thanks to the intervention of an aunt, a Belgian company had commissioned him to sail up the River Congo into the heart of Africa – then known as the 'dark continent', because so much of the interior remained unexplored by Europeans – to find a European ivory-trader named Kurtz. He is an employee of the same company, which has lost touch with him. Marlow feels that he will make a name for himself, have exciting adventures, learn how civilisation is being taken to Africa and return a wiser man. He receives his final instructions in Brussels, where he meets, amongst others, two rather daunting ladies and a doctor. These make him feel rather uneasy even in the excitement of picking up his first appointment as captain, and of speculating about his experiences of the dark continent. He is partly reassured about his journey when he looks at a map of Africa and sees how far European civilisation has already penetrated. He is taken to Africa in another ship and his first sight of the continent is of a French man-of-war shelling the jungle, an incident that Marlow, a very practical man who needs a good logical reason for everything he does, finds inexplicable. The French, who are dying of fever, say that the Africans in the jungle are enemies, but to Marlow it all seems absurd.

Once he reaches Africa, Marlow's expectations of finding good organisation and creative activity are disappointed: he comes across abandoned machinery, a fire-fighting water bucket with a hole in the bottom, a brickmaker with no materials with which to make bricks, and various other examples of inefficiency. Expecting to find the Europeans in Africa humane and enlightened, he discovers that the natives are cruelly ill-treated, abused and exploited. He is eager to press on up-river to explore the little-known interior, but is considerably and frustratingly delayed because his ship is grounded and cannot be repaired for lack of rivets – a major hold-up caused by a comparatively minor problem. His first impressions of European culture in Africa are entirely different from his expectations. After much frustration and hanging about, Marlow and his command, complete with African cannibals and assorted European 'pilgrims', steam up-river through the encroaching jungle. On the way his enthusiasm is at first dampened by an attack from the river bank by Africans; but it is rekindled when he picks up a Russian traveller who knows Kurtz. Marlow becomes increasingly curious about Kurtz as the stories and reports about him get ever more extravagant, and fears that the extraordinary ivory-trader will die before he can meet him. Ultimately he does meet Kurtz, and discovers that the truth of his life is even more fantastic and horrifying than the rumours had been. Not long after their meeting Kurtz dies, summing up his life in the words 'The horror! The horror!' Marlow has promised to return Kurtz's possessions to his fiancée in Brussels, and his story concludes with his meeting with the woman. Instead of telling her the truth, he tells her what she wants to hear, that the dead man's last word was her name. The novel itself ends with Marlow and his audience preparing to sail on the turning tide.

As we have seen earlier in this book, the best way to start making sense of a story is to search for a pattern in the plot. In a Conrad novel you should always be able to discover an opposition between ideals and reality at the core of the text. Think about this in relation to the main character, who also narrates the main part of the story, Marlow. He starts as a young man excited by the prospect of captaining a ship for the first time, and of having wonderful adventures. His expectations of Africa are that he will find good men doing fine work, bringing the best aspects of European civilisation to the dark continent. The reality he discovers is at best stupidity and inefficiency, and at worst moral degeneracy, injustice and cruelty. This is summed up by the fact that the main representative of Europe, Kurtz, lives in a nightmare of horror. The Europeans are in Africa not to bring enlightenment but to get as much wealth as they can, and are willing to exploit the native population in order to achieve their selfish ends. The pattern of the plot shows that the youthful idealism of Marlow meets the dark forces of the reality of greed and power. In fact his story ends with a lie to Kurtz's fiancée. This shocks Marlow himself, as he had begun by believing in the importance of the truth. The reality he met was so strong that it corrupted his ideals.

Even if the novel appears to be obscure at first reading, we can begin to make sense of it by finding the tension around which it is organised. I have tried to show that this is the conflict between ideals and reality, and that by looking at this opposition in the pattern of the plot we can get a firm grasp of the novel.

2 *Select a short passage for discussion and try to build on the ideas you have established so far*

As you begin to think about the way Conrad fleshes out the basic opposition, you will start to develop an appreciation not simply of the recurring characteristics of the work but also of this novel's unique qualities. It usually makes sense to begin by looking at a main character. In this case Marlow is the central character in the novel and I have chosen to examine the moment when he steps onto African soil for the first time. He leaves the ship on which he has arrived, and begins to walk alone to the company station:

> I came upon a boiler wallowing in the grass, then found a path leading up the hill. It turned aside for the boulders, and also for an undersized railway-truck lying there on its back with its wheels in the air. One was off. The thing looked as dead as the carcass of some animal. I came upon more pieces of decaying machinery, a stack of rusty rails. To the left a clump of trees made a shady spot, where dark things seemed to stir feebly. I blinked, the path was steep. A horn tooted to the right, and I saw the black people run. A heavy and dull detonation shook the ground, a puff of smoke came out of the cliff, and that was all. No change appeared on the face of the rock. They were building a railway. The cliff was not in the way or anything; but this objectless blasting was all the work going on.
>
> A slight clinking behind me made me turn my head. Six black men advanced in a file, toiling up the path. They walked erect and slow, balancing small baskets full of earth on their heads, and the clink kept time with their footsteps. Black rags were wound round their loins, and the short ends behind waggled to and fro like tails. I could see every rib, the joints of their limbs were like knots in a rope; each had an iron collar on his neck, and all were connected together with a chain whose bights swung between them, rhythmically clinking. Another report from the cliff made me think suddenly of that ship of war I had seen firing into a continent. It was the same kind of ominous voice; but these men could by no stretch of imagination be called enemies. They were called criminals, and the outraged law, like the bursting shells, had come to them, an insoluble mystery from the sea. All their meagre breasts panted together, the violently dilated nostrils quivered, the eyes stared stonily up-hill. They passed me within six inches, without a glance, with that complete, deathlike indifference of unhappy savages. (pp. 42–3)

It is important to remember that my aim in this book is to illustrate a method of analysis. Rather than accept my interpretation of this extract, try to build your own analysis of the passage. If you do not know where to begin an analysis remind yourself of the five steps I set out in the previous chapter.

Think about what the extract is showing, or telling, us. I would say that the passage records Marlow's first impressions of life in and around the company station. The central tension is between the unexpectedness of the sights for the inexperienced and idealistic Marlow and the harsh reality of what he sees. We can see this in the details of the passage. The first sights to greet Marlow's eyes are the boiler and railway-truck, products of European science and technology, lying, obviously uselessly, in the grass. The boiler is described as wallowing, an action more appropriate to an animal than to a piece of machinery. The truck is specifically compared to an animal, significantly a dead one. This is Marlow's first encounter with what happens to European civilisation in Africa. The unexpected bleakness of his initial impressions is confirmed by further details: decaying machinery and rusty nails; the pointless activity of blasting the rock. Ideally all these should have been producing something constructive, but they appear to be futile objects and actions. The details of the second paragraph of the passage take this idea further by showing that European civilisation is not merely incompetent – although that in itself is against young Marlow's idealistic expectations – but actually cruel and brutal. The details move from a presentation of machinery to men. Marlow first sees that the six Africans carrying earth are almost naked – notice that the rags they wear give the impression that the men have tails, like animals – then that they are practically starving, and finally that they are brutally chained together. This reinforces the idea that the Africans are being treated more like animals than like human criminals. Within the ideals of European justice criminals have rights, and should be treated with some humanity, but these Africans can hardly understand what has happened to them and have a deathlike indifference, the reality of which shocks the inexperienced Marlow, who 'by no stretch of imagination' can see them as enemies.

How do we relate the impression of these details to the novel as a whole? I have tried to show how the passage turns on a central tension between ideals and reality, while at the beginning of this chapter I suggested that *Heart of Darkness* was written partly to challenge its original readers' preconceptions. At the height of British imperialism the kind of passage we have been considering certainly did that. The novel as a whole can still make us think hard about the value of our civilisation when it is placed in a crisis situation. Conrad sees the dark forces of reality lurking beneath the veneer of what we think we are. The distinctive style of the extract supports this interpretation. Marlow himself, the narrator of his own experiences, cannot entirely see, or understand, what is going on. There are dark things he cannot quite make out; the quality of the light makes him blink; he is surprised by the sounds he hears, and then is disturbed by an ominous noise that reminds him of the warship's futile shelling of the jungle. Finally he seems to become invisible as the natives pass within six inches of him without appearing to notice that he is there. The European Marlow seems hardly to exist any more. The reader's own ideals are taken into the story and meet reality through Marlow's eyes and ears.

3 *Select a second passage for discussion*

An analysis of a slightly later experience of Marlow's should now prove productive. He journeys on to the Central Station a little further up-river, where he is to pick up the steamboat that is to be his first command. The boat is grounded and cannot be repaired for lack of rivets. Marlow has his first long conversation in Africa with a European, a brickmaker who cannot get any straw with which to make bricks, and who does not care; Marlow, by contrast, is very frustrated by the delay caused by incompetence:

> I demanded rivets. There was a way – for an intelligent man. He changed his manner; became very cold, and suddenly began to talk about a hippopotamus; wondered whether sleeping on board the steamer (I stuck to my salvage night and day) I wasn't disturbed. There was an old hippo that had the bad habit of getting out on the bank and roaming at night over the station grounds. The pilgrims used to turn out in a body and empty every rifle they could lay hands on at him. Some even had sat up o' nights for him. All this energy was wasted, though. 'That animal has a charmed life,' he said; 'but you can say this only of brutes in this country. No man – you apprehend me? – no man here bears a charmed life.' He stood there for a moment in the moonlight with his delicate hooked nose set a little askew, and his mica eyes glittering without a wink, then, with a curt Good-night, he strode off. I could see he was disturbed and considerably puzzled, which made me feel more hopeful than I had been for days. It was a great comfort to turn from that chap to my influential friend, the battered, twisted, ruined, tin-pot steamboat. I clambered on board. She rang under my feet like an empty Huntley & Palmers biscuit-tin kicked along a gutter; she was nothing so

> solid in make, and rather less pretty in shape, but I had expended enough hard work on her to make me love her. No influential friend would have served me better. She had given me a chance to come out a bit – to find out what I could do. No, I don't like work. I had rather laze about and think of all the fine things that can be done. I don't like work, – no man does – but I like what is in the work; – the chance to find yourself. Your own reality – for yourself, not for others – what no other man can ever know. They can only see the mere show, and can never tell what it really means. (pp. 59–60)

The extract compares the responses of a European who has been in the dark continent for a long time, and those of Marlow, who is a relative newcomer and not yet completely disillusioned. This statement takes us to the central opposition in the passage: Marlow's continuing idealism, his belief in positive values, and the brickmaker's cynical and negative view of reality. Once again the details support the interpretation. The brickmaker changes the subject of the conversation from the practically useful rivets that would allow Marlow to get on with his job of captaining the boat, and expatiates upon yet another example of futile activity – the pilgrims, who are other intruding Europeans, obsessionally trying to kill a natural inhabitant of the dark continent, a hippo. The ideal activity would be to do something creative; the reality is that the pilgrims are interested only in destruction. The brickmaker's final comment implies that, although the brutes cannot be destroyed, the reality of Africa does destroy men. At this stage in the novel Marlow's response is to cling to his idealism, to insist on the value of his own reality – which is found through work, by means of creative activity.

I hope I have shown how the details in this extract help to reflect the tension between ideals and reality that runs through the whole novel. The passage also marks another stage in Marlow's own development. He turns from the brickmaker to his real friend – which is the boat, not an actual person – showing how as a comparative outsider he is alienated from the older colonists. When we look at the distinctive aspects of the style, however, we can appreciate that Marlow has changed since his arrival in Africa. Working on the boat has, Marlow observes, given him the chance to find himself, to know himself rather than the image he projects, the self that other people see. It is part of Conrad's style that we are not quite sure what this reality is, and that the tone perhaps suggests some doubt about its solidity. The boat that now represents his reality is, by Marlow's own admission, a ruined tin-pot affair that resembles an empty biscuit-tin rattling along in a gutter. The idealised reality he was confident of in Europe has been seriously challenged, and Marlow has begun to substitute for it a much more battered one. Conrad does not say this outright – because that is not the way he writes – but we can infer it from the details and tone of the passage.

4 *Select a third passage for discussion*

As Marlow is both narrator and central character, it has been necessary to spend some time considering his role in the novel. Now I should like to move on to the next most important character – Kurtz, the man Marlow has been sent to retrieve from the heart of the jungle. It is an aspect of Conrad's curious style that this very important character actually appears only in a fairly short section of the novel; but his influence is all-pervading. Marlow learns fragments of information about him as he journeys closer to the heart of darkness. I have chosen a passage in which Marlow talks about Kurtz's background and relates it to the report, or pamphlet as he calls it, that Kurtz has written:

> His mother was half-English, his father was half-French. All Europe contributed to the making of Kurtz; and by-and-by I learned that, most appropriately, the International Society for the Suppression of Savage Customs had entrusted him with the making of a report, for its future guidance. And he had written it, too. I've seen it. I've read it. It was eloquent, vibrating with eloquence, but too high-strung, I think. Seventeen pages of close writing he had found time for! But this must have been before his – let us say – nerves, went wrong, and caused him to preside at certain midnight dances ending with unspeakable rites, which – as far as I reluctantly gathered from what I heard at various times – were offered up to him – do you understand? – to Mr Kurtz himself. But it was a beautiful piece of writing. The opening paragraph, however, in the light of later information, strikes me now as ominous. He began with the argument that we whites, from the point of development we have arrived at, 'must necessarily appear to them [savages] in the nature of supernatural beings – we approach them with the might as of a deity,' and so on, and so on. 'By the simple exercise of our will we can exert a power for good practically unbounded,' etc., etc. From that point he soared and took me with him. The peroration was magnificent, though difficult to remember, you know. It gave me the notion of an exotic Immensity ruled by an august Benevolence. It made me tingle with enthusiasm. This was the unbounded power of eloquence – of words – of

> burning noble words. There were no practical hints to interrupt the magic current of phrases, unless a kind of note at the foot of the last page, scrawled evidently much later, in an unsteady hand, may be regarded as the exposition of a method. It was very simple, and at the end of that moving appeal to every altruistic sentiment it blazed at you, luminous and terrifying, like a flash of lightning in a serene sky: 'Exterminate all the brutes!' (pp. 86–7)

The extract begins by giving us a few facts about Kurtz, and goes on to present Marlow's impression of Kurtz's report with some short quotations from it. The central opposition is between Kurtz's eloquence and his desire to bring civilisation to Africa, to exert a power for unbounded good – his idealism – and his notions of racial superiority and inferiority that led him to add the diabolical phrase 'Exterminate all the brutes!' – the reality of the darker social and psychological forces at work in this man who to some extent represents 'All Europe'. The details of the passage, the quotations from Kurtz's report, illustrate this tension; but it is not simply a question of the man starting off as an idealist and somehow going mad along the way. Marlow notes that the seeds of Kurtz's destructiveness were evident right at the beginning of his pamphlet, in the assertion of godlike white racial superiority. The conflict between goodness and the reality of the darker forces is at the very heart of Kurtz's personality. The effect of the report on Marlow is significant too. There is still something of the idealist in Marlow, and Kurtz's eloquence on behalf of altruism appeals to him; the practical sailor tingles with enthusiasm. Yet Marlow specifically states that there are no practical hints in Kurtz's pamphlet. It seems that Marlow's idealism is seduced by the unbounded power of burning, noble words. It is, perhaps, a weakness of idealism that it is to some extent innocent and therefore vulnerable to a dark reality – the brutal truth behind the words – that it is unable to recognise.

We can relate this to the novel as a whole in two ways: by seeing the experience as part of Marlow's personal development, and by seeing Kurtz as a kind of emblem of Europe. Although *Heart of Darkness* is a novel peopled by individuals, it is not a text simply about personal experience. On a wider level all of Europe is involved in the colonisation of Africa (as, politically, it was). The imperialists do not necessarily set off as evil men – Kurtz is a kind of missionary as well as a trader, and may have had genuinely good intentions; but the reality of the imperial experience changes the colonists by bringing out the greed, egoism and destructiveness that is latent and suppressed in a purely European context. One feature of the style here is the irony that Kurtz, the savage exterminator, is an emissary of the International Society for the Suppression of Savage Customs. Marlow remarks that this is most appropriate, and it is difficult to tell whether he means that literally or ironically. Again Conrad is not straightforward in his presentation of Marlow's character and we can only speculate about an interpretation.

5 *Select a fourth passage for discussion*

Having considered Kurtz's ideas we should perhaps now look at the character more directly. I think the most intense passage concerning Kurtz is that describing his death:

> One evening coming in with a candle I was startled to hear him say a little tremulously, 'I am lying here in the dark waiting for death.' The light was within a foot of his eyes. I forced myself to murmur, 'Oh, nonsense!' and stood over him as if transfixed.
>
> Anything approaching the change that came over his features I have never seen before, and hope never to see again. Oh, I wasn't touched. I was fascinated. It was as though a veil had been rent. I saw on that ivory face the expression of sombre pride, of ruthless power, of craven terror – of an intense and hopeless despair. Did he live his life again in every detail of desire, temptation, and surrender during that supreme moment of complete knowledge? He cried in a whisper at some image, at some vision – he cried out twice, a cry that was no more than a breath –
>
> 'The horror! The horror!' (p. 111)

The extract is mainly concerned with describing Kurtz's last moments of life. There is a tension between the watching Marlow, who still has not entirely lost his ideals and who offers the dying man the decent comforting phrase, and Kurtz, who, facing the imminent reality of death, realises a hopeless despair and horror. The language is very vivid, intensifying the significance of the event. Marlow momentarily loses power over his own actions; he is transfixed and fascinated, as though hypnotised, being given a glimpse of something he had never expected to see. The reality he sees is a series of changing emotions registered on the dying man's face: sombre pride is followed by ruthless power, both suggesting strength, but then Kurtz shows craven terror, and that is followed by intense despair, which is expressed in his final words. It seems that reality is even more dire than can be illustrated by the novel as a whole. We have noticed before how the novel seems not to commit itself one way or another on matters of interpretation, and here too an aspect of style is that Marlow is unable to pin down what is actually happening. The narrator observes the changes on Kurtz's face but does not know exactly what causes them, or their meaning. Marlow can ask a question about what Kurtz finally sees, but cannot answer it. This kind of feature was one of the things in my mind when, at the beginning of this chapter, I commented on the apparently deliberately inconclusive nature of the story.

6 *Have I achieved a sufficiently complex sense of the novel?*

I have made a number of points about imperialism, or colonialism, and these reflect the importance of the political aspects of the novel. People who think European imperialism of the Victorian period was bad applaud Conrad for exposing its vices; those who consider that it did more good than harm think Conrad was unfair. That debate will continue, but I think it is interesting that the novel is not merely about nineteenth-century politics: there is a broader historical perspective on the theme of conquest.

Before Marlow starts telling the story of his adventures in Africa he makes an observation about the Thames and London:

> But darkness was here yesterday. Imagine the feelings of a commander of a fine . . . trireme in the Mediterranean, ordered suddenly to the north; run overland across the Gauls in a hurry; put in charge of one of these craft the legionaries – a wonderful lot of handy men they must have been, too – used to build. . . . Imagine him here – the very end of the world, a sea the colour of lead, a sky the colour of smoke, a kind of ship about as rigid as a concertina – and going up this river with stores, or orders, or what you like. Sand-banks, marshes, forests, savages, – precious little to eat fit for a civilised man, nothing but Thames water to drink . . . cold, fog, tempests, disease, exile, and death – death skulking in the air, in the water, in the bush. They must have been dying like flies here. . . . They were men enough to face the darkness. . . . The fascination of the abomination. . . . (pp. 30–1)

Marlow is putting himself, his listeners, and us, in the position of an adventurer of the ancient Roman Empire. The opposition we found in the main story occurs here too: an ideal life in command of a fine ship in warm, calm, friendly waters, suddenly meeting the reality of an uncivilised and extremely inhospitable Britain. All the details

Marlow outlines in his introduction – forests, ferocious savages, a hostile climate, disease, the permanent presence of death, a kind of tin-pot old boat – are paralleled in the main story. The ancient Roman conquerors, like their more recent counterparts, also had to face the darkness of unexplored, dangerous territory. I think Conrad is suggesting a universality and a continuity of human nature – that it is similar, even in its political and social organisation, in different places and times. The stronger society and culture abuses and exploits the weaker simply because it can get away with it, even if the original intention, the initial motivation, was basically altruistic, or idealistic. The darker forces of human nature and organisation are a universal psychological and political reality. The reality of external nature, that which cannot be controlled by mankind, is that it makes men pay for their forays into new, unknown, dark places by inflicting madness and horrible deaths upon them. The historical perspective is that it has all happened before, and therefore that it is likely to occur again. The Roman Empire was mighty but it fell; Britain had been dark and uncivilised, but had risen into light and civilisation. At the time when the novel was published (in 1902) Britain had a great empire, but it had gone into dark places and was likely, sooner or later, to follow the Roman Empire into disintegration. We know that this did indeed happen, but for Conrad's original readers, at the glorious noontide of empire, that was an extremely challenging idea. Whatever you think of my argument, the important point to grasp is that Conrad was not just writing about one time and place and not just interested in contemporary events; rather – and more profoundly – he was interested in the fundamental question of what happens when humanity's aspirations and ideals come up against its own and external realities.

Well, that is my conclusion. Your analysis of the text may lead you to different interpretations. What I do hope is clear at this point, however, is that the method of analysing the evidence here is very simple and straightforward. The controlling principle throughout is to keep to a few ideas, then interpret the details in the light of those ideas. You should then find yourself steadily constructing your own coherent view of the text.

Aspects of the novel

So far the emphasis in this chapter has been on characters and themes in the novel. To discover more, keep considering relevant scenes. For instance, you might want to think about a character that I haven't had room to consider here. The Russian, the character Marlow refers to as the 'harlequin', is an example. He is a great admirer of Kurtz, and throws a slightly different light on him. By looking at a scene or two in which the harlequin appears you should be able to expand your understanding of the novel as a whole.

However, at this stage you may want to move away from direct consideration of characters and themes to a broader issue. You may, for instance, wish to think about the novel's peculiar elusiveness – the way in which questions are sometimes raised but not answered – and the related factor of the way in which the story is told, its narrative structure. The best way to organise your thinking, as with constructing an overall analysis, is to focus attention on short extracts. This will help you to avoid simply offering unsubstantiated assertions that the novel is complex or incomprehensible. You must take a close look at the text in order to understand what is going on, and why. You could begin by considering how Marlow is introduced as a narrator, or storyteller:

> The yarns of seamen have a direct simplicity, the whole meaning of which lies within the shell of a cracked nut. But Marlow was not typical (if his propensity to spin yarns be excepted), and to him the meaning of an episode was not inside like a kernel but outside, enveloping the tale which brought it out only as a glow brings out a haze, in the likeness of one of these misty halos that sometimes are made visible by the spectral illumination of moonshine. (p. 30)

Some readers may think this passage is not important, that any story is just a story. But I think Conrad is telling us that this adventure has to be read differently from others. We may relate what is said here about the narrative form to the tension that is central to *Heart of Darkness* as a whole. There is an ideal way, the traditional method, of telling stories; but this novel deals with a different kind of reality in a different manner. Ordinary tales, according to the extract, have a direct simplicity – crack them open and the meaning spills out obviously, just like taking the kernel out of a nutshell. You have the whole experience complete and in front of you without any doubts or uncertainties. Reality and meaning, however, may not be that neat and tidy. This tale works through odd impressions, a glow here and there in a haze or mist that we cannot see through clearly. Instead of the clear view of the ideal, this novel is going to offer us illuminated incidents and moments that we have to bring together to interpret. The phrase 'spectral illumination of moonshine' indicates that the light will be shifting, and may at times seem unreal – but will nevertheless be revealing a reality, no matter how unusual or unexpected. We do not have a narrator, or author, who knows everything about all the events, and who can see into the minds of all the characters. Marlow has only his own point of view, and what other people tell him from time to time. This is less like the reality of the ideal novel, in which everything is comprehensible; more like the reality we live in, where our knowledge and understanding are incomplete.

The novel is written in such a way as to remind us occasionally that it is Marlow's personal story, in his own words, that we are reading. At one point in the novel Marlow breaks off his narration, by now occurring in the dark, in order to light his pipe, and we read,

> There was a pause of profound stillness, then a match flared, and Marlow's lean face appeared, worn, hollow, with downward folds and dropped eyelids, with an aspect of concentrated attention: and as he took vigorous draws at his pipe, it seemed to retreat and advance out of the night in the regular flicker of the tiny flame. The match went out.
>
> (p. 83)

This passage reminds us that Marlow is the storyteller as well as a participant in the action he is describing. It implies a contrast between the young, idealistic character in the story, and the older man telling the tale, whose face is worn and hollow with the reality of experience. The flaring of the match illuminates the scene momentarily and dramatically, its flickering casts a lesser glow, and finally darkness returns. This reminds us that the novel itself is written in such a way as to achieve just such an effect, the sudden illumination of a scene before it recedes back into a gloom in which we may not be able to understand it.

So, a feature of the form of the book is that it draws attention to itself, whereas the traditional novel often pretends it just exists, that there is no particular author or narrator. The narrative form in this case reminds us that Marlow is the storyteller, that his understanding is limited, and implies that here is one man who, like you, cannot know everything – but think about what he does tell you. You can find other places in which Marlow's role as narrator is highlighted in order to emphasise its importance. It is a central feature of *Heart of Darkness*. When discussing the role of the narrator in the novel, always focus on a passage – the last paragraph of the novel provides further evidence for you to work on – and by analysing it thoroughly you will see how its style works, and in what ways it contributes to the ideas and meaning of the novel as a whole. Conrad is always trying to provoke us into thought, especially about the nature of ideals and of reality.

I hope I have shown that the novel's complex narrative organisation, and the elusiveness of the text at times, is not so difficult or obscure if you set about exploring it systematically. It is easy to be vague, and to fall into the trap of presenting loose impressions rather than a thoroughly argued case. By working through a few passages you should be able to construct a detailed discussion of the issue. What I hope is also evident is the importance of keeping your central ideas clear, and that is quite easy providing you always refer back to the idea of a tension between ideals and reality.

An important topic about which there is disagreement among critics, and which is related to the other points discussed so far, is the language of *Heart of Darkness*. It is all too easy to plunge into this debate with a lot of random observations that leave you no clearer at the end of the process than you were at the beginning. If, however, you tackle the subject systematically by exploring a few passages and using the idea of a tension between ideals and reality you will come out with a coherent argument. One of the features of the novel's language that irritates some readers is the repetition. The novelist, they say, seems more interested in creating atmosphere than in getting on with the story. Once he has said the jungle is dark, they add, it does not need to be reiterated. Generalised observations, though, do not lead anywhere, and in order to appreciate why words and descriptions are repeated you must analyse relevant passages.

Choose a scene in which there are various kinds of darkness, for instance. One example might be when Marlow is walking through the jungle at the edge of the company station:

> Black shapes crouched, lay, sat between the trees leaning against the trunks, clinging to the earth, half coming out, half effaced within the dim light, in all the attitudes of pain, abandonment and despair . . . nothing but black shadows of disease and starvation, lying confusedly in the greenish gloom. . . . These moribund shapes were free as air – and nearly as thin. I began to distinguish the gleam of the eyes under the trees.

> Then, glancing down, I saw a face near my hand. The black bones reclined at full length with one shoulder against the tree. . . . (p. 44)

This does strike me as very atmospheric writing, but I do not think it is atmosphere simply for its own sake. The black shapes at the beginning of the extract are Africans. Partly they are described in that way because in the darkness of the jungle and the dim light they are difficult for Marlow actually to make out; but, more importantly, describing them as indistinguishable shapes emphasises the way in which those men have been dehumanised. They cannot be distinguished from the trees or the earth, they are not upright as men ideally should be, and so they are merely shapes. In the gloom they cannot *have* shadows, but they have *become* shadows – rather than human beings. An ideal of what men are, or should be, lies by implication behind the descriptions. Ideally the Africans should be representatives of mankind; in reality they are almost less than nothing – which is a reflection of the way in which they are treated. The gloom is, I think, not just a feature of the jungle but a comment on the moral atmosphere that has created the cruel brutality that is the main point of the episode. We have to read it as a metaphor, or symbol, because a simple, literal reading does not make sense. The phrase 'The black bones' is not literally true, because we know that in fact all bones are white. The words stress the Africans' thinness, caused by disease and starvation; they have become bundles of bones, living skeletons, scarcely recognisable as human beings.

I am arguing that the repetition of images of blackness and darkness takes the writing beyond physical description, into a metaphorical comment on the reality of the moral depravity Marlow discovers. We read the episode in relation to Marlow's own idealism at this point in the novel, and the ideals of the people who sent him there. All the moral blackness Marlow finds in the gloom of the jungle is a comment on the naïve ideals of his aunt and her influential friends in Europe, those people who have dispatched Marlow as a sort of idealised missionary rather than a practical sailor: 'one of the Workers, with a capital – you know. Something like an emissary of light, something like a lower sort of apostle' (pp. 38–9). In this instance the image is of a light that does not fully penetrate the darkness of the jungle, or what is happening there in reality. The journey he undertakes into the heart of darkness is literally into the centre of the dark – because unknown, unexplored – continent; but it is also a journey into the darkness that exists at the core of European civilisation, and the dark heart of individual people. These are the dark forces of reality.

One of the reasons why I enjoy reading and rereading this novel is that there are so many layers of meaning in it. You do not have to agree with my interpretations, but you must always argue your case from the evidence of the text. If you wish to pursue any of these ideas or issues on your own, choose a passage and work through it systematically, as I have, until you reach conclusions, whatever they are, based on and expressed by coherent argument. In order to achieve that effectively, you need to see that the basic tension in Conrad's fiction is a conflict between ideals and reality: that framework will guide you into an intelligent interpretation of individual passages.

4

Nostromo (1904)

Constructing an overall analysis

Nostromo was Conrad's first long novel to gain serious critical acclaim. When I first read it, as an ordinary reader – before I eventually became a mature student – I found it totally confusing. I also felt that frustration we experience when we know something exciting and important is happening, but cannot quite grasp it. Many years later, returning to the book, I realised that the excitement comes partly from the difficulty. Conrad presents ideas in an elusive way, and in picking our way through them we broaden our own minds. For example, by presenting events in a complicated time sequence, which we have to work hard at to understand, Conrad makes us see things in different ways, from diverse points of view. *Nostromo* is something of an adventure story, partly a political novel; it has elements of romance, and it explores philosophical questions. All these features can be brought together by the kind of analysis we have been conducting in this book. The page references given after quotations relate to the 1981 Penguin edition of the novel.

1 *After reading the novel, think what kind of pattern you can see in the text*

It is worth trying to sort out the plot, since this is presented in a complicated way but will reveal some kind of pattern that we can later develop. The novel was published in 1904, but the action takes place in the latter part of the nineteenth century. The time is not specific but events are written of as having occurred in the not-too-distant past. The story is set in a fictitious country – Costaguana, with a capital called Sulaco – in South America. The country had long ago been settled by Spanish colonists, but the population now consists of native South Americans, the descendants of the Spanish settlers and an assortment of people with English, French and Italian backgrounds – some of them immigrants from Europe, others actually born in Costaguana and having a dual allegiance. German and North American trade and commercial interests are also involved in the country. Like many South American countries of the period – and the novel is still relevant today – it was politically unstable, lurching from one brutal and incompetent dictatorship to another. The regime of Bento Guzman had been particularly repressive and was eventually replaced by one rather less savage led by President Ribiera.

One aspect of the novel deals with the threat to this dictatorship by the opportunist rebel Montero. The Europeans either support the existing Ribierist government or the idea of Sulaco separating from the rest of the country in a bid for independence. A key figure in this decision is Charles Gould, who, against his now-dead father's advice, has reopened the old family-owned San Tomé silver mine. This provides Costaguana with most of its wealth and no government can succeed without controlling it, or without the support of Gould. Gould and his wife believe the wealth of the mine can be used to create social stability and justice. Montero's rebels intend to appropriate the mine and instigate a savagely repressive regime. As the rebels advance on Sulaco a very large shipment of silver is brought down from the mine in the mountains to the town's harbour to be shipped off to California to buy arms and support. As the rebels close in, the silver is sailed out on a sea-going barge, a lighter, crewed by two trusted men: Nostromo, because of his practical skills, and his pride in his reputation as incorruptible; and Martin Decoud, who has convinced Gould that he too has political ideals. Unknown to them they have a stowaway, the German trader Hirsch. He panics and causes the lighter to collide, ironically, with the ship bringing rebel forces into Sulaco harbour. Nostromo and Decoud manage to beach the lighter on an island and bury the cargo of silver in a safe hiding place. In Sulaco everyone, including the rebels, believes the silver to have been sunk and Nostromo and Decoud to have been drowned. Nostromo swims back to the town and for the purpose of fooling the rebels allows everyone to continue thinking that the silver is at the bottom of the sea. As he discovers how the other Europeans have used him, Nostromo becomes increasingly disillusioned with their attitudes. In the meantime Decoud is left alone for several days to brood on events and on his own life, hopes and actions. The isolation drives him to despair and he drowns himself, weighting his pockets with two bars of the silver.

Meanwhile Gould has become disillusioned with politics and politicians of all kinds, and has arranged for the San Tomé mine to be blown up and completely destroyed if the rebels attempt to take control of it. Their inability to find the lost hoard of silver or obtain access to the mine contributes to the rebels' military and political failure. So, the rebels are defeated, law and order is re-established. The buried silver is still thought to have been irretrievably sunk, and the embittered Nostromo lives the life of a rich trader by secretly digging it up a bar at a time. He has a long-lasting arrangement to marry Linda Viola, one of the daughters of Nostromo's friend and admirer Giorgio Viola, but he falls in love with her sister Giselle. Nostromo and Giselle meet secretly at night but are seen by Giorgio, who, in an act of supreme irony, thinking Nostromo an opportunist suitor, shoots him. Nostromo takes the secret of the hidden treasure to his grave.

All of this happens, or at least is narrated to us, in a most convoluted way, the order of events not following a chronological sequence as in most novels. It is further complicated by the fact that there is more than one narrator, so that sometimes the same event is presented in different chapters from different points of view. The switches back and forth in time, and the changes of narrator, can be confusing; but, once the basic plot is outlined in this manner, can you see any pattern in it? Start your analysis by thinking of the possibility of a central tension between ideals and reality. The character who is most trusted, Nostromo, in effect steals the silver and attempts to run off with the sister he is not engaged to – thus also betraying his fiancée and his friend, her father. Nostromo betrays the trust placed in him partly because he thinks his trust in others has been betrayed – that in reality the other Europeans had taken advantage of his ideals – and partly because of the dark emotional forces at work within him. Decoud's ideals are unable to withstand the reality of isolation. The fates of Nostromo and Decoud illustrate the dark realities of greed, betrayal and despair that lie behind Charles Gould's idealist belief that the silver can create justice and happiness. Those characters with ideals, illusions or hopes all meet some kind of reality that destroys what they believe in. This evidence confirms, I think, that an opposition between ideals and reality lies at the heart of the novel.

Having grasped some kind of coherent pattern it is worth testing our ideas by looking at a specific passage of the novel.

2 *Select a short passage for discussion and try to build on the ideas you have established so far*

It is often a good idea to start by looking at a character who appears fairly early in the novel. Although Nostromo gives his name to the novel he is not a major character early in the story, and I have chosen a passage not too far into it that centres on Charles Gould and his wife. Gould's father had closed the silver mine and forbidden Charles to reopen it, because the previous dictator, the greedy and brutal Bento, had imposed increasingly heavy and arbitrary taxes on it. Charles and his wife have been discussing his father's despair and Gould's own belief in the future of both the country and the silver mine:

> 'He did not like to be robbed. It exasperated him,' said Charles Gould. 'But the image will serve well enough. What is wanted here is law, good faith, order, security. Any one can declaim about these things, but I pin my faith to material interests. Only let the material interests once get a firm footing, and they are bound to impose the conditions on which alone they can continue to exist. That's how your money-making is justified here in the face of lawlessness and disorder. It is justified because the security which it demands must be shared with an oppressed people. A better justice will come afterwards. That's your ray of hope.' His arm pressed her slight form closer to his side for a moment. 'And who knows whether in that sense even the San Tomé mine may not become that little rift in the darkness which poor father despaired of ever seeing?'
>
> She glanced up at him with admiration. He was competent; he had given a vast shape to the vagueness of her unselfish ambitions.
>
> 'Charley,' she said, 'you are splendidly disobedient.' (p. 81)

This extract depicts the arguments that Charles Gould uses to justify disobeying his father's injunction – made because of the trouble it had caused and the despair that ensued – not to reopen the San Tomé silver mine. The main conflict is between Charles's idealist belief in the power for good of material interests, the wealth created by the silver, and the social and economic reality that politicians in the past had been robbers. If we look at the details of the extract we can see that against the danger of a robbing government Charles puts the ideals of 'law, good faith, order, security', and believes that these ideals will be realised by material interests. He is not arguing a simple case in favour of capitalist self-interest, because his contention is that the wealth created by the mine will benefit everyone, by bringing security and so promoting justice. He sees the silver as a means of helping all those oppressed by lawlessness and disorder. Charles's idealistic optimism is shared by his wife because it is in keeping with her own altruistic ideals – the possibility of reopening the mine gives a sense of direction 'to the vagueness of her unselfish ambitions'. Both characters share a desire to make the world a better place, to improve reality.

In relating the passage to the novel as a whole perhaps you can see that Charles Gould's decision here is optimistic, and a catalyst for the rest of the novel's action as the silver becomes a major factor in the Costaguanan civil war. The style of the passage expresses the central tension between ideals and reality by using images of light and dark. Charles hopes, and so does Mrs Gould, that the San Tomé mine will become a rift in the darkness, like a ray of light, a 'ray of hope'. This light of hope will shine through the dark political realities that drove Gould senior into despair. I find it interesting that the word Charles uses to describe his economic and political theory is 'faith'. It suggests a blind belief in the existence of something that is not provable. Economics and politics are aspects of the real world, the world we can verify through our experience; but faith is related to an ideal of existence. Here it is an almost religious belief that material interests will bring out the best in mankind. History teaches us that this is not very likely. The minute detail of that single word expresses the central tension between ideals and reality. Once we have learnt to interpret the text we can see, even at this early stage, that Charles's hopes are going to come up against many difficulties in the effort to impose them on the realities of economic and political life. This is a subtle feature of Conrad's style that requires extremely attentive reading, but is exciting when we are able to unlock the clues. We can see a further example of this sublety of style in Mrs Gould's concluding description of her husband as 'splendidly disobedient'. She uses the term admiringly, because his disobedience fits in with her own ideals, but we must remember that he is disobeying a dead father's wishes. That is not really a splendid action, and was even less likely to be thought so when the novel was written. There is a touch of the foolhardy in it, a neglecting of family trust and a casting-aside of the value of the older generation's experience through an idealistic naïveté. The paradox in Mrs Gould's statement should remind us not to accept the words at face value, but to analyse them, and look beyond their surface.

3 *Select a second passage for discussion*

In order to gain a good basis of understanding I have decided to concentrate specifically on characters. As Nostromo is a central figure I have moved a little further into the novel, to a discussion of his character between Decoud, the dandified journalist, and Mrs Gould:

> 'He talked with his usual carelessness, which, if he had been anything else but a common sailor, I would call a pose or an affectation.'
>
> Decoud interrupting himself, looked at Mrs Gould curiously.
>
> 'Upon the whole,' he continued, 'I suppose he expects something to his advantage from it. You mustn't forget that he does not exercise his extraordinary power over the lower classes without a certain amount of personal risk and without a great profusion in spending his money. One must pay in some way or other for such a solid thing as individual prestige. He told me after we made friends at a dance, in a Posada kept by a Mexican just outside the walls, that he had come here to make his fortune. I suppose he looks upon his prestige as a sort of investment.'
>
> 'Perhaps he prizes it for its own sake,' Mrs Gould said in a tone as if she were repelling an underserved aspersion. 'Viola, the Garibaldino, with whom he has lived for some years, calls him the Incorruptible.'
>
> (p. 189)

This extract offers us two views of Nostromo. Decoud is rather caustic, suspecting Nostromo of striking a pose and of actually being an opportunist under the cloak of his apparent disinterest. Mrs Gould states the opinion that in fact is most prevalent in the novel, that Nostromo is a fine character. She expresses this partly as her own view, but also supports it by bringing in the judgement of someone else – Giorgio Viola, who is Nostromo's landlord and friend, a fellow Italian, an old follower of the military and political unifier of Italy, Garibaldi, and therefore a man who should know something about leadership and politics. We can summarise this difference of opinion about Nostromo as that between the view of him as an ideal, unselfish man, and the view of him as a self-interested realist.

The details of the passage clearly contribute to the expression of this central opposition between ideals and reality. Decoud sees Nostromo's pose of carelessness, or disinterest, in economic terms: his prestige is an investment, and one that will grow into his fortune. According to Decoud, when Nostromo spends money he is not so much spending it as investing it, purchasing his power over the lower classes. Nostromo takes risks, in Decoud's opinion, for the same reason. This certainly attributes a great deal of deviousness to Nostromo. Mrs Gould's response is to argue that Nostromo, as an ideal man, may value his reputation and prestige simply for its own sake, and insists that he is 'the Incorruptible'. Relating this conversation to our knowledge of the whole novel we may be able to pick out the threads of irony that make Conrad's fiction both so complex and so rewarding. Nostromo is corrupted, but partly because he feels betrayed by the other Europeans such as Decoud. The irony, then, is that Decoud is partially right in the long run, but is unable to see that he is contributing to the process of corruption. Perhaps Decoud comes over to you in this extract as something of a snob. He uses terms such as 'common sailor' and 'lower classes' in a derogatory way; and his own concern with social position is reflected in his inability to appreciate that anyone else might take it less seriously. In fact, when isolated on the island while trying to get the silver away from Sulaco, Decoud, deprived of his social position, suffers such a crisis of identity as to fall into despair and suicide. There is thus a further irony in the fact that some of the characteristics Decoud attributes to Nostromo in a tone of criticism apply to himself. Decoud is unaware of this reality. We might also argue that Mrs Gould repels Decoud's undeserved aspersion because she wants Nostromo to be an ideal man, for she too has an idealist approach to life: the 'vast shape ... of her unselfish ambitions' that we encountered in the previous extract. Both Mrs Gould and Decoud interpret Nostromo's character in the way that suits their own interests and aspirations; neither is entirely concerned with the reality of the man.

Having established some ideas it is now worth moving on to a later passage in the novel to discover how the themes are worked out in detail.

4 *Select a third passage for discussion*

In considering any aspect of the novel you should look for the opposition between ideals and reality. For instance, you might now consider a character I haven't looked at: Captain Mitchell, for example. If you consider the way he presents his own role in defeating Montero's rebels you may conclude that he has played a heroic, or at least central, part. But when you analyse other characters' opinions of, and attitudes towards, Mitchell you will find a quite different interpretation. Conrad gives us few objective facts, so that part of the fascination of the book is in trying to work out where the truth actually lies. Mitchell perhaps tends to idealise his role, whilst other people are more concerned with what they see as the reality of that tense period of invasion. In any event you can begin to work towards an understanding of any character or situation by using your ideas on a central tension in the text. Approach the situation or character in the light of the way in which it is constructed on or around that central opposition. Sometimes it may seem rather obvious, but that isn't important: what is important in all literary criticism, the quality that will bring your feeling for the novel to life, is the way in which you develop your appreciation of extracts in the light of your basic ideas. All incidents, circumstances and characters will repay analysis. I want to look at the development of Charles Gould, so I have chosen a passage from later in the novel, when it looks as though the political battle will be lost, and he is having doubts about the wisdom of disobeying his father's instructions about the mine:

> His taciturnity, assumed with a purpose, had prevented him from tampering openly with his thoughts; but the Gould Concession had insidiously corrupted his judgement. He might have known, he said to himself, leaning over the balustrade of the corridor, that Ribierism could never come to anything. The mine had corrupted his judgement by making him sick of bribing and intriguing merely to have his work left alone from day to day. Like his father, he did not like to be robbed. It exasperated him. He had persuaded himself that, apart from higher considerations, the backing up of Don José's hopes of reform was good business. He had gone forth into the senseless fray as his poor uncle, whose sword hung on the wall of his study, had gone forth – in the defence of the commonest decencies of organised society. Only his weapon was the wealth of the mine, more far-reaching and subtle than the honest blade of steel fitted into a simple brass guard.
>
> More dangerous to the wielder, too, this weapon of wealth, double-edged with the cupidity and misery of mankind, steeped in all the voices of self-indulgence as in a concoction of poisonous roots, tainting the very cause for which it is drawn, always ready to turn awkwardly in the hand. There was nothing for it now but to go on using it. But he promised himself to see it shattered into small bits before he let it be wrenched from his grasp. (pp. 302–3)

In this extract Charles Gould is thinking about the possible consequences of his earlier decision to reopen the San Tomé silver mine. The earlier conflict between his idealistic hopes and dark political realities is reworked here in the light of subsequent events, especially the apparent likelihood of a rebel victory which would put the mine in their possession. The details of Charles's thought-processes show that he now realises that he is in the position his father so disliked – the possibility of being robbed by greedy politicians. His ideal of defending the common decencies of organised society threatens to collapse into futility, because of the poisonous root of the dark forces of cupidity and self-indulgence. The sword is presented as a relatively honest instrument of warfare, whereas wealth is an insidiously corrupting weapon that may harm its user as much as those it is used against.

This theme of corruption runs through the whole novel. Ideals are consistently corrupted by the reality in which they have to be expressed. Charles feels that the mine had corrupted his judgement: instead of its wealth leading to justice, as he had earlier hoped and thought it would, it had led him into bribery. It had corrupted his morals as well as his judgement. Ideally the silver should have liberated Charles; in reality it traps him. At this stage in the Costaguanan civil war he cannot simply close the mine down. He is trapped into either unenthusiastically continuing to use its wealth, hoping that some good may come of it, or destroying the mine entirely if it looks as though the rebels will take control of it. Ultimately, we know from our reading of the whole novel that Nostromo's hoard of silver, in effect his own personal mine, traps him into certain attitudes and actions, contributing to the corruption of 'the Incorruptible'. For me, the particular distinctiveness of the style in this extract is that Conrad gives us Charles's thoughts from the inside. For once we do know exactly what, and how, Gould is thinking. I am sure this is because Conrad wants us to be aware of the tension inside the character, that the conflict is not only between the man and his situation but also within him. I think Conrad is emphasising that the ideals are coming into contact with a dark and destructive reality.

This transformation of early hope into subsequent disillusionment is a major pattern in the novel, and one I hope you are beginning to recognise for yourself as part of the conflict between ideals and reality. It is worth looking at another specific illustration of the theme.

5 *Select a fourth passage for discussion*

I have chosen a passage directly presenting Nostromo. It occurs after he has metaphorically come back from the dead, after hiding the treasure on the Great Isabel rock. Nostromo discovers the tortured body of Hirsch and then meets Doctor Monygham, who gives him a different perception of the political machinations, and of the part that he, Nostromo, captain or Capataz of the dock workforce, unwittingly played in them:

> And the Capataz, listening as if in a dream, felt himself of as little account as the indistinct, motionless shape of the dead man whom he saw upright under the beam, with his air of listening also, disregarded, forgotten, like a terrible example of neglect.
>
> 'Is it for an unconsidered and foolish whim that they came to me, then?' he interrupted, suddenly. 'Had I not done enough for them to be of some account, *por Dios*? Is it that the *hombres finos* – the gentlemen – need not think as long as there is a man of the people ready to risk his body and soul? Or, perhaps, we have no souls – like dogs?'
>
> 'There was Decoud, too, with his plan,' the doctor reminded him again.
>
> 'Si! And the rich man in San Francisco who had something to do with that treasure, too – what do I know? No! I have heard too many things. It seems to me that everything is permitted to the rich.'
>
> 'I understand, Capataz,' the doctor began.
>
> 'What Capataz?' broke in Nostromo, in a forcible but even voice. 'The Capataz is undone, destroyed. There is no Capataz. Oh, no! You will find the Capataz no more.' (p. 359)

Nostromo is here responding to the revelation that the other Europeans have taken advantage of his reputation for being trusting and incorruptible. There is an opposition between what Nostromo thought he had been doing, undertaking an idealist action to help protect political justice and bring equality between people; and the reality of the adventure, that the other Europeans are prepared to use Nostromo but do not consider him their equal.

The ideas in the extract are partly expressed through images of dream and death. Nostromo feels detached from what he thought was the reality of his status and reputation – detached in a similar way to the dead Hirsch, though he too appears to be listening to Doctor Monygham's revelations. In a sense the old Nostromo is dead. He repudiates his previous rank and identity: 'There is no Capataz.' In this passage Nostromo also shows a strong sense of social hierarchy. He realises the reality of social distinctions, that everything is apparently permitted to the rich and that he, Nostromo – who had identified himself with their political cause – is one of the lower classes. In a previous extract Decoud had described Nostromo as having power over the common people. This development of the circumstances shows Nostromo in a different relationship with them, not as socially superior but as 'a man of the people', all of whom are treated like dogs by the rich. The recognition that his old idealised life is dead – part of the irony of the whole incident is that at this moment everyone except Monygham thinks Nostromo has drowned – and the acknowledgement of his poverty form the crucible from which the new Nostromo is born. His ideals have been betrayed by the dark social and poitical forces of self-interest, and he realises that the reality of the future lies with 'that treasure'. That realisation changes the direction of Nostromo's life and has reverberations throughout the rest of the novel. The style of the extract emphasises the tension within Nostromo: he uses three Spanish phrases, stressing his foreignness, his difference from the English-based Goulds, the French Decoud, the rich American, and the other English such as his work-superior Captain Mitchell and even Monygham, with whom Nostromo is having this conversation. The difference is expressed in terms of gentlemen and dogs, a very marked and emotive contrast. From this point the conflict is not simply between government and rebels; the action illustrates a split within the European community too.

6 *Have I achieved a sufficiently complex sense of the novel?*

I have concentrated mainly on the political framework of the novel, but it is not just a book about politics. There are important threads of romance woven through the story, contributing to the development of the pattern of themes. The romance between Martin Decoud and Antonia is entirely blighted, largely because of the political circumstances surrounding it. At the outbreak of civil war Decoud declines to leave the country, explaining, 'my true idea, the only one I care for, is not to be separated from Antonia. . . . She won't leave Sulaco . . . won't run away' (pp. 185–6). Decoud sees the only solution as getting silver to the United States to buy support. This is why he accompanies Nostromo with the silver consignment, and that adventure ends in Decoud's death. The romance between Nostromo and Linda Viola is destroyed by his falsity to her. The love between Nostromo and Giselle Viola ends tragically in the man's death – paralleling the fate of the relationship between Decoud and Antonia – as her father shoots his friend believing Nostromo to be the vagabond Ramirez. In these illustrations the ideal of love concludes in tragedy as it meets the realities of life, and this complements the general pattern of the book as we have been studying it.

There is, however, an important complication. Charles Gould and his wife begin the story as newly-wed and happy. We have already analysed an early passage in which Mrs Gould sees Charles as fulfilling her own aspirations for the ideal of universal justice. However, we have also seen how Charles falls into disillusionment and taciturnity. The Goulds drift apart emotionally; meanwhile Doctor Monygham responds 'to Mrs Gould's humanising influence', increasingly seeing and admiring the idealist in her. Monygham is not an idealist; he is the thematic opposite of most of the other main characters. The man tortured by the previous regime of Bento and subsequently cast out of the best Sulaco European society had 'an immense mistrust of mankind' and a 'habit of sceptical, bitter speech' (pp. 49–50). The Doctor has already encountered reality, and without belief or illusion has nothing to lose. However, the hint of latent romance never comes to fruition. Although Monygham adores Mrs Gould, and she finds solace in his company as Charles Gould distances himself from everyone through his obsession with the San Tomé mine, the bonds of marriage and honour are maintained. Their friendship, though, does make Monygham less bitter, more inclined to trustfulness; whilst Mrs Gould, despite encountering the harshness of reality, remains 'full of endurance and compassion' (p. 456) and still able to hold onto a modified ideal of life. This relationship in fact goes against the mainstream of the novel, adding a complexity to what otherwise might have been a mechanical arrangement of ideas in which each case simply confirms all the others. It is significant, though, that Mrs Gould and Doctor Monygham have well-established social positions by the end of the novel. As the wife of the man who controls most of Costaguana's wealth Mrs Gould has a respected place in that society, and a powerful one from which to pursue her philanthropic and altruistic aspirations. Monygham, because of his role in the civil war, also gains respect and some power to create a better life for poorer people. They can be generous, both financially and spiritually, because their realities are not too harsh. Conrad is himself a realist.

Aspects of the novel

If you would like to continue exploring the central pattern through analysis of more extracts you should now be able to do so on your own: take a passage, and, bearing in mind the possible tension between ideals and reality, work through the five steps I have been illustrating. (They are set out in detail in Chapter 2.) Having established a method of approach, I should now like to broaden the discussion a little to include a couple of issues I have not yet been able to take up. When I first read *Nostromo* the **time scheme** of the novel completely bewildered me. What I would now call the narrative structure is confusing because events are not presented chronologically, and there is more than one narrative voice – for instance, Captain Mitchell tells part of the story and as he is a participant his narration is not necessarily reliable. This is not to imply that Captain Mitchell deliberately lies, but his perception – like that of all of us – is perhaps coloured by his own involvement. His views to some extent idealise situations, and particularly his own roles in them – or the parts played by those who work for him. His judgement regarding Nostromo, for example, becomes retrospectively suspect when we compare his view – 'Nostromo, sir, a man absolutely above reproach' (p. 24) – with our later knowledge of Nostromo's actions. Indeed, Mitchell repeats his opinion towards the end of the novel – 'Nostromo – a man worth his weight in gold' (p. 434) – and the irony that the statement is nearly literally true (he is certainly worth his weight in silver!) emphasises the unconscious untrustworthiness of the speaker.

Complicating the novel's structure further is the fact that the narrative jumps back and forward in time. Apart from the opening chapter, which imparts some background information, the story element of Part First, for instance, ends in the time and place in which it begins. The whole sequence is not a forward progression, as in most narratives, but more circular. This means the story is working towards something we have already been told about. As it takes out the element of suspense and makes the story more difficult to follow, you might wonder why an author would work in that way. Conrad, however, is not simply being awkward. I think he is trying to divert attention away from the traditional interest in *what* is going to happen – since we know that – to the issues of *how* and *why*. He is interested not so much in merely describing situations as in understanding processes. This is one reason why the difficulties are worth overcoming. The result is a sharpening of our appreciation of change.

Another feature of Conrad's work you may come across in reading critical studies, or in class or seminar discussions, is the question of **symbolism**. The term is usually used to suggest that a writer employs one thing to stand for another. Consider Nostromo's response when he returns to Sulaco after an absence to discover a lighthouse being erected near his buried treasure:

> At this unexpected, undreamt-of, startling sight, he thought himself lost irretrievably. What could save him from detection now? Nothing! He was struck with amazed dread at this turn of chance, that would kindle a far-reaching light upon the only secret spot of his life. . . . It was dark. Not every man has such a darkness. And they were going to put a light there. A light! He saw it shining upon disgrace, poverty, contempt . . . four hundred or so [yards] from the dark, shaded, jungly ravine, containing the secret of his safety, of his influence, of his magnificence, of his power over the future. . . . (pp. 430–1)

The lighthouse that is built at the end of the novel, and which leads directly to Nostromo being shot by Giorgio, who becomes the lighthouse-keeper, may be seen as a symbol of truth casting a light of revelation into the darkness of Nostromo's betrayal of those who trusted him with the silver. Nostromo's own thoughts support such an interpretation. He is not concerned with the actual use of the lighthouse, with its benefits to navigation and the safety of ships – although he has himself been a sailor. He thinks in moral terms of a dark secret being penetrated by a shining light. An illuminating justice will reveal, he fears, the dark criminality that is the source of his wealth and prestige. His position stems from a moral ravine. It is a real lighthouse, too, but the fact that Part Third is entitled 'The Lighthouse' also implies that the thing has an importance beyond its contribution to the plot and the realism of the narrative. Many novelists work in this kind of way, although it is something of a particular feature of Conrad's method. Perhaps you can find other illustrations for yourself.

There is, however, an element of Conrad's work that is more complex than this one-to-one relationship of the lighthouse and the illumination of dark secrets. I think it is helpful if we describe this feature, which I touched on in a simpler form when discussing 'Youth', as **extended metaphor**. A metaphor is a device by which one concept or thing is expressed in terms of another. It is extended when it recurs throughout a novel, accumulating values. This occurs when a factor has a value beyond its simple physical detail or its contribution to the plot, but is capable of more than one meaning. Can you see a realistic detail in the novel that functions in this way? There are several examples – those that spring to my mind first are the San Tomé mine and its silver. Perhaps you have come up with different illustrations, but I shall elaborate the idea in relation to the silver.

The silver is an important part of the narrative realism and the plot. Without it the novel could not exist in its present form. The silver is the main source of wealth in the novel, and that signifies power. The power of the silver, however, is itself complex. In the case of the politicians – Bento, Ribiera, Montero – the silver's power is clearly political. Decoud, too, although not actually a politician, sees the silver in this light, as a means of controlling government. Charles Gould perceives the power the silver gives him as a means of social improvement; as he says in the first passage we analysed, it may provide a 'rift in the darkness', bringing order and justice in the place of chaos and poverty. The silver brings Nostromo wealth and a social status that his reputation alone, although considerable, could never have achieved for him. The silver, then, is more than a symbol capable of only one interpretation; it spreads through the novel with different meanings for a variety of characters.

I think we can take the discussion further than this. The silver is not simply a passive factor that characters have attitudes towards: it also changes and creates attitudes. For Charles Gould the silver begins as something that will enable him to achieve socially beneficial ends, but it becomes a 'cold and overmastering passion' (p. 207), an end in itself – an emotionally destructive obsession. This is not merely a personal characteristic of Gould's, for the silver has a similar potential power over anyone. The novel begins with a story of the ghosts of silver-miners that haunt the mountains in which the metal is found. Nostromo sees this as representative of his, and of many others', experience: 'There is something in a treasure that fastens upon a man's mind ... did you ever hear of the miserable gringos on Azuera, that cannot die? ... There is no getting away from a treasure that once fastens upon your mind' (p. 379).

Nostromo's own buried treasure is like a small silver mine, a parallel to the huge San Tomé mine containing the treasure that dominates the novel. The myth is that the silver will not let the miners die, but in fact they died for it – dying rather than giving up their search. Decloud also dies, literally, by the silver, after he fill his pockets with it, using it to enable him to commit suicide by drowning: 'the brilliant Don Martin Decoud, weighted by the bars of San Tomé silver, disappeared without a trace, swallowed up in the immense indifference of things' (p. 412).

Nostromo describes the silver as 'a curse' (p. 217) and 'a deadly disease' (p. 222), epithets with which Monygham, Decoud, Charles Gould, Mrs Gould and Giorgio Viola all at various times agree. When Nostromo is dying, almost his final thought is 'The silver has killed me' (p. 457). He remembers, ironically, that silver is 'an incorruptible metal that can be trusted to keep its value for ever. ... An incorruptible metal' (p. 251). The irony that silver will not physically deteriorate, or become debased, but is morally corrupting, is emphasised in his very last words: 'Shining! Incorruptible!' (p. 458). It has certainly corrupted almost everyone in the novel. The silver is an aspect of the novel's reality. Every character who has ideals comes into contact with it and is in some way changed. Their ideals – and in some cases their lives – are either destroyed or drastically modified as a result of the reality of the silver.

My argument has been that silver is part of the novel's realist narrative, a physical entity that we can all understand and is essential to the plot; but it is also a pervasive aspect of the thematic development, touching on all the main characters and ideas. We cannot make a simple equation between the silver and one other thing, because it bears several interpretations and values. This does not imply artistic uncertainty, but is a deliberate technique: Conrad is not trying to convince us to accept his views and attitudes but wants to stimulate and provoke us into thinking for ourselves. This is part of the process by, and for, which Conrad shifts the emphasis from *what* happens to *how and why* events occur in the ways they do.

If you look closely at the scenes involving silver you will realise that Conrad does not simply condemn the existence, or the mining, of that metal. He is also aware that it does create a form of wealth. Conrad's refusal to take a simplistic moral stance against material well-being – or on any other issue in his novels – gives his work a feeling of ambiguity, in which it is often difficult for us to know exactly what his own attitudes are. At the same time we can see that Conrad is not a cold, indifferent writer, for there is always a strong sense of sympathy for the people whose ideals are being destroyed. It is never a pleasant process, and usually a moving one, when a vulnerable individual's beliefs and hopes come into conflict with a harsh, and frequently bleak, reality. We shall see this feature of Conrad's work again in the next chapter.

5

The Secret Agent (1907)

Constructing an overall analysis

The Secret Agent was first published three years after *Nostromo*, and if you come to it from that earlier novel you will already have encountered Conrad's curious way of telling stories. The basic story is, in fact, fairly straightforward, but the narration jumps back and forth in time so that we have to keep our wits about us as we read. Once again this factor makes reading the novel both a more difficult and a more exciting experience than it would be if events were described in simple chronological order: there is a wonderful sense of achievement when you have grasped all the complexities of a Conrad novel.

The action of the novel is set towards the end of the Victorian period. The skeleton of the story line is that the secret agent, Verloc, is employed by an unnamed foreign embassy to foment activity amongst *émigré* political dissidents who have sought asylum in the relatively liberal atmosphere of Britain. These people, known either as anarchists or as revolutionists, are tolerated in London because they represent no real threat. They are simply talkers, always ready to condemn various European governments with words but actually too lazy to commit any acts of dissent. The foreign embassy is anxious to provoke the British government into action against the *émigrés*, and therefore orders Verloc, the paid *agent provocateur*, to organise an act of terrorism for which the anarchists will be blamed. As the cover for his activities as a secret agent Verloc runs a small back-street shop selling disreputable smutty magazines and photographs. The shop is also a meeting place for various anarchists, or revolutionists, who think that Verloc is one of their group and therefore trust him, not realising that he is a secret agent for the foreign government they oppose. The anarchists have contact, too, with a man known as the Professor, who is obsessed with the idea of inventing the perfect detonator. Whereas the anarchists are happy to sit around talking about revolution, the Professor is a nihilist, whose only ambition is to annihilate, to destroy, everything once he has invented the perfect detonator. Verloc lives at the shop with his unsuspecting wife Winnie and her mentally retarded brother Stevie – to whom Winnie is a kind of surrogate mother, which gives them a very close and trusting relationship. Verloc arranges for his simple-minded brother-in-law, Stevie, to plant a bomb against the wall of the Observatory in Greenwich Park – an act that will be construed as one of gratuitous and blatant terrorism against a worthy and blameless scientific institution. Stevie is very idealistic, and like his sister Winnie – and the anarchists – trusts Verloc absolutely as his protector. Verloc persuades Stevie that blowing up the Observatory will be an act against poverty and injustice, and will help to create a better and fairer society. Unfortunately, as he is carrying the bomb across Greenwich Park in order to plant it, Stevie trips, accidentally triggers the detonator, and blows himself up.

The remainder of the novel deals with the consequences. The anarchists discover from the nihilistic Professor who supplied the bomb that it was Verloc who had bought it, and so assume that he was the person who died. One policeman, Detective Inspector Heat, wants to pin the blame on the anarchists for personal reasons; his superior, the Assistant Commissioner, is intent on uncovering the truth, although also for personal reasons rather than in the interests of justice. Winnie finds out that her husband was responsible for the death of her brother Stevie and murders Verloc. One of the anarchists, the philandering Ossipon, learns the truth by chance, tricks Winnie out of her money by pretending to help her flee the country, abandons her by leaping off the boat train when he had promised to accompany her to France, and is subsequently conscience-stricken when he learns of her suicide – she jumps off the cross-Channel ferry. At the end of the novel only the nihilist Professor, still involved in his obsessive search for the perfect detonator, has any feeling of satisfaction.

I hope you can see that this is clearly a story dealing with events that can be related to our own times. The novel has been criticised over the years for not having any really sympathetic characters; or that at best the couple of people who may raise our sympathy – Winnie and Stevie – both die during the course of the story. For such critics there seems little point in reading it, yet this is a book that I – and many other people – have read over and over again for sheer pleasure. The ideas in it are interesting, and still entirely relevant today; and the style is a most wonderful mixture of irony and comedy. It is true the tone of the novel is extremely elusive, so that it is very difficult to pin down Conrad's own attitudes. You may remember that in Chapter 1 I remarked that Conrad has been attacked by both left- and right-wing critics, as neither can agree on exactly where he stands. I find this part of the joy of reading *The Secret Agent*: the way in which Conrad discusses serious themes and presents tragic scenes in a manner that pulls us in different directions almost simultaneously. The way through the complexities of the style, the way to grasp what Conrad is actually saying, and the manner in which he is saying it, is to consider in detail a number of particular passages. However, as usual, you should start by thinking about the novel as a whole. The page references after quotations relate to the 1981 Penguin edition of the novel.

1 *After reading the novel, think what kind of pattern you can see in the text*

I have tried to work out the sequence of actual events, for the moment disregarding the order in which they are told, and I have already offered you my summary of that. As with the novels discussed in previous chapters, we can start thinking about a pattern by seeing if there is an opposition in the plot between ideals and reality. Verloc is considered to be an ideal anarchist by the revolutionists, and an ideal protector of the family by Winnie and Stevie. In terms of political realities he is an *agent provocateur* working to discredit the anarchists who trust him. Verloc destroys the family – unintentionally, it is true – by putting Stevie in a fatally dangerous situation in order to get himself out of an awkward position with the embassy that secretly pays him. Similarly, Winnie starts out as an ideally caring daughter, loving sister and acquiescent wife who has within her reality the seed of the dark forces of murder. She is eventually driven to self-destruction by the betrayal of Ossipon, whose own self-projected image of political idealism covers a reality of simple greed. Stevie is an idealist believing in the possibility of social justice, and the ultimate goodness of Verloc. The reality of his destruction brings the achievement of justice no closer, and is caused in part by the dark, selfish opportunism of the man he idealised. The embassy staff and the policemen, who in theory exist to protect decent values and common justice, in reality all pursue their own self-interest.

I think we can say, then, that there is a pattern in which ideals are consistently presented in opposition to the reality of the dark forces that fundamentally motivate men and women to action. We need, however, to test this initial analysis by looking at specific passages from the novel. As usual we start by focusing on a character near the beginning of the novel.

2 *Select a short passage for discussion and try to build on the ideas you have established so far*

Our main task, with any novel, after recognising the central themes, is understanding how those themes are brought to life. Novelists achieve this partly through the characters. If you have read novels by such writers as Dickens, Hardy or Lawrence you will be used to them giving descriptions, sometimes quite lengthy ones, of characters, scenes or places. Although I now greatly enjoy Conrad's novels, at first I found reading his fiction slightly unsatisfying, and eventually I realised that it was because he does not often write such descriptions and that I was looking for something that wasn't there. We have to build up a picture from many small fragments of information; the experience is more like constructing a jigsaw than looking at a completed painting, but once we understand that then the novels become less puzzling. Here, for example, is the first appearance of Verloc, the secret agent:

> Undemonstrative and burly in a fat-pig style, Mr Verloc, without either rubbing his hands with satisfaction or winking sceptically at his thoughts, proceeded on his way. He trod the pavement heavily with his shiny boots, and his general get-up was that of a well-to-do mechanic in business for himself. He might have been anything from a picture-frame maker to a lock-smith; an employer of labour in a small way. But there was also about him an indescribable air which no mechanic could have acquired in the practice of his handicraft however dishonestly exercised: the air common to men who live on the vices, the follies, or the baser fears of mankind; the air of moral nihilsm common to keepers of gambling hells and disorderly houses; to private detectives and inquiry agents; to drink sellers and, I should say, to the sellers of invigorating electric belts and to the inventors of patent medicines. But of that last I am not sure, not having carried my investigations so far into the depths. For all I know, the expression of these last may be perfectly diabolic. I shouldn't be surprised. What I want to affirm is that Mr Verloc's expression was by no means diabolic. (pp. 20–1)

This is the narrator's description of Verloc as the character walks through the busy London streets to keep his appointment at the embassy, to which he has been summoned in his role as secret agent. Verloc looks almost like an ideal late-Victorian man: a mechanic, or artisan, who has succeeded in business and is socially upwardly mobile, a mechanic who no longer works manually himself but employs other people to work for him. The reality is that Verloc is actually a man of moral nihilsm; not an honest craftsman turned businessman, but someone who lives off the vices, follies and fears of mankind. Verloc's outward appearance suggests the ideal, and his expression is specifically not evil; but his inner reality is that of a parasite, an exploiter of other people.

This tension between the ideal appearance and the darker inner reality is reinforced by the details. Verloc's appearance is relatively smart because he is going to see his employers and wants to create an aura of efficiency. But, although his boots have been well-polished, his tread is heavy, emphasising his burly fatness. I think this image of the fat-pig heaviness comically works against the idea of efficiency, suggesting that is is only a superficial quality. The comparisons of occupations are also revealing: in appearance Verloc resembles a picture-frame maker or locksmith, both respectable craftsmen in late-Victorian society; but the reality is that he is like a disreputable keeper of a gambling hell or disorderly house, someone who makes a living out of moral nihilism and other people's weaknesses. Private detectives and publicans, whom Verloc also resembles morally, are engaged in shady affairs too. These details bring out the difference between the ideal that Verloc is trying to project and the reality that he is attempting to conceal. They also remind us that Verloc's official business is the purveying of disreputable magazines and photographs. When we have read the whole novel we can appreciate how this tension between ideal and reality, outer appearance and inner truth, is worked through the text. As an *agent provocateur* among the anarchists Verloc's position depends on his dishonesty, on his being accepted as a revolutionist although he is an embassy agent. The idea of the disparity between appearance and reality is something we can take through the novel.

The tone of the above passage moves from seriousness, when commenting on Verloc's moral nihilism, to comedy as it brings in the ludicrous comparisons with the purveyors and inventors of ridiculous machines and cures. The description of Verloc as being like a fat pig is satiric, and the tone both disapproving and throw-away. Verloc has an ideal of himself as a rather important person, but the language comically deflates him to a realistic level. The way in which Conrad mixes serious comment and a comic style is an aspect of the novel that I shall elaborate in the second part of this chapter. What we can also see here, however, is an example of Conrad's ambiguous attitude to the story. The narrator humorously drags in eccentric inventors, and then claims to know nothing about them. They are an actual feature of late-Victorian society, yet paradoxically they add to the grotesque element of the novel – the aspect that may seem exaggerated and unreal, but is a part of society's reality.

In *The Secret Agent* there is a good deal of talk about politics and political theory, which students sometimes think of as dull or rather abstract for a novel. This is perhaps because it can be difficult to see how such discussions fit into the novel, so that they seem less than interesting. It may therefore be helpful if I take one of these passages for the next step of my analysis and try and show its interest for us as critics.

3 *Select a second passage for discussion*

I have chosen part of a long paragraph from Chapter 4 that deals with the development of political oppositions. It is the chapter in which the Professor is introduced. He and the anarchist Ossipon are discussing their diverse political philosophies. Ossipon is a theorist for radical social change; the Professor replies,

> 'You revolutionists ... are the slaves of the social convention, which is afraid of you; slaves of it as much as the very police that stands up in the defence of that convention. Clearly you are, since you want to revolutionize it. It governs your thought, of course, and your action, too, and thus neither your thought nor your action can ever be conclusive.' He paused, tranquil, with that air of close, endless silence, then almost immediately went on: 'You are not a bit better than the forces arrayed against you – than the police, for instance. The other day I came suddenly upon Chief Inspector Heat at the corner of Tottenham Court Road. He looked at me very steadily. But I did not look at him. Why should I give him more than a glance? He was thinking of many things – of his superiors, of his reputation, of the law courts, of his salary, of newspapers – of a hundred things. But I was thinking of my perfect detonator only. He meant nothing to me. He was as insignificant as – I can't call to mind anything insignificant enough to compare him with –

> except Karl Yundt perhaps. Like to like. The terrorist and the policeman both come from the same basket. Revolution, legality – counter moves in the same game; forms of idleness at bottom identical.' (p. 64)

The Professor is outlining his own political theory, from which his personal obsession with inventing the perfect detonator comes. The conflict of ideas in the passage rests between the ideal of the Professor who wishes to obliterate society with the ideal, perfect bomb; and the revolutionists who pretend to be entirely against social order but in reality want only to change it, to replace the existing system with a slightly different one, rather than destroy it. In this case there is also a further opposition in the passage between the Professor and the police and the revolutionists. Because the revolutionists want to change society, they, as much as the police, need to protect it from the Professor's ideal of complete destruction: therefore he sees a conflict between himself and both the anarchists and the police. This may seem a bit bewildering at first glance, because generally such issues are presented to us in black and white, good and bad, terms. Can you see why both left- and right-wing critics are tempted to denounce Conrad? Usually the revolutonists and the police are presented as opposites, one good and the other bad depending on how you individually feel about them. Here they appear to be on the same side. This is because we are shown them through the Professor's eyes. We are given a new perspective, are made to see – you may remember that in Chapter 1 I quoted Conrad's remark that he wanted to make us '*see*' for a moment our own reality from a different angle. Although the protectors of society – the police and the revolutionists, as the Professor sees them – are motivated by different reasons, the central tension of the extract, from the Professor's point of view, is between an ideal of destruction and the reality of protection. I hope you can see from this example how identifying the central tension, between some kind of ideal and a reality, is helpful in tackling this sort of political discussion in the novel.

The Professor, in fact, brings out his arguments clearly enough, telling Ossipon that he and the other anarchists are slaves to a social system that is afraid of them, and that the police are also slaves of society. He sees Chief Inspector Heat as a slave of his job, trapped by 'a hundred things', includ ng the Professor himself. However, the Professor argues that he himself is not a slave, because he thinks of one thing only: 'my perfect detonator'. The obsessional ideal is a recurrent theme in the novel. Earlier we learnt that Verloc's obsession was his own idleness, 'a fanatical inertness' (p. 20). This gives some credence to the mad Professor's statement that 'revolution' and 'legality' are at bottom identical 'forms of idleness', but the actual description of Heat should warn us against thinking that the Chief Inspector is in reality as idle as Verloc. I think Heat's investigations through the novel as a whole confirm that the Professor is only half right about idleness. Conrad's method here is mainly to present the Professor's ideas in the character's own words. This allows us to see the Professor directly and draw our own judgement about him; we find, for example, that he sees terrorism, revolution and legality as a 'game'. We might want to see those issues more seriously, but we have to bring our own critical judgement to bear; Conrad does not tell us what our attitudes should be. This is one reason why I have come to like reading him so much: he provokes us into thinking, but does not tell us precisely what to think. I think it is also necessary to draw an inference about the Professor's claim that he is not a slave. Ossipon, the character to whom the speech is addressed, does not point it out, but the Professor is a slave to the ideal of the perfect detonator; the reality of the Professor's life is that he can think of nothing else.

Since Conrad looks at things from many sides, at this point it may be a good idea to explore someone else's point of view.

4 *Select a third passage for discussion*

I should now like to look at the policemen's view of all this. Chapter 6 of the novel provides a rich field for analysis of them, and I have chosen part of a paragraph taken from the long interview Heat has with his superior, the Assistant Commissioner. Heat wants to pin the guilt for the bomb on Michaelis, the ticket-of-leave apostle (meaning he was on parole from a prison sentence); the Asssistant Commissioner's wife is friendly with the society lady who had 'adopted' the anarchist and would like the blame to be fixed elsewhere. During the course of the discussion the narrator describes Chief Inspector Heat's thoughts:

> The celebrity bestowed upon Michaelis on his release two years ago by some emotional journalists in want of special copy had rankled ever since in his breast. It was perfectly legal to arrest that man on the barest

> suspicion. It was legal and expedient on the face of it. His two former chiefs would have seen the point at once; whereas this one, without saying either yes or no, sat there, as if lost in a dream. Moreover, besides being legal and expedient, the arrest of Michaelis solved a little personal difficulty which worried Chief Inspector Heat somewhat. This difficulty had its bearing upon his reputation, upon his comfort, and even upon the efficient performance of his duties. For, if Michaelis no doubt knew something about this outrage, the Chief Inspector was fairly certain that he did not know too much. This was just as well. He knew much less – the Chief Inspector was positive – than certain other individuals he had in his mind, but whose arrest seemed to him inexpedient, besides being a more complicated matter, on account of the rules of the game. The rules of the game did not protect so much Michaelis, who was an ex-convict. It would be stupid not to take advantage of legal facilities, and the journalists who had written him up with emotional gush would be ready to write him down with emotional indignation. (pp. 104–5)

These are the thoughts of Chief Inspector Heat on the explosion in Greenwich Park in which Stevie was accidentally killed, and his job of tracking down the people responsible for it. Heat's ideal solution is to arrest Michaelis. There are several reasons for this: upon his release from prison Michaelis had been treated by the press as a martyr, which annoys Heat; as a prisoner on parole he has little legal protection; it would be easy to arrest him; and it would help Heat pursue his inquiries if Michaelis were in jail and the real perpetrators of the outrage felt safe. This plan of action crumbles against the Assistant Commissioner's attitude. The central opposition in the extract is between Heat's readiness to exploit the reality of the situation and his superior's unwillingness to sanction such action. Heat sees the Assistant Commissioner as being out of touch with reality, 'as if lost in a dream'.

The details of Heat's argument revolve around the repeated phrase 'legal and expedient'. The Chief Inspector is in many ways an ideal policeman, yet in reality he is also human. He is concerned with his reputation; he is prepared to put a man who he realises knows little about the outrage into prison simply because it is expedient. Ideally the law should be above expediency; it should be concerned with the pursuit of the abstract virtues of truth and justice. In reality this is clearly not so. We can relate this to another episode in the novel: we know that the Assistant Commissioner's objection to the arrest of Michaelis is not really based on ideals either, but has to do with his wife's connections with a society lady who has befriended the ex-convict as an act of philanthropy.

Although they are not actually malicious, bad or evil men, any ideal of the policemen as guardians of truth and justice comes up against the reality of their personal interests and weaknesses. A point of style that it is worth noticing is the way in which Heat's thoughts echo the Professor's earlier speech. Looking back at the previous passage, can you see a word, a concept, in common? The Professor speaks of politics as a 'game', and here Heat thinks of his job in terms of 'the rules of the game'. In considering the earlier extract I argued that we might find the Professor's use of 'game' to describe terrorist activity as disturbing. To describe the problems of law and order as a 'game' may also be unacceptable. Again, Conrad makes no overt statement about it; we have to draw the two incidents together and make up our own minds about the connection and our attitudes to it. Through the structure of the novel Conrad shows that he is quite clear about the complexity of society and social issues, but the job of the novelist is not to tell us what to think but to make us aware of the complexities of life. Once again Conrad seems to want to make us '*see*', to perceive facets of life and society we might otherwise be unaware of, or approach only through prejudice and preconception.

5 *Select a fourth passage for discussion*

Two central characters we have not yet discussed are Stevie and Winnie, so I have chosen a passage in which they appear. When their mother moves out of the Verloc home, they hire a cab with a very decrepit horse (and cabman) to transport her and her belongings. The poverty of the cabman and his horse appals the unsophisticated Stevie, and as he and Winnie are walking to catch an omnibus home they talk about it. Stevie wonders why the police do not act against poverty and unfairness. Winnie explains that is not the job of the police:

> He had formed for himself an ideal conception of the metropolitan police as a sort of benevolent institution for the suppression of evil. The notion of benevolence especially was very clearly associated with his sense of the power of the men in blue. He had liked all police constables tenderly, with a guileless trustfulness. And he was pained. He was irritated, too, by a suspicion of duplicity in the members of the force. For Stevie was frank and as open as the day himself. What did they mean by pretending then? Unlike his sister, who put her trust in face values, he wished to go

> to the bottom of the matter. He carried on his inquiry by means of an angry challenge.
>
> 'What are they for then, Winn? What are they for? Tell me.'
>
> Winnie disliked controversy. But fearing most a fit of black depression consequent on Stevie missing his mother very much at first, she did not altogether decline the discussion. Guiltless of all irony, she answered yet in a form which was not perhaps unnatural in the wife of Mr Verloc, Delegate of the Central Red Committee, personal friend of certain anarchists, and a votary of social revolution.
>
> 'Don't you know what the police are for, Stevie? They are there so that them as have nothing shouldn't take anything away from them who have.' (pp. 143–4)

Stevie's unsophisticated mind thinks that the police exist not merely to pursue justice in the sense of maintaining law and order, but to prevent injustice in a wider social, political and moral sense from occurring. Winnie's response expresses the more sophisticated truth of the situation. And this is clearly another illustration of the novel's central tension between ideals and reality: in this case, Stevie's idealised view of society and social organisation, and the reality expressed by Winnie.

We can see Stevie's idealism very obviously in the details of the extract. He has 'an ideal conception' of the police, which leads him to trust, and almost love, them. On discovering that they are not primarily interested in suppressing evil, which for Stevie is social injustice and cruelty, he feels betrayed. To his mind the police have been pretending. Stevie's belief in the ideal of the surface appearance of the police as guardians of justice is destroyed by the reality of their actual purpose. It is this collision of ideal and reality that causes Stevie mental and emotional pain.

There are three ways in which we can relate this episode to the novel as a whole. Going back to the previous passage I discussed, we can see that the police are in fact guilty of duplicity, and that the interview between Heat and the Assistant Commissioner partly prepares us for this revelation in Stevie's experience. Going forward in time, we can appreciate that this revelation itself in part contributes to the idealistic Stevie's willingness to plant the bomb, as he thinks that will help bring about an ideal society. We can also see that Stevie's idealistic trust of the police, when it is betrayed, becomes transferred into an idealised trust of Verloc. Unfortunately he too will betray Stevie's ideal trust, a betrayal caused by Verloc's selfishness and leading to Stevie's death. Stevie's death is thus an important element in the ironic structure of the novel: the best of intentions end in the most catastrophic disasters.

In the passage itself the main irony of style stems, of course, from the fact that Winnie decides to tell to Stevie the 'real' truth specifically because she dislikes controversy, and because she does not want Stevie to feel upset. Yet her explanation of the role of the police in society is for Stevie both controversial and distressing, in that it completely destroys his previous view of it. Winnie has a good reason for encouraging the discussion, but the ultimate reality of its effect is that Stevie is blown up. The way in which the details and various parts of the novel fit together is one of the aspects of Conrad that I find so interesting – particularly the way in which he shapes irony out of an interweaving of ideals and realities.

6 *Have I achieved a sufficiently complex sense of the novel?*

I have attempted to get hold of a broad pattern and also some of the particular themes, essentially by approaching them through a number of the main characters. This method may initially leave ideas in the novel undeveloped, but it does provide a coherent foundation on which to build. Perhaps you have chosen different passages, or have interpreted my extracts differently. That is in the nature of literary criticism, and I am not necessarily convinced that my conclusions are always the only ones possible. My main purpose has been to illustrate how it is possible to work from a series of passages to construct a critical appreciation of a novel.

There is an area of the novel that I should like at least to bring to your attention. The novel is firmly grounded in the social reality of London towards the end of the nineteenth century, when there were several actual explosions which the press and politicians labelled anarchist outrages. The atmosphere of the time and place is carefully conveyed, and the physical details of public and private life that are necessary to the story are presented in realistic terms. Yet there is another level to the book, too, a more directly philosophical one, which I have not yet looked at specifically.

When the secret agent is being threatened with dismissal by Vladimir at the embassy, a small incident occurs that seems to have little value to the plot at that point:

> in the silence Mr Verloc heard against a window-pane the faint buzzing of a fly – his first fly of the year – heralding better than any number of swallows the approach of spring. The useless fussing of that tiny, energetic organism affected unpleasantly this big man threatened in his indolence. (p. 31)

Vladimir, the embassy official, has questioned Verloc's usefulness as a secret agent. Verloc has attempted to defend himself, but since he has produced few results he has not been convincing. There is a disturbing silence in the interview at that point. This particular incident may be linked to the social atmosphere of uncomfortableness, and Verloc's psychological state of apprehension. That would be an entirely valid argument, but the episode might lead to a bigger idea too. I see a tension between Verloc's ideal of his self-importance and indolence, and the reality of Vladimir's power over him. Verloc is disturbed by the useless fussing of the tiny fly against the window pane because it brings a different perspective to bear on himself. His actions as an *agent provocateur* are in a sense a fussy buzzing against glass; they are meaningless in a context of the wider issues of the nature of life and existence. Verloc can no more see beyond the glass he is buzzing against than can the fly. At the same time the details of the passage, in which the fly's tininess is stressed against the largeness of the fat Verloc, add yet a further perspective to the scene. The big man is not literally or physically threatened by the 'energetic organism', yet it affects him unpleasantly. The useless activity of the fly is a philosophic challenge to the lazy human who is being pressured into action. His sense of importance and significance is disturbed.

By relating this idea to the novel as a whole we can perhaps extend the notion of insignificance to many, maybe all, the characters. It is when people take themselves, and their ideals, too seriously that the perspective of reality threatens them. Another particular case is that of the Professor. He is literally untouchable and impregnable, carrying in his pocket his ideal of existence, a bomb he can detonate at any moment. At the end of the book he is described as 'a pest' (p. 249). This links him to the earlier energetic fly. He is less important and significant in a wider scheme of thought than he imagines. If you find this a little difficult to accept, think about the function of such elements as the fog and darkness. They certainly contribute to the seedy atmosphere, but the idea of various characters casting about in moral or psychological or philosophical mists without a sense of direction or even knowing what is around them is a recurrent one – more, perhaps, than is demanded by purely realistic detail. Conrad works consistently in this way, pushing the realistic details into carrying the ideas of the text. In order to get a clear line through some of the central themes I have largely ignored this feature of the novel, but it is there for you to pursue further on your own. A great novelist can always be read on different, and complementary, levels. It is never a bad idea, however, first to build up a firm foundation, from a few substantial ideas that can be articulated in detail from the text.

Aspects of the novel

You will be aware by now that I regard *The Secret Agent* very highly. I admire the way in which the ideas are worked out, and the manner in which the story is told and information fed to us, so that all the pieces fall together to reveal a complex mosaic of misunderstandings, intentions and actions. By such means a basically simple story about a group of more or less incompetent people failing to do something is made riveting. Despite this artistic achievement some writers on the novel do criticise it, and the setters of examination questions, whilst acknowledging the novel's greatness, sometimes ask students to consider what they see as its faults, weaknesses or limitations. I have mentioned, in passing, one or two of the political objections to the book that have been raised; and the belief that either the characters do not engage our sympathies, or that if they do Conrad kills them off. There is also a view that Conrad is a rather dreary, heavy-handed writer who has a miserable outlook on life: a kind of melancholy mid-European who sees us all eventually being blown up, and that therefore nothing is quite worth the effort. You might have come across some of these opinions in discussing the novel with other people, or even felt them yourself. I can sympathise, because my own first readings of Conrad were fraught with difficulties, and my enjoyment came only after I stopped wanting him to be a different kind of novelist and accepted his achievement for what it is: elusive and complex. Fortunately many other readers feel the same.

These varied responses to the novel might reflect your own views. Perhaps you enjoy the complexity of the narrative, and the way in which we learn about events, but feel that the characters are exaggerated and therefore unrealistic. Such a response, however honestly felt, is not as it stands an analytical one. So, if you did want to argue for the validity of that response, you would have to work closely from extracts that provided substantial evidence with which to support your view. On the other hand, you might feel that the characters are realistic in the context of the society in which they are shown, and that Conrad is making a point about the way in which social environment can influence attitudes and thinking. Once again you would need to substantiate your argument by working from an analysis of particular passages, showing how they lead you to draw your conclusions about the book.

I have said that the novel is elusive and complex. I hope the complexity has become apparent through my discussion of specific passages, but I should like now to consider more closely the elusive nature of Conrad's tone. This is probably the best means of countering assertions that the novel is miserable or the style dreary. Instead of taking each objection individually, and arguing against it, let's take a positive attitude and by analysing how Conrad writes show how very good the style is.

For the rest of this chapter, then, I shall concentrate on Conrad's style. Look for a passage that strikes you as particularly interesting or intriguing. I have chosen this extract from the beginning of the novel, in which Verloc's disreputable back-street shop is described:

> customers were either very young men, who hung about the window for a time before slipping in suddenly; or men of a more nature age, but looking generally as if they were not in funds. Some of that last kind had the collars of their overcoats turned right up to their moustaches, and traces of mud on the bottom of their nether garments, which had the appearance of being much worn and not very valuable. And the legs inside them did not, as a general rule, seem of much account either. With their hands plunged deep in the side pockets of their coats, they dodged in sideways, one shoulder first, as if afraid to start the bell going.
>
> (p. 13)

Anyone who can write with such a deftly satiric touch, such a sense of amusement, cannot, to my mind, be described as dreary or miserable. That, as it stands, however, is simply a personal assertion. In order to make it into a real critical judgement I need to substantiate the case from a close analysis of the passage.

I have argued before that Conrad never puts in realistic detail simply to create atmosphere, although such descriptions may contribute to the novel's mood, but that everything in some way reflects the book's main ideas. You might argue here that Conrad is setting up a tension, in a comic way, between appearance and reality – which is certainly a central, and serious, theme in the novel. The customers want to buy the mildly pornographic goods – remember that this is in the late-Victorian period, and attitudes in general were not as liberal about this kind of trade as they are now – but are ashamed of doing so, or afraid of being seen doing it. This is seen in the description of the young customers hanging about, pretending they are not interested in the shop, and then 'slipping in suddenly'. The satire seems to me to be against the hypocrisy involved, and the humour arises from the young men trying to conceal an intention that must be perfectly obvious. The passage is more specific about the men described as 'of a more mature age'. This is not, I think, just a long-winded way of saying 'older'; rather, Conrad is using 'more mature' ironically: these men are older, and that is the polite way of expressing it, but by bringing in the idea of maturity he is drawing attention to their immaturity. Do truly mature men need to buy what have previously been described as 'photographs of more or less undressed dancing girls'?

For me, one of the great joys of reading Conrad is his use of language. These men of a mature age themselves look as disreputable as the merchandise they are buying, but the narrator does not say directly that they look seedy. Again, the reason for his being slightly roundabout is not that he is long-winded, but that he wishes to draw our attention to the detail in a comic manner. The older customers are not described as impoverished, but are said to be 'not in funds'. The use of this genteel phrase is incongruous, for normally only a middle-class man temporarily hard-up for cash would be described in that way. These people are not middle-class: even the bottoms of their trousers slouch and droop in the mud of the streets. Again, the term 'much worn' is also one that would be used of a threadbare garment belonging to someone of the middle classes who had fallen on hard times. However, the suggestion that the customers' legs are not very impressive is almost surreal. How can we tell what legs inside trousers are like? Does it matter? The overall picture of these men is that almost no part of them can be seen, their faces are almost covered and even their hands are thrust out of sight. Like the young customers they too are ashamed of entering the shop. This is not said directly, but is conveyed indirectly and humorously by the description of them entering sideways – the verb 'dodged' emphasises their desire not to be seen. Indeed, they are almost afraid to alert the shopkeeper that they have come into the shop, a factor that highlights the absurdity of the situation. There is exaggeration here, and it is deliberate. Because Conrad laughs at these men it does not follow, though, that he lacks any sympathy for them. Look what happens to the young men who find they are being served by Winnie:

> Then the customer of comparatively tender years would get suddenly disconcerted at having to deal with a woman, and with rage in his heart would proffer a request for a bottle of marking ink ... which, once outside, he would drop stealthily into the gutter. (p. 14)

There is a certain pathetic quality about these customers which prevents us from seeing them just as objects of satire. Instead we are aware of how their actions point up the gap between social respectability and the reality of the human behaviour that it hides. This disparity is ironically conveyed by Conrad's summary of the shop 'in which Mr Verloc carried on his business of a seller of shady wares, exercised his vocation of a protector of society, and cultivated his domestic virtues' (p. 15). Verloc is an ideal husband and a bastion of the social establishment, but it is all based on the sale of goods people are ashamed of buying. The justaposition of these three factors shows how big a chasm there is between them. Again the actual choice of words is wonderfully accurate: 'exercised his vocation' is the kind of portentous phrase the self-important Verloc might use of himself, but in reality he is a dishonest secret agent because he is too lazy to do a decent job; and 'cultivated his domestic virtues' is a grand description to cover his disinterest in what actually happens at home. I hope you can see that the language far from being heavy-handed or dreary, is actually ironically comic. Conrad uses a deliberately pretentious style designed to deflate self-importance by suggesting something different from what it literally says, so bringing out the comic side of his serious perception.

In view of my analysis and argument, why do some readers still think of Conrad's style as dreary and humourless? I think it is partly due to a failure to read the text closely, a desire to 'get on with the story' and ignore the style of it, so that the nuances of the language are lost. There is also a lurking belief that any novelist who tackles serious ideas, and perhaps especially ones presented in a political context, cannot be much fun. These are all preconceptions about what a novel should be. Conrad wants us to read carefully – that is one reason why he tells the story in such a convoluted way, so that we have to think about what we are reading all the time; he also wants us to appreciate the absurdity of self-importance. The comic satire is not against people in general, as I attempted to show above, but against a society that implicitly encourages moral duplicity, and particularly against those involved in political activities, those who consider themselves important enough to try to organise and interfere in other people's lives.

Our sympathies are, I think, engaged on behalf of the victims. The problem, though, is that we have to be alert as readers, not mentally passive, because the novel's tone can change subtly, with serious and comic blending elusively into one another. Towards the end of the novel, for example, after Winnie has discovered that her husband is responsible for Stevie's death, Verloc argues that Winnie's own attitudes contributed to the tragedy. He is completely unaware of the depth of his wife's feelings, and thinks of himself as the victim of her emotional and domestic oppression:

> He was tired, resigned in a truly marital spirit. But he felt hurt in the tender spot of his secret weakness. If she would go on sulking in that dreadful overcharged silence – why then she must. She was a master in that domestic art. Mr Verloc flung himself heavily upon the sofa, disregarding as usual the fate of his hat, which, as if accustomed to take care of itself, made for a safe shelter under the table. (p. 209)

This is on one level a very serious passage which in the narrative serves as a bridge between the revelation for Winnie of the reality of her brother's death and her murder of her husband, which leads to Winnie's own suicide. It is indeed a bleak exploration of the empty life of the Verlocs. And, although it is true that Conrad does not in general have a lot of sympathy for Verloc, the situation here is shown from his point of view. But the paragraph ends comically with that surreal picture of the hat taking on a life of its own, diving under the table for shelter from the impending catastrophe. The comedy springs partly from the incongruity: the hat does not roll under the table; it 'made for' that position with a deliberation that is not realistic. The language, moreover, suggests that this is not a coincidence just in this particular case, for Verloc disregards his hat 'as usual', while the object seems 'accustomed' to being abandoned.

The ideas of the hat having a fate, and taking care of itself, are surely also comic – giving the hat far too much importance, and conveying a feeling that it is in some way in control of its own destiny. The whole incident of the hat is absurd, but in laughing at the hat scurrying for shelter we are looking at a parallel to the fate of Verloc, Winnie and Stevie, all of whom seek some kind of shelter, and a form of control over their destinies, and all of whom fall victim to dark forces of reality beyond their dreams of an ideal existence. We are pulled between sympathy for Winnie, momentarily seeing the situation from Verloc's point of view, and the comedy of the scene focusing on the hat. We have to take the episode seriously, but acknowledge that the business with the hat is absurd.

Winnie and Stevie die not because Conrad wants to 'kill them off' through loss of interest or lack of sympathy, but because they are victims, vulnerable people who are caught up in forces more powerful than themselves. If Stevie and Winnie had been allowed to survive and live happily ever after, the detractors of Conrad would have complained – and I would have been one of them in this case – that he had rigged the ending to produce a cosy happiness that does not truly belong to the story. This is part of the realism of Conrad's vision of life; it does not, however, necessarily mean that he is an unduly pessimistic writer. The harshness of the reality that destroys the characters is partly offset by the comedy.

Verloc's bowler hat continues in the novel almost as though it were a character, and is later twice associated with his murder. After plunging the carving knife into her husband's breast Winnie rushes for the door in order to escape, knocking over the table:

> Mrs Verloc on reaching the door had stopped. A round hat disclosed in the middle of the floor by the moving of the table rocked slightly on its crown in the wind of her flight. (p. 214)

It is a comic image to conclude a grotesque episode that leaves Verloc, on the sofa, stabbed through the heart by his wife. The hat's attempt to find shelter has failed, and it is left exposed by Winnie's panic. It is her last sight of the scene – a sight not of her dead husband, but of his rocking, as though alive, hat. The image recurs when Ossipon later stumbles across the truth. Entering the room in the dark he seems to see Verloc asleep on the sofa – although at that point he still thinks the secret agent has been blown up by the explosion in Greenwich Park:

> But the true sense of the scene he was beholding came to Ossipon through the contemplation of the hat. It seemed an extraordinary thing, an ominous object, a sign. Black, and rim turned upward, it lay on the floor before the couch as if prepared to receive the contributions of pence from people who would come presently to behold Mr Verloc in the fullness of his domestic ease reposing on a sofa. (p. 230)

The bowler farcically, and tenaciously, reappears – each time in a different guise. Now it is like a busker's hat, yet ominous, a sign to Ossipon that everything is not as simple as he thought, or hoped, it to be. The hat seems almost the last living remnant of the murdered man. It is a grotesquely comic image that encapsulates the incongruous horror of the situation. Without this absurd, surreal element it would be difficult to express the incident other than melodramatically. Again the language is rather pompous, but in order to make a point rather than drearily so. Verloc would have liked to think of people coming to venerate him. He liked to see himself as domestically respectable. The gap between Verloc's appearance and the actual action that has caused it emphasises the wider ironic relationship between ideal and reality. Verloc's pomposity is deflated by the style; the enormity of Winnie's crime – murder – is partly softened by Ossipon focusing on the hat rather than the body. We are encouraged to see the scene in a wide perspective rather than passing a simplistic moral judgement on a murderess.

I hope I have shown how and why Conrad slips from one tone to another without warning, fusing serious, comic, ironic and satiric styles so as to present an intricate pattern that requires very close and careful reading. Whether or not you agree with my interpretation is not important, although you should be able to follow my argument and method. My main concern in this book is to illustrate how you can build up, and express, your own coherent view of a novel by looking analytically at a number of passages. My analysis has led me in a particular critical direction, but you should now have enough confidence to examine your own evidence from extracts you have chosen. Whether you see the novel overall predominantly as tragic, comic, ironic or satiric I hope you can see that all these factors are present to some extent, and that they are all related to one another through Conrad's interest in the tension between ideals and the dark forces of reality. What makes Conrad so challenging, and therefore so very exciting and rewarding, is the complexity of narrative style, the subtlety of his tone, and the power of the language. I have attempted to illustrate how all of these aspects of the novel work, and you might continue the process for yourself by following the pattern of analysis. If you take these ideas as your starting points they should enable you to explore how the central concerns of the novel are fleshed out, and also allow you to come to terms with Conrad's marvellously rich style.

6

Victory (1915)

Constructing an overall analysis

MY CENTRAL idea in this book is that the most efficient way of approaching one of Conrad's novels, or anyone else's, is to start from a basic overall pattern. You can then consider several extracts, as many as you find helpful, from the novel, analysing them in the light of the pattern you have worked out. It is fundamentally a straightforward method, and will lead us naturally into a text's complexities. Sometimes the basic line of this method may seem to have been lost as I tried to pursue interesting issues in Conrad's fiction, but in this chapter I return to the basic approach. I am not going to follow any particularly obscure line into *Victory*; I simply want to illustrate how looking closely at the detail of the text will help you clarify your own interpretation of it. As usual, the best place to begin is with your ideas on the pattern that can be seen in the plot. The page references given after quotations relate to the 1980 Penguin edition of the novel.

1 *After reading the novel, think what kind of pattern you can see in the text*

If you have read other Conrad novels you will be used by now to the idea of a story not being told in chronological sequence, and the fact that the first task is to work out the actual order of events in the story. The main character is a Swedish baron, Axel Heyst, who lived many years in London with his father, an intelligent but bitter man who convinced his son that the world is full only of disappointment and unhappiness, and that the ideal life is one of isolation in order to avoid those experiences. After his father's death Axel Heyst pursues that advice, wandering around the islands of the southern Pacific Ocean, mostly alone. One day he meets by chance a casual acquaintance, Morrison, who is threatened with financial ruin by some corrupt harbour officials who have confiscated Morrison's ship because the unwisely generous captain – who is therefore a poor businesman – cannot pay a fine. Heyst, in an act of spontaneous generosity, immediately lends Morrison the money to pay the fine, and Morrison is so overcome with gratitude that he makes Heyst his partner in business. Morrison has discovered that coal can be mined on a certain island (it was an extremely important and valuable mineral at that time) and shares his good fortune with Heyst. This forces Heyst to give up his ideal isolation. After Morrison dies in England, where he has set up the Tropical Coal Belt Company, Heyst becomes the local manager of the company on the island of Samburan. For various reasons, however, it is not successful, and the business is closed down. Nevertheless Heyst remains on the island with Wang, a Chinese servant, as his solitary companion, once again pursuing the ideal life of isolation.

Because he is a solitary wanderer, and now almost a hermit on the coal island of Samburan, and because the Tropical Coal Belt Company was an economic threat to some of the coal-traders, Heyst is viewed with a mixture of curiosity and suspicious enmity by most of the other Europeans in the southern Pacific Ocean area. One man in particular – Schomberg, a German hotel-keeper – is very scornful of Heyst, even spreading malicious rumours that Heyst caused the death of Morrison. On one occasion when Heyst has to visit the mainland he stays at Schomberg's hotel when a visiting female orchestra is also there, playing for the entertainment of Schomberg's customers. Heyst notices that one young woman is being bullied by the wife of the man who runs the orchestra, and from a feeling of spontaneous sympathy – the same feeling as had led him to help Morrison out of debt – befriends the victim. She is a young English woman called Alma, although later Heyst renames her Lena, who is both poor and friendless. She is also extremely unhappy, as the repulsive Schomberg, despite having a wife, thinks he is in love with her and insists on forcing his attentions on the young woman. Heyst helps the woman escape from both the unwelcome attentions of Schomberg and the gruelling oppression of the orchestra, taking her back with him to his isolated island. This spontaneously generous act again goes against the advice of Axel Heyst's father. As in the case of Morrison, it also earns Heyst the undying gratitude of the person he has saved. Lena's sole motivation in life, her ideal, becomes her devotion to Heyst.

Schomberg discovers what has happened, which increases his

hatred of Heyst, and at the same time he is troubled by some very disturbing customers. These are Jones, who is a footloose criminal and professional gambler of upper-class background; Martin Ricardo, who travels as Jones's secretary but is in fact a killer whose job it is to take care of the violent side of their adventures; and the servant they have for all the manual and menial tasks, Pedro, who is always described as being more like a gorilla than a man, and is treated as such by the naturally vicious Ricardo. Schomberg fears these men will create trouble for him in the hotel, and, through arousing their greed by telling them that Heyst has a fortune hidden on his island, both gets rid of them, as they sail off to rob Heyst, and thinks he will have revenged himself on the Swede for having stolen, as he sees it, the young woman he desires.

In the meantime Heyst and Lena are unaware of all this activity, and living in ideal peace and happiness on their isolated island. Their only contact with the outside world is through the occasional visit of a passing ship captained by a man called Davidson, who keeps a discreet eye on their welfare. The idyllic atmosphere is destroyed by the arrival of Jones, Ricardo and Pedro. The Chinese servant Wang, fearing the outcome of the strangers' visit, steals Heyst's revolver and runs away to the far side of the island, leaving Heyst and Lena without any effective defence against the murderous thieves. Heyst wants Lena to escape to another part of the island too, but she stays with him. Lena has a hope that she can trick Ricardo into parting with his killer's knife, which would partly disarm him and at the same time give Heyst a weapon of his own.

The conclusion of the novel deals with the outcome, in which Jones and Ricardo quarrel with one another and Wang secretly returns to the scene of the action. Wang shoots Pedro dead in self-defence. Jones accidentally shoots and kills Lena while she is tricking Ricardo into trusting her with his knife. Jones was in fact trying to kill Ricardo because of a quarrel, and later does succeed in murdering his former accomplice. Jones is eventually found drowned, but no one knows if it was an accident or whether he committed suicide because he obviously could not escape legal justice. Baron Axel Heyst, in a state of grief over the death of Lena, commits suicide by setting fire to his bungalow, burning both their bodies to ashes.

As we have seen, the plot of any Conrad novel may be approached by looking at the tension between ideals and reality. It may occur to you here that in Heyst's life the theme begins in the young man's relationship with his father. His father teaches him that reality is harsh, and therefore the ideal life is one of isolation – as far from worldly reality as it is possible to get. Although Heyst pursues this ideal apparently with considerable success, it breaks down on two critical occasions. The first time is when he saves Morrison from financial ruin, the second when Heyst rescues Lena from servitude and unhappiness. On both these occasions Heyst breaks out of his isolation to help someone worse off than himself, a person who is encountering the harshest circumstances of reality. What may strike you about this is that Heyst acts from the very best of motives, and without thinking of the possible consequences, simply reponding to a fellow human being in need. I think this gives the book a tragic dimension: the best of intentions leading to the worst of consequences.

These actions bring Heyst's life into conflict with the worldly reality surrounding him – that of other people who are less generous both in money and in spirit. You might, for instance, consider Schomberg. His reality is vanity and sexual greed for Lena, who finds his desire for her repulsive. When his greed is thwarted by Lena's escape with Heyst, the reality of Schomberg's existence becomes centred on jealousy of, and a desire for revenge against, Heyst. Although Heyst attempts to go back into isolation – though now with Lena – on his island, Schomberg's hatred does not allow it. The German hotel-keeper sends Jones, Ricardo and Pedro to Heyst's ideal island partly to get them away from his hotel, but mainly as an act of revenge, since he knows that Jones and Ricardo are murderers who will think nothing of killing Heyst and anyone else who gets in their way. The criminals go because their only value is money, and they believe Schomberg's story that Heyst has a large treasure. So, the island of Heyst's happy isolation is invaded by the dark forces of revenge and greed. The conclusion is that the ideal state of isolation is destroyed by human violence, while the symbol of that ideal, the bungalow in which Heyst and Lena live, is literally consumed by fire. The instrusion of reality leaves nothing at all of the ideal existing.

Lena's devotion to Heyst leads to Schomberg's jealousy. Her attempt to save Heyst from the murderers, instead of running away when she has the chance, brings her ideal life into conflict with the harshness of their ruthless greed. She, too, is destroyed by dark forces. In these ways the novel clearly presents a tension between the people who are attempting to live in an ideal way, and those motivated by selfish opportunism. Where we have found the main challenge in appreciating Conrad, however, is not so much in the ideas as in his style, in the language and the tone through which the themes are expressed. The most effective way of approaching any difficulty in this aspect of a novel is by means of close analysis of particular passages, and we should now move on to do that.

2 *Select a short passage for discussion and try to build on the ideas you have established so far*

Up to now I have been concerned with identifying an overall pattern in the novel. This is the right way to start, but your feeling for the text will begin to come to life only as you consider particular incidents and scenes. In this case we can start by looking in some detail at the main character. I have chosen a passage that describes Heyst's feelings after Morrison's death, when the Swede has to visit the mainland to transact some essential business:

> It was not in Heyst's character to turn morose; but his mental state was not compatible with a sociable mood. He spent his evenings sitting apart on the veranda of Schomberg's hotel. The lamentations of stringed instruments issued from the building in the hotel compound, the approaches to which were decorated with Japanese paper lanterns strung up between the trunks of several big trees. Scraps of tunes more or less plaintive reached his ears. They pursued him even into his bedroom, which opened into an upstairs veranda. The fragmentary and rasping character of these sounds made their intrusion inexpressibly tedious in the long run. Like most dreamers, to whom it is given sometimes to hear the music of the spheres, Heyst, the wanderer of the Archipelago, had a taste for silence which he had been able to gratify for years. The islands are very quiet. . . .
>
> Perhaps this was the very spell which had enchanted Heyst in the early days. For him, however, that was broken. He was no longer enchanted, though he was still a captive of the islands. He had no intention to leave them ever. Where could he have gone to, after all these years? Not a single soul belonging to him lived anywhere on earth. Of this fact – not such a remote one, after all – he had only lately become aware; for it is failure that makes a man enter into himself and reckon up his resources. And though he had made up his mind to retire from the world in hermit fashion, yet he was irrationally moved by this sense of loneliness which had come to him in the hour of renunciation. (pp. 67–8)

This extract is about Axel Heyst's feelings at this stage in the novel: his friend and partner Morrison having died, the Swedish baron is again alone in the world. The narrative describes Heyst's contemplation of his situation. Throughout this book I have emphasised one study guide: that the best way of analysing a passage is by approaching it through the ideas you have already established. In looking for an opposition we might see that Heyst's ideal state is on his island, living 'in hermit fashion', but that is in conflict with his feeling of loneliness. This echoes, and confirms, the tension between ideals and reality we identified in considering the novel's overall pattern.

The details of the extract should, if my argument in earlier chapters is valid, reinforce the expression of the central opposition. The first point of detail you might observe is that Heyst is thinking about the island, but is actually on the mainland. He is meditating on being a hermit whilst staying in a busy hotel with many customers. The island is associated with an ideal of isolation, but the hotel is full of social reality. Although Heyst spends the evenings sitting apart from the hotel's other customers, his contemplative ideal is invaded by the sight and sound of the hotel's entertainment. The decorations are garish, and the sound is 'rasping'. Heyst is described as a dreamer who has an ideal of silence, but the reality of the noise from the orchestra pursues him even into what should have been the ideal privacy of his bedroom, destroying all tranquillity and thought, until it becomes 'inexpressibly tedious'. Heyst seeks inner peace and harmony but mentally, and literally, finds only discord. The fact that it is a critical point in Heyst's life is emphasised by the irony that the sense of loneliness occurs not a long time before or after his decision to seek an ideal of isolation, but in the very 'hour of renunciation' of social reality. Two contradictory impulses occur almost simultaneously. Even the thought of the ideal is invaded by an aspect of reality.

We should be able to relate this theme and passage to the novel as a whole. In doing so it is worth thinking further about the way in which the effect is partly achieved through an ironic style, which, as we have seen, is a recurring feature of Conrad's writing. For instance, at this point Heyst, staying in Schomberg's hotel, does not know that the German hates him, and in trying to escape from the music is unaware that his destiny will shortly be changed by one of the musicians who is being pursued by the hotel-keeper. Heyst is dreaming of his ideal whilst literally positioned between two of the people who will contribute, although in different ways, to his destruction by the reality he wants to shun. We can note the irony in the language too. Hest had once been 'enchanted' by the 'spell' of the islands, which suggests that he had no conscious say in his destiny, like a man bewitched. Now he has 'no intention' of leaving them: he has made up his own mind about that, taking control of his future. Relating this episode to the novel as a whole, I think it is ironic that this thought occurs just at the moment when he is about to lose control over his fate, through his spontaneous act of rescuing Lena. Heyst is also dwelling on the idea that nobody anywhere on earth belongs to him, and is doing so whilst unable to escape from the plaintive music that Lena – of whose existence he is ignorant at present – is helping to make. As we have seen in looking at other novels, Conrad's style is often ironic – appreciating it is part of the sheer pleasure of reading him – and this passage is no exception. The irony largely stems from the idea that the character is contemplating a lifetime of tranquil, if lonely, isolation, but that actually he is on the brink of an involvement with reality that will erupt in terrible violence.

3 *Select a second passage for discussion*

At this point in the process of analysis you might want to go on to consider the relationship of Heyst and Lena, but I prefer to leave that for the next stage. The reason is that I want to approach later events through a slightly wider perspective, and therefore I am going to look now at the German hotel-keeper, Schomberg. I have chosen a passage that describes his attitudes to Lena both before and after her escape with Heyst. The narrative has just commented that Schomberg has reached the age of forty-five, when some men behave recklessly:

> Her shrinking form, her downcast eyes, when she had to listen to him, cornered at the end of an empty corridor, he regarded as signs of submission to the overpowering force of his will, the recognition of his personal fascinations. For every age is fed on illusions, lest men should renounce life early and the human race come to an end.
>
> It's easy to imagine Schomberg's humiliation, his shocked fury, when he discovered that the girl who had for weeks resisted his attacks, his prayers, and his fiercest protestations, had been snatched from under his nose by 'that Swede', apparently without any trouble worth speaking of. He refused to believe the fact. He would have it, at first, that the Zangiacomos [the husband and wife who ran the orchestra], for some unfathomable reason, had played him a scurvy trick, but when no

> further doubt was possible, he changed his view of Heyst. The despised Swede became for Schomberg the deepest, the most dangerous, the most hateful of scoundrels. He could not believe that the creature he had coveted with so much force and with so little effect, was in reality tender, docile to her impulse, and had almost offered herself to Heyst without a sense of guilt, in a desire of safety, and from a profound need of placing her trust where her woman's instinct guided her ignorance. Nothing would serve Schomberg but that she must have been circumvented by some occult exercise of force or craft, by the laying of some subtle trap. His wounded vanity wondered ceaselessly at the means 'that Swede' had employed to seduce her away from a man like him. . . . (pp. 89–90)

Here we are given a description of Schomberg's thoughts as he reflects on his own failure to gain Lena's affections, despite trying for weeks, and Heyst's success in apparently doing so very quickly. Since the extract is partly concerned with Schomberg's attitudes, I think the main tension rests between his view of himself and what he actually achieved. Schomberg has an ideal view of himself in which he is an 'overpowering force' full of 'personal fascinations'. That vision of himself comes into conflict with Lena's 'desire for safety': Schomberg sees himself as irresistibly attractive, but Lena perceives him as a menacing threat. The reality that Lena finds him repulsive and prefers to trust the Swedish baron is not easy for Schomberg to accept. The destruction of Schomberg's ideal view of himself by that reality is what causes his humiliation and fury.

The description of the unfortunate Lena before her escape also contributes to the central tension. When she shrinks and lowers her eyes, Schomberg's vanity never allows him to consider that Lena finds him intimidating. He interprets her attitude as submission to the force of his personality. Schomberg is so egocentric that he cannot see the reality, although it is fairly obvious: that Lena is an impoverished and refined young English woman without a friend or protector (and remember this takes place in the early part of the twentieth century) literally thousands of miles from home. She naturally feels very vulnerable. Schomberg himself is middle-aged and married. The reality is that Lena is terrified by his attentions. The style emphasises that Lena could do little to protect herself – she *had* to listen to him, because she was cornered, like an animal, at the end of an empty corridor from which no help would come if she offended Schomberg and he physically attacked her.

The details of Schomberg's reaction to the reality of the situation, and the style in which they are expressed, reveal Conrad's attitude to the character. Schomberg's first response is disbelief, preferring to think it is 'a scurvy trick', an underhand practical joke by the Zangiacomos. Having eventually to lose that illusion, Schomberg creates another: that Heyst has used a form of witchcraft to entrap Lena. This is so ludicrously far from the reality – the truth being that Lena felt vulnerable and simply trusted Heyst to protect her – that I think we can say it is satire against Schomberg. In the vanity of his ideal self-image Schomberg just will not face up to the reality of his own unattractiveness. The satiric style comes from the tension between Schomberg's obviously unrealistic idealising of himself as an irresistibly powerful and attractive personality, and his inability to see, or accept, the truth of the situation: that Lena finds him repulsive and frightening. If you do not think the style here is satiric and working against Schomberg, you will obviously not agree with my analysis. In that case you will want to work out your own views, and argue the reasons for them, but, as long as you always base your argument on the evidence of the text, you will be able to build a coherent case.

It is perhaps now time to look closely at the novel's central relationship, to see how this reflects the main themes and how it is presented.

4 *Select a third passage for discussion*

The relationship between Heyst and Lena is not an easy one to understand, and if you attempted merely to summarise it your observations would quickly become generalised and limited. This is a good reason for working from close analysis of an extract, to give your views a sound foundation and keep them specific. The passage I have chosen to explore relates to the early days of Heyst and Lena's life together on the isolated island of Samburan:

> 'Why are you looking so serious?' he pursued, and immediately thought that habitual seriousness, in the long run, was much more bearable than constant gaiety. 'However, this expression suits you exceedingly,' he added, not diplomatically, but because, by the tendency of his taste, it was a true statement. 'And as long as I can be certain that it is not boredom which gives you this severe air, I am willing to sit here and look at you till you are ready to go.'
>
> And this was true. He was still under the fresh sortilege of their common life, the surprise of novelty, the flattered vanity of his possession

> of this woman; for a man must feel that, unless he has ceased to be masculine. Her eyes moved in his direction, rested on him, then returned to their stare into the deeper gloom at the foot of the straight tree-trunks, whose spreading crowns were slowly withdrawing their shade. The warm air stirred slightly about her motionless head. She would not look at him, from some obscure fear of betraying herself. She felt in her inner-most depths an irresistible desire to give herself up to him more completely, by some act of absolute sacrifice. This was something of which he did not seem to have an idea. He was a strange being without needs. (p. 170)

The extract describes Heyst and Lena as they sit in a forest clearing on the island of Samburan, each still unsure at this early stage of their relationship of the feelings of the other person. The tension here is very subtle: both people are living an ideal life of mutual love, but they are neither of them sure how to express their happiness or love in reality. So, the ideal is the love of two people who are not used to loving or being loved, the reality their unsureness about the other person, and their inability to show their own deep feelings.

I hope you are able to appreciate how this theme – of an ideal love that cannot be expressed in reality – is part of the wider tension between ideals and reality that we have been discussing. What makes ideas memorable in any novel, however, is the way in which they are given life in the text. This is a touching, poignant scene of two people deeply happy but unable to communicate it. Heyst can only sit and look at Lena. The details of his conversation show that he is awkward in speech, speaking without diplomacy and being content mainly with silence and waiting. He feels a divine enchantment, 'the fresh sortilege', at the novelty of having such a woman to care for, but he cannot express his feelings actively or in words. Lena is in a similar position: she would rather stare into the gloom of the forest than look at Heyst. More than this, she is positively frightened of betraying herself. Why do you think this is so? The reason seems to be that she thinks of her love for Heyst as a revelation of something best concealed because he does not appear to need her love. The last two sentences of the above extract show that Heyst seems to her to have no idea what she is feeling. Because Lena feels she cannot show it in any other way, therefore, her ideal can be expressed only through 'some act of absolute sacrifice'.

By relating the passage to the novel as a whole we know that Heyst is also devoted to Lena. Sacrifice becomes an ideal to them both, and one that leads to the reality of death. Lena dies because she refuses to run away when Heyst is in danger, and it is her attempt to save him from being murdered by Ricardo that causes her death. Lena's sacrifice prefigures Heyst's suicide, the sacrifice of his own life being a consequence of her act of absolute sacrifice. The sombre mood of the episode suggests, I think, that tragedy awaits these isolated idealists. The style itself emphasises this tragic sense in, for instance, the detail that Lena does not look upward, towards the light, where the sun is appearing above the tops of the trees, but downward into 'the deeper gloom' at the foot of the trees. The darkness there appears deeper because of the sunlight beginning to enter the clearing from above. In fact Lena is not merely looking into the gloom – she is specifically staring into it, as though absorbed or obsessed by it. The language stresses her stillness, partly through the description of her motionless head, but also by contrasting her immobility with the apparent mobility of the trees. The trees are described as 'slowly withdrawing their shade', but we know that this is a figure of speech rather than a literal truth. The trees are stationary; it is the sun's movement that is causing the retreat of the shade; but that suggestion of the trees moving, and the increasing light in the clearing, emphasises, I think, how very still and preoccupied with the darkness of the forest Lena is. Even at a time of ideal tranquillity and light Lena is concerned with a gloomy darkness. We know from our wider knowledge of the novel that the dark forces stemming from human jealousy, revenge and greed are at that moment pursuing Lena and Heyst. Our analysis of other Conrad novels has led us to an appreciation of the fact that he rarely uses detail merely in order to create atmosphere: it usually also contributes to the development of the novel in some way. Here, then, it is possible to argue that Lena's contemplation of the gloom, and the almost death-like silence and stillness of the scene, present a poignant foreboding of tragedy, of an impending conflict with reality that is both inevitable and ultimately catastrophic.

The relationship of Heyst and Lena is complex, and if you are studying the novel in preparation for an examination you will probably want to look at other episodes involving them. No matter how elusive the ideas around them may seem, or how subtle the style, you should always be able to relate the relevant passages to the central tension between ideals and reality. You should also consider the language and tone as aspects of Conrad's style, and try to express, through close analysis, how they are created and how they contribute to the overall effect and pleasure of a scene or incident.

Although we could discuss Lena and Heyst further, I should now like to move on to consider further developments.

5 *Select a fourth passage for discussion*

I think it is a good idea to look at the intruders who precipitate the final crisis, in particular Mr Jones, the former gentleman and now ruthless outcast criminal and professional gambler. When Jones, his vicious accomplice Martin Ricardo and their servant Pedro arrive on the island the relationship between Heyst and Lena is put under enormous pressure. Heyst tells Lena to hide in the forest – although in fact she arranges a meeting with Ricardo in order to trick him into parting with his deadly knife – and he goes to see Jones in order to try to resolve the situation and avert the danger. Heyst does not realise, however, that the murderous Jones has arrived on the island in ignorance of an important fact. The two men face one another in near darkness, talking of the information Schomberg had fed the criminals:

> On his right hand the doorway incessantly flickered with distant lightning, and the continuous rumble of thunder went on irritatingly, like the growl of an inarticulate giant muttering fatuously.
>
> Heyst overcame his immense repugnance to allude to her whose image, cowering in the forest, was constantly before his eyes, with all the pathos and force of its appeal, august, pitiful, and almost holy to him. It was in a hurried, embarrassed manner that he went on:
>
> 'If it had not been for that girl whom he persecuted with his insane and odious passion, and who threw herself on my protection, he would never have – but you know well enough!'
>
> 'I *don't* know!' burst out Mr Jones with amazing heat. 'That hotel-keeper tried to talk to me once of some girl he had lost, but I told him I didn't want to hear any of his beastly women stories. It had something to do with you, had it?' . . .
>
> One could see the eyes of Mr Jones had become fixed in the depths of their black holes by the gleam of white becoming steady there. The whole man seemed frozen still.
>
> 'Here! Here!' he screamed out twice. There was no mistaking his astonishment, his shocked incredulity – something like frightened disgust. . . . 'It is possible that you didn't know of that significant fact?' he [Heyst] inquired. 'Of the only effective truth in the welter of silly lies that deceived you so easily?'
>
> 'No, I didn't!' Mr Jones shouted. 'But Martin did!' he added in a faint whisper. . . . 'He knew. He knew before!' Mr Jones mourned in a hollow voice. 'He knew of her from the first!'

> Backed hard against the wall, he no longer watched Heyst. He had the air of a man who had seen an abyss yawning under his feet. (pp. 308–10)

In this extract Heyst inadvertently gives Jones the information that he has Lena living on the island with him. Jones has earlier refused to listen to Schomberg's talk about Lena, because of his profound aversion to women, and Martin Ricardo has deliberately kept the information from him. The passage describes the deep effect the news has on Jones. He begins the confrontation with Heyst thinking of only one thing, an ideal solution that will give him without any trouble or delay the treasure that he thinks Heyst has in his possession. This ideal solution is destroyed by the reality of which Jones has until now been ignorant. What is more, he has not just lost the immediate ideal, but realises that Martin Ricardo has betrayed him by not telling him of the reality of the situation on the island. The immediate implication of this betrayal is that the relationship of Jones and Ricardo is over. Jones's dream of his ideal future – of easy wealth, with Martin Ricardo around to do any violence required to keep it – is destroyed, and facing that reality he is like a man standing on the brink of a yawning abyss. We have already seen different variations on the central opposition between ideals and reality, and in this incident I think we see how Jones's shock also contributes to this theme.

As by now we would expect, the details of the passage are not there merely for decoration or atmosphere, but add something to the meaning of the novel, and our understanding of it. Here they indicate that something powerful is happening. At the beginning of the scene Heyst and Jones are locked in a combat of wills, and I think the detail of the storm outside, the incessant thunder and lightning, mirrors the tense conflict. But during the course of the confrontation the style shifts as the detail focuses on Jones in particular, as he suffers a kind of emotional and brain storm. We know from the novel as a whole that the knowledge Jones has just received causes him to murder Martin Ricardo, and in the process inadvertently kill Lena too. The reality, the knowledge of Lena's presence, that destroys Jones's ideal of his future is like a storm hitting him. If we look at the language we see that Jones speaks with 'amazing heat', but he 'seemed frozen still'. The contrast between these two states help to illustrate the contradictory tensions within Jones. The main conflict, or storm, at this point is not between Heyst and Jones, but within Jones.

Part of the sheer pleasure of reading Conrad's fiction, once we have understood how to appreciate it, comes from the way he writes, the manner in which what he is saying is integrated with the way it is expressed. In looking at the style of the extract quoted above it is worth noticing, too, how Jones's speech expresses this conflict – not just what he says, although that is obviously important, but also how he says it. He screams twice and shouts, but a moment later is reduced to a faint whisper. Again he shows contradictory impulses. This is also expressed by the paradox of his eyes, the gleam of the whites of which becomes steadier and more pronounced as his eyes sink deeper into the black holes that are their sockets. Jones seems to be retreating from the encroaching reality, the knowledge that he cannot, after all, trust his murderous partner in crime. At the end of the extract Jones is literally backed up against the wall, but he also metaphorically has his back against the wall. He does not bother to watch Heyst because the abyss he sees is more dangerous: if Jones cannot trust Ricardo, he must kill him before he is murdered himself.

6 *Have I achieved a sufficiently complex sense of the novel?*

It could be argued that, like all Conrad's fiction, this novel seems to explore an unremitting tension between ideals and reality. This is not to imply that the situation is simple, for the recurrent theme is developed in many different ways in Conrad's work, and a further complication occurs because every individual reader will understand the issues in his or her own way. The fundamental purpose in constructing your own response from a selection of passages is to enable you to define, and articulate clearly, your own distinctive interpretation of a text. When I first discovered Conrad as an author I was immensely impressed by the great variety of his novels. After reading a lot of novels that all seemed to be set in England I was greatly excited by these works that covered the whole world, and I realised that the differences between the novels added another dimension to the challenge of understanding them, and to my enjoyment when I thought I had achieved that.

In thinking about *The Secret Agent* I was struck by the fact that Winnie is associated throughout that novel with family and domestic responsibilities, living a humdrum existence that does not require imagination or contemplation. My response to Lena in *Victory*, on the other hand, is that she is a sensitive, rather highly-strung young woman whose harsh experiences in life have made her defensive, meditative and introverted. She is a musician, alone in the world, and you might remember that in a passage quoted earlier Heyst reflects on her 'habitual seriousness'. Conrad's presentation of these two women helps us to understand in part the difference between the novels they appear in: Winnie is generally maternal and resilient, whereas Lena seems always about to break down under the stress of the situations in which she finds herself. Both these novels might appear to be ordinary adventure stories from a superficial summary of their plots, but novels with such complex central characters can be read and reread with pleasure. The interest moves from the simple story line to trying to understand the complicated characters. Both the women ultimately act paradoxically, and the drama of their actions arises from the idea that they appear to be behaving out of character. The quiet, homely, peaceful Winnie murders her husband; and the frightened, vulnerable, mainly passive Lena succeeds in gaining power over and outwitting a ruthless professional killer, the vicious Ricardo. At the time they do these things the women are in a state of crisis, and therefore become capable of extraordinary acts. One of the reasons why Conrad is, for me, such a great writer is that he understands the profound emotional reality that can lie deep beneath the surface of apparently placid, socially ideal characters. These people are almost always shown as victims of forces they cannot understand or control, and this illustrates an aspect of Conrad's compassion for the characters trapped in circumstances that bring out those dark forces. It is this factor that makes Conrad a moving and very human novelist.

These are my responses. Yours might be different and you might think I am stretching the evidence too far to be convincing. In that case, as ever, you must continue to look at passages and construct your own view until a coherent pattern of ideas emerges, and you get a full and clear sense of the text as a whole in your mind. I realise that my own analysis is not complete: the enigmas of Heyst and Lena would repay further examination, and the characters of Jones, Ricardo and Schomberg as studies in three different forms of evil need more detailed exploration. This work would be interesting in itself, and help to expand some of my ideas about the novel. However, I hope that by now the basic method of approaching a text is plain, and that you can take the analysis forward on your own by looking in detail at extracts.

Aspects of the novel

There are many ways in which *Victory* could be discussed. We could again look at extended metaphor (see Chapter 4), or follow up further the theme of greed that recurs in much of Conrad's fiction. He is the most cosmopolitan of writers in English, and often depicts a conflict of different nationalities, races and cultures – which in this case is carried out by the interplay of English, Swedish, the German, Portuguese and Chinese characters, the virtually brutish Pedro, and the Samburan natives.

In this section, however, I do not intend to explore any particular theme. I have outlined in the other chapters ways in which *Victory*, or any novel, might be discussed. What I want to do now is look at a couple of extracts in order to reach an appreciation of the fineness of language and texture in Conrad's writing, because for me this is a source of great pleasure and a central facet of Conrad's greatness. I hope the exercise will also reinforce my argument that the most effective way of understanding Conrad's themes is through analysing specific passages.

Almost any page could be used in this way. I have chosen two pieces that are rather different from one another in order to illustrate the range of Conrad's style. The first is a description of what Schomberg calls 'my concert-hall':

> The uproar in that small, barn-like structure, built of imported pine boards, and raised clear of the ground, was simply stunning. An instrumental uproar, screaming, grunting, whining, sobbing, scraping, squeaking some kind of lively air; while a grand piano, operated upon by a bony, red-faced woman with bad-tempered nostrils, rained hard notes like hail through the tempest of fiddles. ... In the quick time of that music, in the varied, piercing clamour of the strings, in the movements of the bare arms, in the low dresses, the coarse faces, the stony eyes of the executants, there was a suggestion of brutality – something cruel, sensual, and repulsive. (p. 69).

In normal circumstances a concert hall is something we might ideally associate with harmony, taste, refinement, an epitome of civilised behaviour and values. In reality Schomberg's so-called concert hall is an extension of himself: loud, crude, tasteless, barbaric. We can see how this relates to the central tension of the conflict between ideals and reality, but the point I want to stress is that Conrad does not express it as simply and baldly as I do in my comments above. It is by looking closely at the language that we can appreciate how Conrad powerfully gives life to the theme.

First of all he emphasises the makeshift nature of the building. It is not a real concert hall, but like a temporary barn, put together from boards. The sound is described as an uproar, and later as a piercing clamour, although it is supposed to be 'some kind of lively air'. The reality is quite different from the intention, as is conveyed by means of a piling-up of verbs – 'screaming, grunting, whining, sobbing, scraping, squeaking' – all of which express a form of noise, but none of which is usually applied to the making of concert music. The noise is related not to the creative achievement of human art, but to the violent and destructive elements of nature: hard rain, hail and tempest.

All this discord is also emphasised by the appearances of the people involved in making it. The ideal classical musician of the European concert halls, of which this is Schomberg's pretentious and totally inadequate copy, is refined in dress and behaviour, as well as musicianship. This touring ladies' orchestra has a quite different reality. The pianist attacks her instrument – operates on it – rather than plays it, and her features depict her personality. The other members of the orchestra are coarse and disinterested, and, although their dress, low-cut at the bosom and with bare arms, is intended to make them attractive and alluring, the overall effect is entirely the opposite: 'cruel, sensual, and repulsive'.

Other ideas connected to this passage could be discussed, and by relating it to a slightly wider context we could analyse the appropriateness of the fact that Heyst first sees Lena in this scene, and the irony of her being brought to the attention of her eventual rescuer, Heyst, by the bullying of the aggressive pianist, Mrs Zangiacomo. My purpose here, though, is to illustrate how what might appear to be an unimportant scene, designed merely to advance the plot, does express the main themes of the novel, and how the specific language used gives the passage interest, and force. It is the writing of an author who is in control of the material, and knows clearly the effect he is trying to achieve. You might look for other illustrations of this skill.

The scene of Lena's death conveys a very different mood, through a different use of language. Lena has triumphed over the vicious Ricardo, persuading him to give up to her the knife with which he intended to murder Heyst. Jones aims a shot at Ricardo, but it hits Lena instead. Davidson, the ship's captain who comes in unexpectedly to help, and Heyst are trying to care for the mortally wounded Lena:

> They stood side by side, looking mournfully at the little black hole made by Mr Jones' bullet under the swelling breast of a dazzling and as it were sacred whiteness. It rose and fell slightly – so slightly that only the eyes of the lover could detect the faint stir of life. Heyst, calm and utterly unlike himself in the face, moving about noiselessly, prepared a wet cloth, and laid it on the insignificant wound, round which there was hardly a trace of blood to mar the charm, the fascination, of that mortal flesh.
>
> Her eyelids fluttered. She looked drowsily about, serene, as if fatigued only by the exertions of her tremendous victory, capturing the very sting of death in the service of love. (p. 323)

Whereas the previous extract was full of harshness, this, it seems to me, is very delicate. It is not the horror of death that is emphasised in the scene, but the tenderness of love. There is a contrast between the apparent insignificance of the bullet hole, and its awful consequences. Despite the wound in it, Lena's flesh still has charm, but we are reminded that it is also mortal. The juxtaposition of 'charm' and 'mortal' in this context brings out the poignancy of the episode, and avoids the kind of melodrama we often find in inferior writers when they deal with violent death. The emphasis here is not on the sensationalism of the event, but on its human consequences, and the novelist's compassion for the victims – in losing Lena, Heyst is a victim too – of the dark forces of destruction that have caused the tragedy.

The language expresses the silence, the reverence, of the moment. Heyst and Davidson are mournful, Heyst is calm and moves noiselessly to perform a practical act of compassion. Lena is hardly breathing, and although on the point of death looks 'serene', which we can relate back to the description of her appearance, 'as it were sacred'. 'Sacred' and 'serene' are reverential words, perhaps bringing a heroic tone to Lena's death, and we are reminded that she has achieved a 'tremendous victory', and so may not ultimately have lived a meaningless life. The nature of her death might be compared to the awful numbness of her life in the touring ladies' orchestra, vulnerable to the vile desires of Schomberg. We have seen how elusive Conrad's tone is in other novels, and that feature of his writing is here too. Lena captures 'the very sting of death in the service of love' – what do you understand that to mean? I think it has two interpretations. On a literal level the thing that carries the sting of death is Ricardo's murderous knife, with which he intended to deliver the sting of death to Heyst. Lena has captured the knife from him, and so saved Heyst from it. But metaphorically Lena herself has caught the sting of death, the bullet from Jones's revolver from which she is about to die. I think Conrad intends us to hold both these interpretations of the phrase; it is part of the irony that in saving Heyst from death at the hand of Ricardo she starts the chain of events that will end in Heyst's suicide – setting fire to the bungalow after Lena has died from the sting of that fatal bullet. Lena has expressed her love for Heyst, but it is achieved only through the sacrifice of death. It is simultaneously both a victory and a loss. An aspect of Conrad's power as a novelist is his ability to present paradoxes, to encourage us to see events in two different ways at the same time.

This kind of complexity illustrates Conrad's exciting subtlety. That is something I have stressed throughout this book – how Conrad's style works on several levels at once so that we are aware of the rich fabric of events and of their complexity. The only way to arrive at this complexity is to work on passages and to think about what Conrad is doing, and how he achieves it. A book of critical appreciation written by someone else can give you only that person's views, but if you work out your own response and analysis it must lead you to develop your own ideas. There is also a further advantage to this process, in that you will also be building up a collection of critical notes and material that will be useful in writing your own essays. The following chapter will take up this point.

7

Writing an essay: *The Shadow-Line* (1917)

ONE feature of studying English that makes it quite different from many other subjects is that your success depends not only on your understanding of the texts, but also on your ability to show that understanding through the writing of a good, literate essay. Be determined from the beginning, therefore, that you will write good essays – work that markers and examiners will not find faults in, but will want to reward with high grades. Obviously most students want to achieve good results, but go about the task in different ways. Some approach the subject casually in the hope that they will get 'lucky' examination questions that will enable them to do well without much work or thought, or that they will become inspired on the day. Others don't bother too much because they believe you are either born with the ability to write good essays or not. In fact, as any examiner will tell you, luck and inspiration have little to do with convincing essays or exam answers, and no one is born with the ability to write anything at all – that is something we all have to learn. So, if we have to learn to write any kind of essay we may as well learn to write good ones. That comes from only one source: developing an efficient and effective method for producing interesting and intelligent essays.

If you are still trying to develop your own planned approach, what I can do here is guide you towards a useful method. You may find that my advice is slightly different from that of your teachers, and of other people, because everyone has his or her own individual preferences. But if our advice differs in some details it will nevertheless be fundamentally similar, for the ground rules of good essay-writing are not disputed by teachers or examiners. First you must be clear about what you are attempting to do in an essay. The basic factor is that **in a critical essay, which includes an examination answer, you are building a rational and coherent argument from the evidence of the text with which you are dealing.** This is a simple statement of the formula, and your approach to an essay should be just as straightforward. It is important that you do not confuse writing an essay containing complex and deep content with having a complicated design for it. Complex thoughts are most clearly conveyed through a simple essay construction. The key must be good organisation. Obviously that will not be achieved by just sitting down and writing everything that comes into your head, which is one of the main reasons why even students who do understand the texts they are dealing with sometimes get low marks. Before you begin to write anything you need to understand what the question is asking, and therefore have an outline of the shape of your answer. I do not mean that you need to know exactly what you are going to write, but that you do need to have an idea of how many paragraphs you will be writing and roughly how long they will be.

I shall go into more detail on these points during this chapter, but first I shall summarise these introductory points, just to emphasise how straightfoward the organisation of a good essay can, and must, be. First, realise that you are being asked a question and, therefore, that you are required to construct an answer. This does not mean stating your total response in your essay's opening paragraph. That would leave you no substantial points to develop your essay; and is also likely to lead to a sense of confusion in your answer as you attempt to cram too much into it too soon. The first paragraph should be introductory, clarifying what you think the main issue is that the question raises. This helps you get a clear approach to it, and shows the examiner or marker that you have thought about the question.

Having tackled what the question is about, the second stage is to start developing an answer. There is only one place to find that answer: in the text. But you cannot discuss the whole text at once, so you must select a part of the text to focus on. It therefore makes sense to begin your second paragraph by examining a particular scene in the novel or story. I will elaborate on ways of doing this later in the chapter, but your immediate aim should be to establish a point from the scene you have chosen that is central to the question you are considering. Once you have made a valid point, and substantiated it from the evidence of the scene you are dealing with, you can conclude the second paragraph and go on to the third, again arguing from analysis of a particular episode or perhaps a short quotation. Working in this way you will build your essay in paragraphed blocks, and after you have covered five or six incidents or passages, and analysed them in relation to the question under discussion, you should have developed a coherent line of argument.

The reader will be able to see how each paragraph has established a logical step in constructing your argument, and that it is based on evidence from the text. That is what you must aim for. The remainder of this chapter simply elaborates my basic advice, relating it to a specific question of a kind you might meet in school, college or university.

The question

As I said earlier, many students fail to answer the questions examiners and teachers have taken the trouble to set. Asked, for example, a carefully worded question on 'the function of imagery and symbolism in *The Shadow-Line*', most students will merely write down as many examples as they can of imagery and symbolism without bothering to consider whether, even in the light of the fact that the question suggests that they are different, imagery and symbolism may be slightly different aspects of the novel; and they will also fail to think about, or tackle, the issue of function – why Conrad uses particular images and symbols, what they add to the novel's ideas, how they help to develop its themes. Always be sure that you are answering fully the question you have been asked. To do this you must start from a recognition that the question is posing you an issue, or problem, to explore.

What do you make of the following question on *The Shadow-Line*?

> Discuss the view that Conrad always places his characters in the harshest of circumstances merely for dramatic effect.

There isn't simply a right or a wrong answer to such a question. Whatever your own view it must be argued from textual evidence, and in any case you are here required to discuss the issue, which will mean considering different points of view. There is no such thing as an easy, a difficult or a trick question. All questions are designed to make you think about the central ideas or conflicts in a text. The examiner's focus on a particular aspect should help you construct your response, so that in this instance you must concentrate first on the characters and their circumstances; but at the same time your essay must show an awareness of the scope and interests of the novel as a whole. This might appear daunting to some students, but all through this book I have emphasised the importance of seeing a broad pattern in any text, and this is what is required of you now. This is all that is meant by 'an awareness of the scope and interests of the novel as a whole'. What you are being asked to do here, in terms of the novel, is explore analytically **the relationships between characters and their circumstances, and the purpose Conrad puts them to.** Can you see that this question might be approached in terms of characters with ideals about life meeting the reality of experience? Recognising that the question involves the broad pattern of conflict between ideals and reality, which is a central opposition in Conrad's fiction, will help to give your answer a sense of direction. It will also help you to appreciate that the question is related to the central themes of the novel, rather than merely asking you for descriptions of the main characters and their various circumstances.

The first paragraph

Don't worry if my summary of the question did not occur to you independently. The main point to have grasped is that most questions about Conrad can be related to a broad conflict between ideals and reality. Recognising this will give you a starting point for thinking about the question. In any event, it is not necessary to sort out every point in detail before you begin, as the process of thinking about, planning and writing the essay will in itself help you discover the right kind of answer. Your opening paragraph should be used for sorting out the question's main issue. An introductory paragraph on this question, for example, might take something like the following form:

> In *The Shadow-Line* the main character, who is unnamed, tells his own story. We see him in two different sets of circumstances, first on shore and later at sea as captain of his ship. He encounters the worst circumstances whilst at sea. His ship suffers terrible weather conditions, and while nearly all the crew are struck down by fever, some are made delirious and almost die. Only the narrator and Ransome, who is the ship's cook and has a weak heart anyway, escape illness. So, the characters are placed in very harsh circumstances. But the question asks whether this is merely for dramatic effect, and a detailed look at what effect the circumstances have on the characters will help to uncover the answer.

In this brief introductory paragraph, I have had to show an overall grasp of the novel. I have also restated, to show that I understand, the main point of the question, but I have not tried to answer it yet. Your opening paragraph should be as brief and relevant as this, and if you find it isn't you are probably losing a sense of direction. That sense of direction comes from clearly defining the subject of your answer.

The second paragraph

If there is one single key factor in the writing of good answers it is probably the effective use of paragraphs. I noted above the necessity for a concise and clear opening paragraph, one that establishes your view of what you intend to do. Every paragraph that follows should be based on a similar pattern, well organised and adding to your analysis. Think about the overall shape of your essay: in your introduction you set up the areas for discussion, and in your final paragraph you will draw your conclusions; between them, in the body of your answer, you need five or six paragraphs to act as stepping stones, each making a specific point, with argument from the text, that advances the previous points and leads on to the subsequent ones. Very long paragraphs are often a sign that a student has lost control over his or her sense of direction, while paragraphs that are very short frequently indicate that points are being made in a flimsy way, so aim at somewhere about a half to two-thirds of a page in length for each of the main paragraphs. Remember that examiners see the overall shape of your answer before they start to read it in detail, and if they see a well-laid-out pattern of an opening paragraph followed by a body of five or six paragraphs of fairly uniform length, rounded off by a neat conclusion, they will be extremely surprised if the content is poor. Clear layout and coherent thinking usually go hand-in-hand.

Start to get into the text itself when you begin the second paragraph. Although I suggested earlier that most of your response to the question on *The Shadow-Line* above will be concerned with events on the ill-fated ship, the first third of the novel takes place on shore, and you might begin by looking at the way in which Conrad introduces the themes he later develops. In this instance a second paragraph might show a sense of this by starting, 'The introduction to the narrator leads us to believe that he has given up the sea, that he is a man who has decided to change the circumstances of his life.' In most other chapters of this book I have quoted long passages, but that obviously isn't possible in an exam. You can, however, relate in a lively way the episode you have chosen. Then start to examine the features you can see that are relevant to the question. In this case the narrator thinks he is going to change his circumstances, but immediately he learns about the command of a new ship he abandons his earlier desire to leave the sea. He little realises that this change has been arranged for him and so Conrad is able to distance us from the narrator by irony. At the same time we can see that Conrad is interested not just in presenting us with extreme events, but in illustrating and making us think about how people react to circumstances. By showing us the narrator on shore beforehand Conrad is able to strike up an effective contrast with later events which are wild and desperate. But he is also able to establish a certain irony that allows us to think about people's responses.

Can you see how I have started to shape an answer here? I have looked at the opening and begun to suggest that, while Conrad is interested in dramatic events, he is also interested in more than just dramatic effects. Notice how my paragraph does reach a conclusion, that I do try to pull my analysis of the opening together around the question. It is important to end a paragraph with this kind of summary of your argument and conclusion. These two or three sentences will keep your answer relevant, and ensure that your discussion moves along – instead of merely repeating points already made – by providing you with a springboard for your next paragraph. In this instance it would be logical, having considered the way the narrator's circumstances are changed, to look at what happens after he has assumed command of the ship. The only effective way of achieving that is to select an incident from the relevant section of the novel which appears to be helpful in answering the question.

Building your discussion on textual evidence is a method you can use to approach the writing of any essay on Conrad's fiction. It is also worth remembering that an essay is a self-contained piece of work in which you are presenting a convincing case to your reader, whether he or she is a teacher or an examiner, so there is no point in writing along the lines of 'The discovery that begins on page 111 proves that ...' unless you go into proper detail. Merely quoting a page or chapter number does not convey to the reader that you have a real sense of the text, that you have actually analysed and thought in detail about the evidence on which your argument is based. Giving a clear sense of the text, and expressing it persuasively, is vital. Students sometimes worry about style and try to cultivate a particular kind of style, but, provided you write grammatically, clearly and coherently, your own style will emerge interestingly. It is mainly a matter of thinking ahead: if you know roughly what a sentence is going to say before you start writing, it will usually come out right. Bad style is unclear style. Confused and meandering sentences indicate to an examiner that the student is fishing about for a point, rather than having a strong sense of essay direction.

The third paragraph

This sense of direction comes partly from each paragraph leading naturally to the next. For paragraph three I suggested above that an incident which occurs during the time the narrator is commanding his ship would be appropriate. There are several suitable choices, but I am choosing the incident in which the narrator discovers that the vital supply of quinine has been sold by the previous captain, that the jars he expected to contain the life-saving medicine are full of some useless powder. The thing to do here is to outline the episode, then bring out all the features that seem to you relevant to the question. It does not matter if you cannot remember the chapter number, or give a long quotation, but any details or phrases that come to you might be helpful; and using them efficiently will help to bring your answer to life, to give a real sense of the text. For instance, you might recall how the narrator, on discovering the truth, lets the jars slide through his fingers one by one so that they break on the floor at his feet. That action tells us something about his response to the terrible, and dramatic, information he has just learned: it is *dismay*, rather than the anger and rage of hurling them down melodramatically. To conclude the paragraph, write two or three sentences drawing your ideas together. Regarding this incident you might consider that Conrad does not go for the big dramatic effect of rage, and that the point of the experience is that the narrator learns for the future to take nothing for granted as reality teaches him to be prepared for the worst. If you build up your essay carefully, summarising your main points at the conclusion of each paragraph, you will find the novel's central themes are emerging in your response. It might occur to you here, for example, that Conrad is interested in what his characters learn from their experiences, their confrontation with circumstances, harsh or otherwise. I have repeatedly pointed out in this book that Conrad works around a central conflict between characters with ideals and the reality of circumstances, and I hope you can see how that is relevant to the experience of the narrator of *The Shadow-Line*.

Continuing to build

When you have finished a paragraph with a summary of its main argument, think for a moment about the next step. Is there another angle to the question? Is there a further feature of the novel not yet covered in the answer? You should always consider these kind of possibilities as you advance through your essay. At this point in the answer I am developing it might be possible to find a further contradiction to the argument that the narrator is placed in harsh circumstances merely for dramatic effect. Or it might be relevant to apply the idea to other characters. You might, for example, want to explore the character and experience of Burns, the ship's chief mate (or second-in-command). The fever sends him almost mad, and you could look at one of the scenes in which he raves about the old, dead captain putting a curse on the ship. Burns is certainly placed in harsh circumstances. But it is not necessary to keep slavishly to a format of dealing with only one incident in each single paragraph. You could expand this discussion to compare Burns's delirium with his eventual recovery, and the incident when, although terribly weak, he crawls on deck to offer the narrator moral support and companionship. Your final sentences in this paragraph would need to draw a conclusion about these two different aspects of character and experience. The delirium is not used just for dramatic effect, you might argue, but illustrates how close a basically good and sane man is to madness, to losing control over his circumstances and actions when under pressure – in this case from the effects of fever. But whatever your argument, conclude your paragraph properly with a summary of the main points. You should never end a paragraph with a quotation. At the conclusion the reader should always feel that you are in control of the material, that you have substantiated your own argument.

After considering the character of Burns, who suffers most from the fever, you might want to move on in the next paragraph to analyse the role of a character who avoids it – for example, the ship's cook Ransome, who becomes the narrator's right-hand man as the rest of the crew fall prey to the fever. It is always necessary to begin by choosing a specific incident, and there are many in which Ransome helps care for the sick. In particular he looks after and calms the raving Burns, is always ready to help his captain, sees to the running of the ship, and even assists in heavy physical tasks despite the fact that he is not supposed to do so. But there is an ironic complexity: Ransome is not threatened with death from the fever, but he is permanently living in the shadow of death because he has a weak heart. The final scene of the novel sees Ransome leaving the ship because of this. The man who is so resourceful when everyone else is weak and suffering finally gives in to a fear of death. I would argue that Ransome's circumstances of living are permanently harsh rather than dramatically so, and ultimately he tries to change his circumstances in order to bring his ideal of a life at sea into line with the reality of his health. The crucial thing, however, is what *you* think of the text.

Bringing out the complexity of the text

Roughly two-thirds of the way through your answer you may want slightly to change the direction of your essay. In the essay I am outlining I have spent four or five paragraphs constructing a reply to the suggestion that Conrad writes merely for dramatic effect. I have tried to do this by showing how characters are sometimes thrown into harsh circumstances, lose control of them and sometimes of themselves, but then emerge as in some way better, stronger people, or as men with greater self-knowledge. The point of modifying the direction of your essay towards the end is that it will add another dimension of interest to your work, especially if you try to bring out the complexity of the novel more fully. In the earlier section of your answer you will have presented a broad view of the text, looking at it in a particular way, but at this stage you can begin to bring out some of the complexities and subtleties. Just at the moment this might sound confusing, and contradictory, advice. So I shall now work through an example of the kind of thing I mean, arguing that what appear to be the facts of the circumstances are themselves thrown into some doubt, and cannot be taken entirely at face value. In effect this means picking up and elaborating a point I made in passing in the introductory paragraph of my essay.

Because the story is told in the first person rather than the third, by someone telling his own story rather than by an author who knows everything that occurs, why, and what all the characters are thinking, no one is able to verify the circumstances that the narrator describes. (You might remember that Conrad used the same narrative style in 'Youth', and that Marlow's narrative of his own adventures in *Heart of Darkness* is similarly nightmarish and not fully substantiated.) There may be moments when the story has the quality of a nightmare and it is difficult to believe that the narrator's account is accurate. At times the narrator himself seems to have difficulty in believing what is happening. You might consider, for example, the scene of immense darkness, in which, because water gets into them, even the binnacle lamps are put out. You might remember the kind of phrases the narrator applies to the experience in order to express his incomprehension – phrases such as 'impenetrable blackness', 'inconceivable terror', 'inexpressible mystery'. The experience has become something the narrator cannot really articulate, except in negative terms that suggest that, like a nightmare, it can never be rationally understood. You might explore one or two of these and relate the idea to the conversation the narrator has with the doctor when the ship finally reaches port. The doctor appears not to believe the narrator's claim to have been on deck for 'seventeen days', during which he is not sure whether he has slept. Can we be sure, then, whether or not he has dreamt some of the incidents he describes?

What I am arguing is that the harshness of the circumstances creates a state of mind in which the character himself is not sure in retrospect what has happened. Conrad's purpose in setting up this situation is not merely to exploit any possible dramatic effect, but to explore the intangible nature of the reality of experience. The narrator suffers a kind of split consciousness, as we do when experiencing a nightmare, when what we are dreaming seems as real as any waking physical sensation, but is only a figment of an overactive imagination. The harshness of the circumstances described in the novel is used, you might argue in this case, to enable Conrad to explore a theme of the uncertain nature of reality, especially the reality of our own experience, which only we can have, and for which there are not always independent witnesses to verify our feelings or suspicions about what has occurred. I hope I have illustrated how modifying the direction of your essay, or adding another perspective and argument to it, during the final third will create an extra dimension of interest to your work.

The concluding paragraph

In a sense, if you have constructed a careful and coherent response to the question you are answering, you might feel there is not much left to say by the time you reach your conclusion. If you have taken the right approach you will have built up your own confidence, and will be writing fluently and therefore won't consciously worry about drawing your points together in a final paragraph. The conclusion is just a matter of finally answering the set question. My argument has been that Conrad explores his characters' responses to harsh circumstances in various ways; and that it is not merely for dramatic effect but always to illustrate something about vulnerability, resourcefulness, moral and psychological weakness, strength and complexity. This is partly illustrated by the narrator's own maturing during, and through, his experiences: he begins by stressing his youth, and ends by emphasising that he has lost his youth, telling Captain Giles that he feels old. Your conclusion may be different, but as long as it is logically argued from the evidence of the text a difference of interpretatation is not important.

Use the format of your essay to help you think

Having read through this chapter you might object that I have, in a way, cheated by choosing my own question – a privilege that you do not have. My argument, though, is that the format outlined in this chapter will help you answer any question, and, more than that, present your reader with a very good essay. This is because the method used here will actually help you organise your response to any question that is set.

For instance, how would you approach a question on symbolism in *The Shadow-Line*? Your opening paragraph might recognise that symbolism pervades the novel, and, since the story is mainly concerned with a voyage, much of it is related to the sea and ships, but at this stage the meaning and purpose of it is not obvious. In your second paragraph look at a particular episode. As you are discussing symbolism you might like to give an example or two, perhaps working from a very short quotation. On this basis you can argue your first substantial point. Subsequently you can look at further incidents or scenes, expanding your discussion and always building each paragraph on the foundation laid by the previous one.

Then, just as I have illustrated in my earlier answer, in the last third of your essay you might change direction, perhaps by arguing that not all the symbolism is connected with the sea and ships, and that a central idea is the narrator's crossing of the shadow-line between youth and manhood, which is applicable to all men, so that maturing is a universal experience rather than just limited to seamen. Your change of essay direction will be concerned, then, with the fact that the novel is not a simple tale of a disastrous voyage. Indeed, part of the complexity is that the journey is both a literal, external one, and on a more symbolic level an internal journey: an exploration into the mind, and perhaps soul, of the narrator. (You might consider this idea in terms of 'Youth' and *Heart of Darkness* too.)

Essay-writing is very much a matter of organising your thinking in a logical manner, moving in small steps from one clear observation to the next logical one. Although it is in itself a formula, the method outlined above is not one that restricts your thinking. In fact one of its main advantages is that the system allows you more easily to express your own ideas, and your own appreciation and enjoyment of a text, providing always that they are based on sound textual evidence. And with the security of a good and efficient method of working you should feel confident about expressing yourself, about discovering and expanding your personal responses, because you will know they are organised and based on a sound approach to the text.

Further reading

SOME students spend more time reading books about novels than they spend reading the set novels themselves. They are not usually the students who come out with the best understanding of literature. There is sometimes a lurking belief that if you study enough critical books you will find 'the answer' to the meaning of a novel. Throughout this book I have reiterated the idea that no single correct interpretation of any novel exists. You can read two different critics who each have a persuasive view on a novel, yet are totally opposed to one another. That does not necessarily mean that one is 'wrong', but rather that each of them has emphasised different aspects of the text. This is one reason why it is important for you to reach some conclusions of your own before you read academic criticism. Critical texts can be valuable as a complement to your own understanding, in expanding the thinking you have started to do from your reading of the novel. When you are writing an essay a teacher or examiner will not be impressed by a mere catalogue of other people's ideas. Your argument will have weight only if it is firmly based on your own response to the text.

Nevertheless, we have all come across a story or novel that simply does not make sense to us. In that case an introduction that clearly draws out the novel's main themes can be extremely useful. All the fiction I have discussed, and many other of Conrad's stories and novels, are available in Penguin editions with more or less helpful introductions. These also usually print – as do the World's Classics editions – the Author's Note that, in many cases, Conrad wrote to accompany a reprinting of his work, and which gives an indication of his original intentions. Although these are introductions, probably the best way to use them is to read them *after* the novel concerned. They can validate your response, confirming that your own first impressions are proceeding in a productive direction; or they can help to guide your thinking in directions that are useful. In any event, do not waste time actually seeking out very unusual or even eccentric critical texts. That is not the kind of originality that ultimately leads anywhere interesting. You need to get a substantial grasp of the story or novel, and to extend that logically and sensibly. The introductions I have mentioned above demonstrate the kind of intelligent approach to develop.

If you are able to work out the central ideas for yourself you probably do not need critical texts. Do not be afraid to spend time rereading a novel, or sections of a novel: the fact that you have already read it does not mean you cannot get any more out of it. Time spent thinking is also valuable, because all the ideas won't spring ready-made out of the text. You do not have to be reading new material in order to be making progress in formulating your response. Sometimes, however, working very hard on a text on your own can lead to your wanting to know even more about it, and the way other people see it. This is a good time to turn to academic criticism, which can expand your thinking either by going further along the lines you have been pursuing, or by challenging your ideas, forcing you to articulate a defence, or to amend your position on the text. This is part of the cut and thrust of intellectual debate that is such a thoroughly enjoyable aspect of studying literature. Before going on to mention a few specific critical books I should like to summarise my main points on the use of critical texts. Never use criticism as a substitute for your own reading and thinking; if you want to use critical texts, do so after you have read the set novel and have begun to formulate your own opinions on it, only using criticism to make sure you are going in a useful direction; and use critical texts as a stimulus to additional thought after you have done a lot of work on your own.

One factor that may help you apprec ate Conrad's fiction more fully is an understanding of the period in which he was writing. In Chapter 1 I indicated that it was a time of change, and also of international conflict, particularly between the powerful European nations. Conrad's writing period starts with the Boer Wars, in which British dominance of Southern Africa was established, while the other European countries squabbled over other parts of what they called the dark continent. The fiction I consider in this book goes up to the First World War, or Great War as it was known then, in which the peoples of Europe were tearing their own continent, and one another, apart. This was clearly a period of some importance. A good, relatively brief, guide to the political, cultural and intellectual background of the period is contained in volume 7 of *The New Pelican Guide to English Literature*, edited by Boris Ford: *James to Eliot* (Penguin, 1983). This also includes an essay on Conrad's early fiction.

A book of excellent basic scholarship on Conrad's life and work is *Joseph Conrad: A Critical Biography* by Jocelyn Baines (Weidenfeld and Nicolson, 1960). This links Conrad's own life with his stories and novels, and also provides an interesting critical commentary on the fiction. There are two works by Norman Sherry that follow a similar pattern: *Conrad's Eastern World* (Cambridge University Press, 1966), and *Conrad's Western World* (Cambridge University Press, 1971). Probably the fullest account of Conrad's life is in *Joseph Conrad: The Three Lives* by Frederick R. Karl (Faber and Faber, 1979). Conrad certainly had an interesting life, and all these books contain insights into his working methods, but in the end you are concerned with the stories and novels themselves, the finished products rather than the processes of their production. You might, therefore, find books containing critical essays from several different writers useful and interesting. Reading such collections of critical texts will ensure that you see more than one critical point of view. The Macmillan Casebook series is very good in this respect, and it includes two books of essays on Conrad's novels: *'Heart of Darkness', 'Nostromo' and 'Under Western Eyes'*, edited by C. B. Cox (Macmillan, 1981); and *The Secret Agent*, edited by Ian Watt (Macmillan, 1983).

One of the features of Conrad criticism you will discover as you read through it is the diversity of approaches to his fiction. In Chapter 1 I mentioned that some critics with strong political beliefs praise certain novels and dismiss others, while readers of different political persuasions take opposite views of the same novels. On this basis any one novel is likely to have both supporters and detractors. Much recent criticism has tended to explore Conrad's complex and elusive style of narration. In this respect you might find it interesting to read *Conrad and the Paradox of the Plot* by Stephen K. Land (Macmillan, 1984), in which the critic discusses recurring situations and character types throughout Conrad's fiction, and relates that pattern to the themes of the stories and novels. Jakob Lothe, in *Conrad's Narrative Method* (Clarendon Press, 1989), applies some of the most recent post-structuralist critical theories to the way Conrad organises narrative time, and his storytelling techniques. Conrad's particular technique of irony is considered broadly in *Culture and Irony* by Anthony Winner (University Press of Virginia, 1988), and there are specific chapters on *Nostromo* and *The Secret Agent*. There are at present no thorough feminist studies of Conrad's work, but you might find it interesting to read *Critical Practice* by Catherine Belsey (Routledge, 1980), and extend soge of the theoretical ideas there to such characters as Winnie and Lena, who appear to be victims of an unfair social system. You might also consider the more elusive female characters such as Mrs Gould and Antonia in *Nostromo*, and the very shadowy figure in *Heart of Darkness* of Kurtz's Intended.

There are literally hundreds of books on Conrad, but I do not think it is especially useful for me to outline them all here. The ones I have noted above deal with the central issues, but as articles and books are being published all the time anything new might add something to your understanding and appreciation of this great and challenging writer. Do remember, though, that when you approach a critical text it must be with caution, absorbing the sound ideas that are based on firm textual evidence but not accepting points simply because they are in print. All critics have their own preconceptions and limitations when approaching complex fiction. Be confident that your own views, provided they are based on good textual evidence and are organised into a coherent argument, in the ways that I have been suggesting, are as valid as those of any other reader. Always work from a close analysis of the text. In fact a good way of testing the quality of a critic's work is by whether or not it stimulates you to return to the original story or novel to read and think about it again. Your own essays should aim to have that effect on your reader.

'Tis All Lies, Your Worship'

About the Author

Mary Kotsonouris served as a judge of the Dublin Metropolitan District for nine years. A graduate in history and in law of the National University of Ireland and of Trinity College, Dublin, she is the author of *Talking to Your Solicitor, Retreat from Revolution: The Dáil Courts, 1920-1924* and *The Winding up of the Dáil Courts, 1922-1925*. She lives in Castleconnell, County Limerick.

'Tis All Lies, Your Worship'

Tales from the District Court

Mary Kotsonouris

The Liffey Press

Published by
The Liffey Press
Ashbrook House, 10 Main Street
Raheny, Dublin 5, Ireland
www.theliffeypress.com

A catalogue record of this book is available from the British Library.

ISBN 978-1-905785-97-1

Printed in the United Kingdom by MPG Biddles.

Contents

For my children, Vassily and Anna.
and my friend Maeve.

Acknowledgements

It is not possible to acknowledge individually all the people who contributed to this book: there were so many. Without doubt, at the head of any list must be the twenty-seven men who set out in the midst of a civil war, without experience, preparation or guidelines, to establish the rule of law in communities who could have no certainty that the new order would survive the conflict. Happily, it did, and the District Court also survived to create its own narrative, its legends and myths, its dramas and comedies. Improvised scripts have been played out in venues all over the country with a new cast of characters daily for the past ninety years, and I am very grateful for the chance I was given to participate.

Thanks are indeed due to judicial colleagues and court staff, not only for their friendship and support when I worked with them, but also for the patience with which they have pursued the answers to many questions in recent times. This is equally true of Brendan Ryan and Helen Priestly of the Courts Services, of Gregory Ryan of the National Archives, and of Sean Aylward, Oonagh

McPhillips and Brian O'Neill of the Department of Justice, Equality and Law Reform.

I appreciate the time all kinds of people – laity, lawyers and court personnel – took to talk to me of their experiences and of the stories they had heard.

There is great gratitude due to Dolores O'Neill of the President of the District Court's office, not only from me for her friendship, phenomenal memory and tireless energy, but I know on the part of every district judge who has come and gone during her time there. She has the gift of remaining an abiding link between old comrades.

I am gratified that a scholar of Gearóid Ó Tuathaigh's eminence would be so gracious as to write the foreword. Jonathan Williams has always been a lighthouse on a rock with other work, but never more so than in this endeavour when he guided my path through the ragbag of notes, newspaper cuttings and all kinds of material in order to put some form on it all. Any recidivist lapsing into incoherence is wholly my fault. I should like to express my thanks to the publisher, David Givens, for his attention and help in bringing the book to publication.

Foreword

Gearóid Ó Tuathaigh
Professor Emeritus of History
NUI, Galway

Some years ago large commercial hoardings in public places, advertising a certain Sunday newspaper with a reputation for the saucy and the scandalous, carried a simple legend: 'All human life is here'. This motto might more appropriately refer to the drama of the District Court in Irish life during the past ninety or so years. Certainly, the editors of Irish local newspapers (and, indeed, some national journals also) have good reason to be profoundly grateful to the District Courts for providing them with such a vast quantity of excellent copy down through the decades. The public appetite for such 'tales' seems insatiable. Apart from enjoying the intimacy of local reference or personal acquaintance with any of the dramatis personae, the readers of these court cases may take pleasure in recognising stock characters and classic situations: the curmudgeonly and eccentric judge; the incorrigible rogue with an inexhaustible repertoire of utterly improbable excuses and explanations; the elaborate 'extenuating circumstances'; the character witnesses and the ever-dutiful gardaí with their arcane language for describing the scene and circumstances of the crime, arrest and demeanour of the accused.

The District Court is the first point of reference beyond that threshold where social disapproval encounters the law and its administration, where certain actions of which society disapproves are translated into legal categories of 'crime and misdemeanour' and those accused face the due process of the law. It is the crowded (sometimes literally) foyer of the formidable edifice of the law and its administration. The remote origins of these lower or petty courts go back to the reign of Edward III in England (its immediate antecedent during the Union era in Ireland was the Petty Sessions) and the emergence of the District Court during the revolutionary years (1919-21), and its incorporation into the judicial structure of the new Saorstát Éireann is a tangled and fascinating story, summarised with impressive concision here by Mary Kotsonouris, herself a distinguished legal historian and author of a seminal monograph on the Dáil Courts (1920-24). Mary Kotsonouris, a solicitor by profession, 'did time' as a District Justice, and her experiences, familiarity with the record and folklore of the proceedings of the District Court (including a trove of newspaper accounts of various sittings from courts throughout Ireland), and general reflections on the law and society as they appear from the bench of a District Court, form the basis of this most engaging book.

Her disarming reference to 'scraps from a magpie's hoard' scarcely hints at the sharp insights and warm sense of humour that Mary Kotsonouris brings to her pithy observations on judges, gardaí, court dress, the physical surroundings of the various court locations, the folklore of solicitors and barristers, and the chronicles of human ingenuity, endurance and, at times, misery, that constitute her 'tales'. There is no settling of scores, no recriminations in these tales, though Mary Kotsonouris is far too shrewd not to appreciate that gentle chiding can be folded in the most innocuous of anecdotes. Most striking of all, however, is the steady, humane gaze that informs these engaging observations on all the trials, idiosyncrasies and foibles of the colourful cast of the drama of District Court life.

An attractive tone of self-deprecation does not inhibit Kotsonouris from expressing firm and forthright views and opinions. The sense of historical context is important throughout, not least in the author's comments on several of her fellow judges. A number of reputations are rescued from unjust neglect (and not exclusively judges), and Kotsonouris is not slow to remind the reader of the range of talents and accomplishments of earlier District Court judges – as published dramatists and novelists, historians and antiquarian scholars – and 'all pursued their academic and literary interests in tandem with their judicial careers'. Kotsonouris's own scholarly credentials as a legal historian are firmly established and universally respected, and her commentary on the evolution of the District Court system and on many aspects of its operation demonstrates independent judgment and a first-class mind. In this book, the former judge wears her learning lightly and dispenses her wisdom with deliberate calm; but, as they might say in Limerick, when she has an important point to make, she doesn't baulk her tongue!

Despite regular complaints about procedural shortcomings and anachronisms (including dress and ritual), the courts and the issues with which they deal must inevitably reflect the changing circumstances and values of the society that they serve. With her assured sense of historical context and social change, Mary Katsonouris repeatedly reminds us of this truth in her observations on the case lists of an earlier era, when compared to more recent times, and in her lucid comments on many of the episodes and incidents recounted in this book: the cause célèbre of the Rose Tattoo prosecution of the late 1950s; the bizarre case of Malcolm McArthur; the difficulties suffered by early evangelising Jehovah's Witnesses; the increasing importance of EU law and directives at every level of the Irish judicial system; the growing presence of drug-related cases at District Court level. The expanding jurisdiction of the District Court in recent decades is reflected in her acute commentary, both on specific cases and on general trends.

The expanding jurisdiction of the District Court is not simply a matter of the monetary level of fines, redress and penalties rising in tempo with inflation, cost of living and general economic conditions. The changes in the categories of complaint, crime and social problems that occupy the attention of the District Court prompt Mary Kotsonouris to some of the more interesting, and disturbing, observations in this book. In particular, her comments on the heart-breaking cases relating to domestic violence, family disputes and the care and custody of children will leave readers in no doubt about the genuine distress that many district judges experience in having to deal with such human tragedies. Indeed, in writing of the criminal (as distinct from the civil) business of the District Court, the author properly reminds the reader that, 'While there are "funny incidents" which catch the eye, there can be drama, fury and despair too'. Likewise, in the light of some of the sad cases referred to in this book, it is difficult to argue with her verdict that, 'Nothing perhaps better illustrates how difficult it is to legislate for the human condition than a long afternoon in a family court'.

These tales from the District Court may be enjoyed, so to speak, *idir shúgradh agus dáiríre*. They are written with wit and elegance by a wise and humane observer of the human condition. They will entertain. But they will also prompt a more reflective response. The Courts are a vital site of discourse on our values and standards as a society. What is done and said, what is determined and declared, what is 'conducted' in the courts, resonates within the wider society, affirming or calling into question its notions of what, in colloquial terms, it considers 'right' and 'wrong'. Those who preside in our courts are human and fallible, yet they must exercise authority in a manner that assures and affirms the public in its shared sense of fairness and justice. For a former judge to provide an insight into the world of the District Court, to reveal a personal perspective, make observations and express opinions on that world, in a gentle yet thought-provoking manner, may be considered a public service of real value. It is also a most pleasurable read.

Introduction

THE DISTRICT COURT WAS IN operation for almost two years before it was formally established by legislation. The Provisional Government was in a position to sanction its beginnings by virtue of the powers transferred to it by the British government under Article 17 of the Treaty and the Provisional Government (Transfer of Functions) Order 1922. This was the mechanism used to appoint twenty-seven men as temporary resident magistrates under the Constabulary (Ireland) Act of 1836. The announcement was made in *Iris Oifigíuil* on 28 October 1922, and two days later, in the same official gazette, it was noted that the residual jurisdiction of the courts set up under the First Dáil had been brought to a close. The new appointees were to be called district justices and, with surprisingly little fuss, they seemed to have slipped quickly and efficiently into the role, place and title of the justices of the Dáil district courts, although that had not been the primary intention of those who had appointed them. The Constitution establishing the Irish Free State was passed on 6 December and the Adaptation of Enactments Act, which followed, gave official recognition to the office of District Justice.

Although the Constitution had outlined the judicial system to be established, including 'courts of local and limited jurisdiction, with a right of appeal as determined by law', the Courts of Justice Act was not passed until May 1924. For a year and a half, the justices had to carry the administration of the law throughout the country without a framework of higher courts for the purpose of appeal or to send serious crimes forward for trial; neither were there Rules of Court. Anti-Treaty forces frequently tried to kill the justices or disrupt their courts. Once the legislation had been passed, there was a Supreme Court consisting of the Chief Justice and two others, a High Court of six judges and a Circuit Court of eight. The number of justices of the District Court was not to exceed thirty-three, but four assistant justices could be appointed. Its jurisdiction in civil matters was limited to claims not exceeding £25 in contract and £10 in tort. It could try minor criminal matters, but would send the more serious forward for trial before judge and jury in the Central Criminal Court or the Circuit Court. In the latter half of the twentieth century, there was a considerable increase in the number of judges in all courts, as well as changes in the jurisdiction of the Circuit and District courts.

On the following pages are two documents which signal the foundation of the District Court: the prototype letter of nomination to each of the twenty-seven men who were appointed to be the first justices, and the oath they swore on taking office. They are reproduced with the kind permission of Mr. Sean Aylward, Secretary General of the Department of Justice, Equality and Law Reform.

THE SECRETARY,
MINISTRY OF HOME AFFAIRS,
UPPER MERRION STREET,
DUBLIN,

AIREAĊT UM ĠNÓĊAÍ DÚIĊĊE
(MINISTRY OF HOME AFFAIRS),
UPPER MERRION STREET,
DUBLIN.

29th October, 1922.

A Dhuine Uasail,

I am directed by the Minister for Home Affairs to notify you that he has been pleased to nominate you to hold temporarily the office of District Justice (Magistrate) for the areas comprised in the Counties named in the attached Schedule.

Your appointment will be temporary and will be held at the Minister's pleasure during the present transition period pending the reconstruction of the Irish Judicial and Magisterial system, which is intended at an early date.

The salary of the office will be at the rate of £1,000 per annum and will cover all duties whatsoever which you may be called on to perform in virtue of your office and will include all subsistence and bonus allowance. A commuted allowance of £200 per annum to cover all travelling expenses will be paid in addition to the salary abovementioned. The appointment shall not carry a pension allowance nor any right to compensation for abolition of office or loss of office by reason of change of Government or reconstruction of the existing Judicial and Magisterial system. The foregoing salary and allowance shall be accepted by you in lieu of all salaries, bonus, allowances and pensions payable under any of the statutes relating to Resident Magistrates in Ireland or any rules, orders or regulations made thereunder.

You will be required to reside within the area to which you may be assigned and in a convenient locality to be approved by the Minister and to attend in person on the days and at the hours and places which shall be laid down by direction of the Minister from time to time and not to absent yourself from the said district without the permission of the Minister having first been sought and obtained.

Your jurisdiction will be the jurisdiction of a Stipendiary Magistrate under the Constabulary Acts.

Upon hearing from you that you are prepared to accept the appointment on the foregoing conditions, the Minister's Warrant of Appointment will be immediately proceeded with.

Mise le meas agat,

RUNAIDHE.

W. D. Coyne, Esq

OATH - DISTRICT JUSTICES.

"I William Dowrd, Coyne / Liam D. O Caidin ....do swear that I will well and truly serve the Irish Free State (Saorstat Eireann) in the Office of District Justice without favour or affection, malice or ill-will; that I will see and cause the peace to be kept and preserved; that I will prevent to the best of my power all offences against the same; that while I shall continue to hold the said office I will to the best of my skill and knowledge discharge all the duties thereof in the execution of Warrants and otherwise faithfully according to law, and that I do not now belong to, and that while I shall hold the said office I will not join or belong to any political Society whatsoever or any Secret Society whatsoever.

So help me God!

Signed W. D. Coyne
Liam D. O Caidin

Made and subscribed before me
this 28th. day of October in the
year Nineteen hundred and twenty two.

Signed J. O'Curran Commissioner for Oaths.

Constabulary (Ireland) Act 1938

Chapter 1

A Short History of the District Court

THE DISTRICT COURT WAS CREATED on the fly and on the sly. By sleight of hand and practically overnight, two separate jurisdictions were melded by an announcement in October 1922 that the provisional government had appointed twenty-seven lawyers as resident magistrates under the Constabulary (Ireland) Act of 1836. Under the British administration in Ireland, the courts of Petty Sessions were manned by resident magistrates, appointed at the pleasure of the Lord Lieutenant, and by honorary justices of the peace; neither group was composed of professional lawyers. As the name implies, these courts were concerned with civic administration and minor offences carrying prison sentences of less than six months. Resident magistrates were hated by tradition and by rote as the local enforcers, along with the Royal Irish Constabulary, of the will of Dublin Castle. It had become exceedingly difficult, however, for the authorities to impose their will from 1919 onwards by an extraordinary phenomenon manifesting itself all over the country.

It began in the county of Clare and quickly spread. Local communities, inspired by self-confidence and a spirit of can-do, set up local tribunals to settle land disputes, determined that agitation and violence about land were not going to mar the prideful march towards self-government which was everywhere evident. On 21 January, the Sinn Féin members who had won seats in the general election of 1918 had met in the Mansion House in Dublin and established Dáil Éireann, claiming themselves to be the legitimate government of the Irish Republic. Within its executive was a Ministry of Home Affairs, with a programme to establish a system of courts. Although there was a group of lawyers drafting reports and working on ideas, it was not until 29 June 1920 that a decree was issued establishing civil and criminal courts, the latter element a contradiction of the benevolent principle of agreed arbitration which was Arthur Griffith's ideal of the administration of justice in the new Jerusalem. However, it has to be said, in passing, that it was not totally without foundation in the early days. To give only one example, the *Limerick Leader* of 11 June 1920 reported that two men, exiled by a makeshift court to a deserted island in the Shannon for an offence of demolishing a wall, had repelled the police coming to their rescue by hurling stones at their boat and shouting out that they were 'prisoners of the Irish Republic'.

It is foolish to hope that a revolutionary government might prove to be more efficient in advancing its programme than any other, and by the time Home Affairs got around to issuing its decree and publishing the rules of court, the war of independence was raging and civic life was so disrupted that there was little chance of implementing its grand plans. Briefly, the proposed system of courts was to include one in every parish; the justices were elected locally by a combination of voluntary bodies, such as Cumann na mBan and the Sinn Féin Clubs, as well as representatives of labour and employers. Above them was a hierarchy of superior courts, to be presided over by lawyers, of whom only four were eventually appointed. The applicable law was that in force on 21 January 1919, the date of the inauguration of Dáil Éireann. The takeover of the ad hoc courts and tribunals already operating in towns and villages was accomplished almost imperceptibly, and was the consequence of the remarkable acceptance by most people of the authority and reality of the Dáil.

While it was impossible during the worst of the Troubles to maintain any open contact with the ministry in Dublin, justice continued to be administered through an underground system of secret meetings, false identities and elaborate *maquis*-type arrangements. In spite of arrests, raids and occasional shootings by the Crown forces, a sufficient framework survived to the extent that, with the advent of the Truce in June 1921, these courts came to dominate the legal landscape under the central control of the Ministry of Home Affairs. Cahir Davitt, the most prolific of the professional judges, recalled that in circuit sittings around the country he had heard over 135 cases, most of them very substantial claims. They were suits for:

> … administration of estates … for specific performance and to set aside and rectify deeds, actions for breach of promise of marriage and for judicial separation, actions for assault, slander, trespass, trover and conversion, breach of contract … and so forth and so on.

This was heavyweight stuff, and litigants were prepared to take these matters to an administration of justice which had so recently emerged into the light of day and was illegal by any objective standards.

In the months following the Anglo-Irish Treaty of 6 December 1921, these courts became even more entrenched in public perception. Not only were they making use of official prisons and courthouses, but all prosecutions by local authorities for breach of regulations and the non-payment of rates were conducted there. As far back as mid-January, the provisional government had issued a proclamation that the law courts which had operated under the British government would continue to do so until the Irish Free State was established, but it did nothing to support the magistrates or the Crown-appointed judges of the system and they faded almost out of public sight. The Dáil Courts were immeasurably strengthened, and were increasingly used by corporate bodies, as well as by individuals. Lists of circuit sittings were advertised in the local press, juries were summoned and barristers condescended to appear on behalf of litigants. The looming shadow of civil war appeared to be having little effect on their busy operation but, in fact, they survived the outbreak of hostilities by a bare fortnight.

It was decided at a government meeting on 10 July that 'sittings of the Republican Courts were to be restricted as far as possible and ultimately stopped altogether'. The terminology is interesting: the reference is to the Dáil Courts but the distancing had already begun. The following day the professional judges on circuit in various venues were recalled to Dublin. The Supreme Court, where its President, James Creed Meredith, was sitting, was brought to an abrupt end by an order from the assistant minister. There was mayhem in the legal establishment, fury and bafflement among the populace, and utter consternation when it was announced that the minister 'with the concurrence of the Cabinet of Dáil Éireann' (a parliament that had not even been convened, never mind in session) had rescinded the decree of 29 May 1920 under which the Dáil Courts had been established.

The reason for the diktat was a habeas corpus application which had been made on behalf of a George Plunkett, who was captured in the ruins of the Four Courts. Judge Crowley had made the usual conditional order that the prisoner be produced by those holding him, and that they show cause for his detention within seven days. The government was having none of such legal niceties: it sent a messenger out to Crowley on the evening of the sixth day with the news that his court no longer existed. Of course, he sat the following morning and when there was no appearance on their behalf, issued warrants for the arrest of General Mulcahy, Minister for Defence, and of the governor of Mountjoy Prison. Crowley was picked up in the street shortly after and was thrown into jail for doing his judicial duty. Admittedly, it is not the start of a brand new democracy of which we might be proud, but then neither is a civil war in which worse things happened. There was now a very serious dilemma facing the government: it had left itself without any effective courts. Michael Collins expressed his concern from Beggars Bush Barracks: 'What will be the procedure for bringing men to trial before a civil court and what civil courts are there to bring them before?'

The answer to both questions was, 'None'.

It had already been decided that the days of the resident magistrates were not merely numbered: they would not be allowed to sit again. Yet no one had the grace to tell them so. It was left to them to infer it by the official silence with which they had been met at every turn since the Treaty. The draft constitution, with its provision for a new court system, had already been finalised, but the Irish Free State would not come into existence until it was passed on 6 December. So some kind of a structure, or rather an arrangement, had to be cobbled together because the provisional government, as its name implies, had no power to pass legislation. It had, however, power under the Transfer of Functions Order 1922 to appoint new magistrates, as the Lord Lieutenant could have done, and so twenty-seven lawyers were named as resident magistrates to replace those who were hastily pensioned off. However, the government shrewdly did not use the hated title: they were referred to as District Justices, the nomenclature of the Dáil Courts. It was a remarkable sleight-of-hand which worked. It is clear from reports in the provincial press that the new District Justices slipped almost unobtrusively into a niche prepared by the former tribunals known as the parish and district courts. Their success in this was not down to government cunning, but to the courage, character and good sense of the men themselves; they somehow managed to seem as if they had always been there.

Who were these men? They were a mixture of solicitors and barristers – most of whom were quite young, and none of whom had previous judicial experience, unless in Dáil Courts. Some were to have surprising career changes. Tom Finlay became an assistant secretary at the Department of Justice in 1924, and within a few years was a Dáil deputy and senior counsel. Philip O'Donoghue, after a spell as the senior official in the Attorney General's office, was appointed a judge in the European Court of Human Rights. Among them were men already distinguished in fields other than the law and who continued to produce an extraordinary amount of work. Both Kenneth Reddin and Louis Walsh were novelists and playwrights, Dermot Gleeson a respected historian and Liam Price an eminent antiquarian. James Crotty published the seminal work *Practice and Procedure in the District Court* in 1959, and Richard Johnson had a play produced at the Abbey in 1961; and none of them (unlike the present writer) gave up the day job!

These were temporary appointments and remained so for almost two years. Civil war was raging in the countryside in which they travelled and they frequently came under attack from anti-Treaty forces, but the government was unable to afford them much protection. When Kevin

O'Higgins, as the responsible minister, raised the matter in cabinet, the curt command was that they 'were to be directed to continue their duties as usual'. It was necessary, after all the sudden upheavals and conflicting signals thrown out by their rulers regarding legal arrangements, that the public be reassured. So, as well as dodging bullets, the justices stressed from the beginning that they were of a different calibre to those of the old regime, and more in the tradition of their immediate predecessors. At the first sitting of the District Court in Ennis, Justice Dermot Gleeson said 'that they were the servants of the people, and not their masters and he paid tribute to the magnificent and gratuitous manner in which Parish and District Justices had carried out their duties', according to the *Clare Champion* of 19 November 1922. In similar fashion, Justice Fahy in Wexford stressed that 'the justices came from the people and were akin to them in their feelings, hopes and wishes, that they were the people's servants in dispensing justice to all parties, irrespective of creed and class.'

The bullets, however, were real. Eamonn O'Donoghue, whom I knew as the Chief Clerk of the District Court, told me that, at a statutory meeting of District Justices in the 1950s, the newest appointee was being introduced to his brethren. He looked keenly at one of the older ones and said: 'The first time I saw you was through the sights of a gun. I was with a bunch of the lads behind a ditch when you came into our area. We had planned to shoot you but we changed our minds.'

There were no Rules of Court (they did not come until 1926), and there were no higher courts to which the justices could send forward persons accused of serious crimes. They had constantly to explain that litigants could not continue any cases from former regimes in their courts. Public house licenses, for which the law has always had an inordinate respect, were in a mess and had to be untangled regardless of any civil war. It is greatly to their credit that within a short time, as is clear from provincial newspapers, it was as if the justices had always been an integral part of the community

The District Court was formally established under the Courts of Justice Act in May 1924, but not before a relentless crusade about its status was waged by deputies and senators, who were determined that the justices would not hold office at the pleasure of the Minister for Justice; that they would be judges and not civil servants; and that their salaries would be paid from the Central Fund, like the rest of the judiciary. In other words, they would have to be wholly independent of the executive. The Department of Finance had advocated that they could be dismissed at will by the Minister for Justice, but Hugh Kennedy, Attorney General, was adamant this would not happen: 'You may take it that everything that savours in the very least of the old RM's [Resident Magistrates] and the pollution of justice by Castle interference will be opposed tooth and nail and indeed I personally will not stand for anything of the kind.'

Seanad Éireann sent the Bill back three times to Dáil Éireann to have the title of 'District Justice' amended to that of 'Judge'. It was the only skirmish the legislators lost, although the change, under the Courts Act 1991, was effected some sixty-seven years later! Tom Johnson, the Labour leader, was a lone voice in pleading that an element of lay involvement in the administration of justice – a defining characteristic of the Dáil Courts and also of the Petty Sessions – be preserved, but nobody was listening to him. The way the legal regime of the District Court emerged from their efforts will be discussed in the next chapter.

Chapter 2

Development of the District Court after 1922

THE HASTY THROWING OF A handful of lawyers into the judicial mix was only a stop-gap measure to fill the void the government itself had created. It was conceived to be temporary and would put some sort of sticking plaster in place to tide civic society over the hiatus until the Free State was created and its constitution in place. All this would be happening within two months on 6 December 1922. The final draft of the constitution had been approved, and the first native courts in Ireland since Brehon times could begin; that is, of course, if one did not count the Dáil Éireann courts, recently suppressed and, it was hoped, forgotten. Simultaneously, with its decision to close them, the provisional government had issued a direction to the Minister for Home Affairs and the Law Adviser 'to prepare a code for Courts in Ireland'. Under Article 64 of the 1922 Constitution, the brief reference was to 'courts of local and limited jurisdiction, with a right of appeal as determined by law'. So the establishment of the courts themselves would have to await legislation and, although it was decided to set up a 'judiciary committee' in September 1922, it did not have its first meeting and a body in place to sketch out a scheme until the end of January. In the meantime, James Creed Meredith, late President of the Dáil Éireann Supreme Court, tirelessly turned out a stream of papers and suggestions. Everything he did seems to have been taken for granted, including his dignity, when it was decided to shut down his court even while he sat there. In other jurisdictions he would have been cherished but, to date, no legal historian has written as much as a monograph on this remarkable soul.

The Judiciary Committee was appointed with none other than Lord Glenavy, a former Lord Chief Justice, as its chairman; as Attorney General, he had refused legal representation to the leaders of the Rising in 1916. Its work was coordinated through the office of Hugh Kennedy, the Attorney General, so the correspondence is with his papers in the UCD Archives. William Cosgrave addressed a bracing letter to the members in January 1923, declaring that there was nothing more prized than the liberty to constitute 'a system of judiciary and an administration of law and justice according to the dictates of our own needs and after a pattern of our own designing.' A preliminary conference of the members was held early in February in Government Buildings. However, months before, the Law Adviser (Kennedy's then title) was inundated with advice on the subject of local courts, urging that the defining characteristics of the Dáil Courts be preserved. Louis Walsh, shortly before his appointment as a justice, wrote:

> Apart from the necessity of Irishing them, you know what slaves of words we are in this country, as the rubbish that has been talked since the 7th Decr. [the day after the Anglo-Irish agreement in London] shows. For instance, if you are appointing professional minor Justices, don't call them R.M's or you will damn the whole system. Call them 'leas-breithimh' [deputy judge] or something … [the new courts] must be as expeditious and convenient as the Dáil Parish and District Courts.

Other letters echo the same sentiment: these court structures had suited the people and should be retained, particularly the involvement of lay justices.

The final report of the committee was submitted to cabinet on 17 May 1923, Glenavy having left the address of his London club with the Secretary in case he needed to be reached on any point of urgency! The Courts Bill, based on the report, was drafted by Arthur Creed Meredith KC, who had been pressed into service because Arthur Matheson, the sole parliamentary draftsman, was harried and distraught and up to his eyes in drafting the act to wind up the Dáil Courts. The hope that these troublesome courts might be forgotten had not been fulfilled – indeed, far from it.

The litigants in 5,000 cases left stranded by the peevish and abrupt closure of the forum into which they had been coaxed and pushed refused to go gently into the night, and had not ceased to insist that something be done about their legal rights. So a judicial winding-up commission was to be created which, in effect, revived the Dáil Court jurisdiction and allowed their cases to be finalised. The Bill to set up the commission was ready to go before the Dáil and was introduced by the minister, Kevin O'Higgins, on 19 July. It was passed on 31 July, following a very bad-tempered debate, albeit one in which only two other deputies took part. On the same day, W.T. Cosgrave was waiting with considerable impatience to introduce the Courts of Justice Bill, confident that it would be passed swiftly and with little debate; he was to be sorely disappointed. He touted the Bill as 'being as free from offence as was possible ... and all concessions would be willingly assented to'.

Cosgrave was hoping that it would have passed into law within a week because the Dáil was due to be dissolved for a general election on 9 August. The House was not minded to oblige him so it had to be reintroduced in September and, contrary to his expectations, it was seven months before it was passed. The proposed institution of a Circuit Court caused great fury among the lawyer-deputies with its promise of cheaper and speedier litigation, and was the subject of a constant flow of amendments. However, on the issue of the District Court, there was blue murder. The proposals in the report had been altered so as to insert considerable executive control on justices – such as tenure, parliamentary or executive oversight and salaries to be paid by the Houses of the Oireachtas and not through the Central Fund like the rest of the judiciary. This latter would have meant that decisions of individual justices could well end up being criticised in the Dáil when the estimates were debated. The overall effect would be to make them the equivalent of resident magistrates. The proposal of the officials in the Ministry of Finance that their tenure should be at the pleasure of government had already been rejected by Hugh Kennedy. It is impossible to understand why it was not foreseen that any like suggestion was guaranteed to raise the hackles of every deputy. 'Now Castle government has gone, let us make sure that it has gone with a vengeance and that it cannot return under another name,' thundered Professor Magennis.

It was an extraordinary clash between the executive and parliament, all the more so given that there was no official Opposition because those elected deputies who opposed the Treaty did not take their seats. Cosgrave became increasingly frustrated and threatened to withdraw the bill and take it to a plebiscite. He made the threat when the bill moved to the Seanad and confided that he had 'been obsessed in reading in the Press for some time an extraordinary disposition to belittle, to reduce the status of the Executive Council of the State and its officers in every possible way.'

Now the same arguments were raised and the same amendments were proposed as in the Dáil, and an attempt to prevent the Seanad passing an amendment on how the salary of justices was to be paid infuriated the senators and provoked a constitutional crisis. A special committee was set up to consider 'the most important question to come before the Seanad in reference to its powers'. Numerous amendments were sent to the Dáil and forty-two were eventually accepted, although not the one which proposed that the title of 'judge' be substituted for 'justice'. As already noted, that metamorphosis took another sixty-seven years. It is puzzling that the battle in the Houses of the Oireachtas was allowed to rage for so long, or why the Executive Council would feel so strongly that it dug in its heels in a doomed effort to retain control over the lowest court. It is noteworthy that it was the cohort of barristers in both chambers who made sure that this did not happen. Another anomaly was the non-appearance of Kevin O'Higgins, the responsible minister. Undoubtedly, he was absent because of other pressures of state on a wider stage, so it was left to William Cosgrave and Hugh Kennedy to face the battering from the members.

In the meantime, the District Court had become an accepted feature of rural life. It had not yet been established in the capital, where the Dublin Metropolitan Police Force remained in existence and the Dublin police courts dispensed summary justice. Court proceedings were reported in the local press; indeed, over the years, they, with reports of local authority meetings or agricultural fairs, made up the backbone of the content of provincial papers right up to the 1960s. If nothing else, they disprove the pompous and vacuous condescension of Sir James O'Connor in his introduction to the 1925 edition of his *Irish Justice of the Peace*:

> With the arrival of dapper and efficient District Justices, something of the joy that comes from

> the highly dramatic instinct of the Irish people will be gone.

O'Connor had also taken the opportunity to advise these nattily turned out bureaucrats that they should generally accept the evidence given by police. In many ways, a reader would not have perceived a great deal of difference with the Petty Sessions of former times. The accounts can be amusing, mundane, quite often enraging. One gets the impression, as the years went by, that the young men who had embarked on their judicial duties with enthusiasm and courage had acquired something of the aura of the fusty middle-class respectability of those justices of the peace who had once presided over the local administration of justice. At times, it seems that the poor and uneducated were forced into a subservient role in sheer self-defence. There was no legal aid, of course, but, disgracefully, many prosecutions were brought by the injured parties themselves and not by the gardaí.

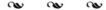

The *Limerick Leader* in 1934 told of a summons which had been brought by a daughter against her father who had tried to choke her when he discovered that her mother had used some of her old-age pension of £5.10s. to buy clothes for the girl. He knocked out two of the daughter's teeth. The man was not in court but, surprisingly, a garda gave evidence on his behalf that he had never been in trouble and that he did not drink. It was left to her solicitor to inform the court that this paragon of virtue had taken the £300 which the daughter had received as compensation for the loss of an arm while working in a laundry in England. He went on a trip to France and spent the money within the year. Justice Gleeson issued a warrant for his arrest. It is interesting that the newspaper chose not to publish the father's name. And the same newspaper in the same year decided that

> ... the cases for hearing at Glin District Court on Wednesday were of no public importance. They had references to the lighting-up regulations, wandering animals etc.

❧ ❧ ❧

Again, where two schoolboys were assaulted by their teacher, it was the parents who brought the summons and obtained the doctor's evidence. The assault must have been pretty severe because, although the justice hedged his decision with elaborate circumspection and expressions of solidarity with the teacher in his support for 'reasonable' physical punishment, he still awarded damages and costs totalling five pounds between the two children.

❧ ❧ ❧

There was a noticeable increase in traffic cases as we moved into the 1930s and, naturally, a decline after 1940 because of petrol restrictions in the Emergency years. They were lifted for some occupations, including that of a district justice. Justice Johnson of Kerry was driving home from court to Tralee on a dark evening when, near Rathkeale, he came across two men with a tractor which was stranded in the middle of the road. He parked and went back to see if he could help; they had run out of fuel.

'Why on earth are you out on a tractor in the dark?' he asked.

'Because we have cleats on the wheels and there is a hoor of a district justice in Kerry who is death down on using cleats on the road,' he was told.

Justice Johnson fetched a petrol can from his car to give to them and the two men were overcome with gratitude. Nothing would satisfy them but that they would return the petrol in spite of his refusals. Just to get away, he was forced to give the address of a shop in Tralee where they could leave it. He hurried back to his car.

'But who will I say it's for?' shouted one of the men.

As Dick Johnson lowered himself into the driver's seat, he called back, 'Tell them it's for the hoor of a district justice.'

Another thing that comes out from these accounts of driving offences is a greater tolerance, combined with the courteous and helpful attitude of the gardaí, towards those whom they were actually prosecuting for motor offences, so it was not a question of a blind eye being turned. In Ennistymon, two dangerous driving cases went on late into the evening, the people leaving in almost total darkness, because 'the Courthouse is not provided with electrical current', according to the *Clare Champion*. (I wonder what happened to that courthouse.

I took a court in Ennistymon in 1984 and my memory is that it was held in the office of the Credit Union.) Although two doctors, no less, gave evidence that the defendant was capable of driving, the garda said he smelled of drink, was incoherent and lay behind the wheel like a log, apart from the fact that he had been driving on the wrong side of the road when he collided with a car. Michael O'Loughlen, a local witness, had been enlisted to drive the car to the barracks and afterwards to take the man home, who, he explained to the court, had a high cockney accent and it was hard to understand him, drunk or sober.

The justice asked, 'You have heard him in both conditions?'

The witness replied, 'The funny thing about it is that the Sergeant and Guard Cummins were not capable. I don't mean that they were drunk but they are not able to drive.'

❧ ❧ ❧

In his history of Tullamore Garda Station, *From Civic Guard to Garda Siochána*, Michael Dalton recalled one of the old-timers with a remarkable turn of phrase.

> Garda Joe Hanly, the driver of the patrol car at Tullamore in the 50s, had a gift of never being stuck for words and of making up a few of his own. One day, while in the witness box in a traffic accident prosecution, he was asked by the district justice if there was much damage to the vehicles and Joe replied, 'Your Honour, they were melodionated'.

❧ ❧ ❧

It is difficult to imagine the following newspaper headline appearing today:

> 'Life Disqualification Preferred to Prison Sentence. Counsel's Offer accepted by Judge.'

It seems two Limerick gardaí were cycling in William Street when a car came out of a minor road, suddenly stopped, reversed and knocked one of them off his bicycle. The garda gave evidence in the District Court that the driver had got excited and asked, 'Where is the other man I knocked down?' He had to be reassured that there was only one casualty. He got a month's imprisonment and appealed to the Circuit Court. His counsel offered that he be disqualified for life in exchange for the lifting of the sentence, and the judge accepted the offer. Surely, no one could complain that that particular plea bargain in January 1951 was in any way *sub rosa*?

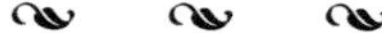

One wonders if the former Lord Justice O'Connor ever availed of the opportunity to revise his opinion on the sobering effects of the new district courts. If he did, the following report in the *Clare Champion* of 11 January 1936 might have shaken his faith in prophesy:

> John Linnane was charged with the larceny of one turkey, three ducks and two hens. The poultry owner and the accused lived near each other but they were not on speaking terms over goats. When he searched the accused's premises, a Garda witness had found footprints made by boots

> over which bags had been worn. He had made a sketch of the footprints he had found in the fowl owner's yard. A Garda from Kilrush, who was a foot print expert, gave evidence of making a plaster cast of the heel of one print which compared in every way with the heel of Linnane's left boot. The Justice said someone in Lisdeen must have been reading detective stories and went out to rob a henhouse with two odd boots wrapped in sacking. From the Garda's evidence he got the impression that it would be impossible in future to rob a hen roost in Lisdeen without the aid of stilts. In his defence, Linnane said he had borrowed a boot from his brother as he had a sore toe. He got sentenced to 21 days' hard labour.

There is no need to think of these characters as something from whimsical folklore. It would be a foolish punter who would wage a substantial sum that a district judge of the twenty-first century could not match that story for general lunacy.

Chapter 3

The Widening Jurisdiction

THE SETTLING-DOWN OF CIVIC LIFE in the new state, after its shaky and violent start, allowed the court system to establish rules and routine and, over time, to build up its own narrative of practice and precedents. From 1924 on, there was a steady progression of Courts of Justice Acts, some of them increasing the number of judges at every level. The District Court was always more flexible and more accommodating to the occasional need for extra judges, because the Minister for Justice had the power to appoint up to four additional justices. Under the 1991 Act there was a complement of forty-five allowed for and by 2004 it had increased to fifty-four, plus the President. Its monetary jurisdiction expanded enormously since the 1924 figure of £25, an expansion which took inflation into account as well as convenience. It had risen to £2,500 in 1981, and ten years later to £5,000 (now €6,350). If the parties agree to it, the civil jurisdiction of the District Court has no limit – which means that a claim for a million euro could be made there at a considerable saving in legal costs.

We constantly marvel at how much the world changed in the last quarter of the twentieth century. It is a phenomenon that affected the happenings in the District Court just as in every other institution. An onlooker sitting at the back of a rural court around 1937 would not have noticed a great difference in the run of cases had he also been present at the Petty Sessions there in 1907. The late John Casey, a well known solicitor in Ennis, was kind enough to tell me what court practice was like when he qualified:

> I began to practise as a solicitor in July 1941. In the beginning I appeared for itinerants, many of whom I knew personally and who were charged with being drunk and for 'begging'. Never for stealing or assaults. Mugging was unknown. There were summonses for cycling without lights, for having no dog or wireless licences. I remember the arrival of the first wireless in my native parish. There were summonses for 'after hours', summonses for driving with one light and no rear lights and, occasionally, for speeding, careless or dangerous driving. There were common assaults, more verbal than physical; robberies were very rare except from orchards. There were applications for dancehall licences and transfers of pub licences. I remember cases of trespass, animals wandering on the public road, unlicensed bulls. The sad and shocking cases would, in my opinion, relate to violence in the home and family law cases with little children, young and old, involved. I had to deal with only

> two cases of violence in the home. I never had a family law case; I had one bigamist. You could liken the many clients I appeared for to 'the poor player that struts and frets his hour upon the stage and then is heard no more'.

Motoring offences took up an increasing amount of court time at every level as more people became drivers and more roads were rolled out. What made the greatest difference, however, was the introduction of a scientific test for drunken driving, particularly Section 49 of the Road Traffic Act 1961. The prosecution no longer had to rely on a garda's observation of the general appearance and behaviour of the defendant, but on a laboratory reading of the amount of alcohol in his system. The obligation to provide the blood or urine sample fell on the person arrested and, depending on the result, he might be charged in due course with driving 'over the limit', as it came to be called.

The procedure was straightforward, impersonal and absolute; there could hardly be much to argue about. To think thus is to overlook the endless ingenuity of lawyers. Decisions of the District Court can set no precedent, but there have been hundreds of decisions that have been the precedent, in another sense of the word, of an equal number of Supreme Court judgments, in which a District Court summons has been examined in the most minute detail as to its service, issuing, punctuation, the status of the justice, of the clerical staff and the locality of the courthouse. I have no idea of the statistics: it seemed to me that most of the judgments to which I was referred, and therefore read, had their origins in a conviction for drunken driving.

As a matter of undoubted fact, in the course of a judicial review of one such conviction, the appointment to office of a particular District Justice was challenged and found to be faulty. So, naturally, he had to go. All or any of these challenges could have been made in other prosecutions, but they would not have been cheap to mount and it demonstrates the lengths to which an appellant was prepared to go to retain his licence. Quite apart from money, some were also prepared to throw their bodily privacy to the winds to keep on driving. I have, in my day, been asked to state a case that a man could not form an intention to drive if he were engaged in sexual intercourse at the time; and, on another occasion, counsel questioned the doctor as to whether or not the urine sample might have been contaminated by his client's venereal infection. This was at a time when actual disqualification, in the case of a first offence, usually lasted no more than six months.

Section 50 of the Road Traffic Acts had rather jesuitical undertones to it, I always thought. Roughly speaking, a driver had to be in charge of a car, with the intention of driving it, although not driving, and to be over the limit. A further refinement was that the defendant was required to show he had no such intention. During a very cold spell, a garda observed a man fast asleep in the driver's seat of a car, which was blanketed in snow parked in Dublin's Leeson Street. It was after midnight. The garda's evidence was that he found it well nigh impossible to wake up the man. He succeeded only after ten minutes of shouting, banging on the window and shaking the door handle. When the man woke up, he was arrested and eventually charged under Section 50. I could not for the life of me see how someone could form an intention while he was fast asleep, or how a third party could intuit that he had any intention at all. Although I was initially asked to state a case, it was not pursued by the State.

It would, mercifully, surprise our children to realise the pockets of almost primitive bigotry which existed in Ireland in the past, and how its flotsam washed up in our secular courts. Whatever about fears of world communism – rational or irrational – something of the same infection greeted the arrival of Jehovah's Witnesses come like St Patrick to spread the word. It is difficult to understand what could have provoked such vindictive, ugly behaviour.

There was a case in 1956 where two of them were assaulted and the Attorney General prosecuted a Father Ryan in the District Court in Limerick, much to the chagrin of the local Catholic Bishop of Killaloe, who wrote to the then Taoiseach strongly protesting at this *lèse-majesté*. The Attorney General should have known better than 'to proceed against one of my priests for upholding and defending the fundamental truth of our treasured Catholic Faith'.

Across in Wexford, some years later, the State Solicitor struggled to obstruct the prosecution of three local priests. His helpful suggestion was that if the evangelists did not leave the town of New Ross, they were the ones who should be prosecuted and bound over. The poor man probably just wanted a quiet life. In fairness to the common sense of most ordinary people, I have a strong memory of the anger loudly expressed when a district justice convicted some Jehovah's Witnesses of a breach of the peace and not the solid citizens who had attacked them.

~ ~ ~

In a recent judgment, the Chief Justice outlined some of the changes in the District Court wrought in the past half-century, and his words highlight the sharp contrast to Mr. Casey's memories which opened this chapter. If I may quote from that judgment:

> The legal environment in which the District Court exercises its criminal jurisdiction had changed a lot since 1962. This included the aggregate time of imprisonment that could be imposed from one to two years and the introduction of new offences, many of them arising out of the introduction of modern regulatory regimes and often emanating from EU legislation. In addition, dealing in and supplying illicit drugs was virtually unknown in the 1960s, as was the offence of possessing child pornography (*Carmody* v. *Minister for Justice*).

At the time of Ireland's entry into Europe, we hardly imagined the extent to which the imposition of EU regulations would become part of standard court proceedings, as the Chief Justice has observed. Some of them were still novel in my time. One rather sad one was a prosecution that had to do with animal feed and alfalfa dioxin contamination. There was very professional evidence from government scientists and inspectors from the Department of Agriculture, but I will always remember the succession of farmers giving their evidence. It was heartbreaking. Because their young pigs were not thriving, they kept 'feeding them up' as they thought, but it was the feed that was slowly killing them.

On the other hand, there was the steady stream of prosecutions about tachometers which had something to do with measuring the hours spent driving long distance trucks. Most of these cases were defended, but one that is engraved in my memory was of a lorry driver who felt so aggrieved that he had taken the device out of his lorry and brought it in to show me. It was a civil court where the witness stand was right beside the bench, on the same podium. The lorry driver had a sports bag which he placed at his feet and unzipped it. He said something along the lines of, 'I'd like to show you this', and proceeded to lift up what looked decidedly like an old-fashioned alarm clock with a profusion of different coloured wires dangling from it. This was during the worst times of the Northern troubles. My heart stopped. I glanced quickly at the garda inspector who was leaning over looking with mild interest at the device, the same interest which, to varying degrees, was shared by the lawyers in the front row. It was obvious that I was the only one there who knew with absolute certainty that we were all about to be blown up, but I am from a generation that was taught not to make a fuss. Just as well because it was, of course, a tachometer and not a bomb – but it could have been . . .

Another EU regulations case provided even more of a contrast, but in a pleasant way. It was a fishery prosecution and was being heard in Court No. 6 of the Dublin Bridewell where the accustomed fare was drugs, assaults, robberies and more drugs. The lovely small court out in Howth had been closed down, so here were these handsome sailors in their gleaming uniforms and white caps with anchors and braid, talking knowledgeably about ships and knots and tides and the boarding of vessels on the high seas. I learned about cod ends – the very narrowest part of a net – and the proper keeping of logbooks and charts. It was a whole other world – you could almost smell the ozone and feel the sea wind.

There was another occasion in which Europe figured, but the consumer was determined that it would be only in a negative mode. Edam is a town in Holland famous for its cheese. A customer had bought a piece of Edam cheese as being made in Ireland, because it was so labelled, but when he unwrapped it, he found a further label stating that it had come from Holland. He did not want to be passed off with any foreign stuff, so he complained to the Director of Consumer Affairs, and the supermarket was duly summonsed under the Description of Goods Act. The offence was to sell an item as Irish when, in fact, it was an Edam cheese from Edam in Holland. However, the customer had his apology, the state a nominal fine and history recorded another entry in the glorious annals of Irish Bulls!

Chapter 4

First Impressions

My appointment to the District Court in 1981 was somewhat chaotic. While visiting my family in County Limerick, I received an urgent call from an official in the Department of Justice to say that the government had decided to offer me an appointment, but if I accepted I must return to Dublin and be sworn in the next day. The August Bank Holiday was the following weekend and I would be required to take the sittings on the Monday in Tullamore. And, oh, what was the Irish version of my name? For a brief interval, it seemed the invitation might be withdrawn on linguistic principles and I found myself murmuring that we had, over time, come to regard the name of de Valera as native Irish, a point that was conceded after some reflection. In any case, neither the President nor An Taoiseach, who jointly signed the warrant of appointment, nor the Chief Justice before whom I made the statutory submission in the Supreme Court, seemed to harbour any misgivings and so on the Monday I set out for Tullamore.

The gratitude I feel for the good luck that Hugh Carr was the official in charge of the court that day has not lessened. I knew his name as a playwright, of course, but had not met him. He was kindness itself and presumably had long experience of guiding neophyte justices. He was relaxed and knowledgeable and outlined the list of cases to be heard. Hugh also advised me that there was a newly qualified solicitor who would be appearing for the first time and that it was customary to say a few words of welcome. (Come to think if it, I was never welcomed in any court, even in my native Limerick.)

It reminded Hugh of a similar event featuring Donagh MacDonagh who had been his justice for several years. Hugh had mentioned to him before they went out that there would be a new solicitor in court that morning. As soon as he sat down, the justice expressed some welcoming words to the beginner who, in fact, had not yet arrived. The hearing of the list proceeded and at some stage the young man made his appearance. At a suitable juncture, Justice MacDonagh was informed quietly by his registrar that Mr So-and-So was now in court, whereupon he snapped, 'I don't put my cabbage down to boil a second time. Get on with the list.'

Later I would also come to appreciate the good luck that I happened to be appointed in such a hurry to fill in for August. The District Court is closed for its regular business during that month, but there must be a sitting in each court area once a week. By September, when more serious business was the order of the day, I had acquired some familiarity with the procedure, but it was undoubtedly a baptism of fire. I was dashing around the country taking two courts a day – Clonmel in the morning, Limerick in the afternoon, Cork and Dungarvan, Tralee and Dingle and so on. Driving breathlessly up the streets of unknown towns and haranguing passers-by through the car window: 'Do you know where the courthouse is?' Most did not, and there was not a garda in sight; they were all in court. When I finally found it, I had no idea where the actual courtroom was so I would join the end of the queue of people waiting to speak to the court clerk and when it was my turn whisper that I was Justice Kotsonouris. The response was invariably, 'You are what?' Nobody was expecting me and few had ever seen a woman judge. Because of the hasty nature of the enterprise, there never was an announcement of my appointment.

In Waterford, when the registrar opened the door leading into the court, I saw a table and chair directly ahead and made a beeline for it. The punters, struggling with their initial consternation, stood up and then sat down again when I was seated. The Garda Superintendent detached himself from the front row and came forward gesturing upwards with his pencil. For a wild moment I thought there must be some tradition peculiar to Waterford where a new judge was required to go into the witness box and retake the oath which I had already made in the Supreme Court the previous week. When the red mist cleared, I glanced back and saw there was a huge wooden structure behind me and the further sight of the miserable face of the registrar, leaning against the wall, clutching the huge court ledger confirmed that I was sitting at his desk.

I rose, everyone else rose, and I turned and walked up the mountain of stairs leading to the bench and sat down. Then everyone else sat.

As the morning went on, there was little reason for anyone in court to feel reassured that the administration of justice was in competent hands. There was the distraction of a man sitting at the end of a row engaging in a loud and animated conversation with a woman standing beside him who was holding a beautifully dressed little girl. I told him severely that he had to be quiet, that this was a court of law and not a friends' meeting house. In that I was wrong; some time later I caught a reference in a newspaper that the Waterford courthouse was being repaired and that, in the interim, courts were being held in the Friends Meeting House! However, after a short pause, the man continued to talk and I suggested that he take himself outside and stop distracting other people. A grin split his face, he jumped to his feet and then I noticed that he was dangling a smaller prison officer from his right wrist. He was the first prisoner I ever saw, but it was to become a familiar sight; the wife or girlfriend, with the children dressed to the nines, all availing of the chance to see their father. For them, the court *was* a meeting house.

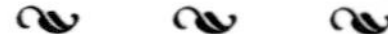

From the very early days, I had the benefit of some spiritual advice. Father Austin Flannery, OP took me aside at a party to impart an object lesson. When his friend Jack Dowling was a young army officer in Athlone, soldiers who were up on minor charges would be paraded before him by the sergeant-major. They all had excuses for their conduct and Jack would listen sympathetically to their stories and offer words of encouragement. It slowly dawned on him that the sergeant-major was getting red in the face and struggling to contain his outrage. He suddenly bellowed: 'Permission to speak, sir?'

'Yes, Sergeant-Major?'

'Sir, the way the men look on officers is that they are either effin' bastards or effin' eejits. You better make up your mind smartly which you are going to be. Sir!'

After he finished his story, Austin said to me: 'And you are going to have to make up your mind too, Mary.'

Of course, I succeeded only in being both.

There were times when even Austin, the most forgiving of men, would have sighed in despair. Some years later, in a country town, two good-looking men in their thirties appeared before the court. They were very well-dressed in matching tweed jackets, pink shirts and smart ties. Not only that, they were identical and they had the same surname. No advantage was being taken of the resemblance, as the charge – a minor fishing offence – was admitted. I then asked the question, which, doubtless, astounded all present with the brilliance of my insight: 'Are you two brothers?'

Later, I drove home overcome with shame at the memory. I had the good fortune at a party that evening to find myself sitting beside a charming man to whom I blurted out my humiliating stupidity and felt relieved to have found a sympathetic ear. Was ever a girl so deceived?

Two days later, a colleague, Brian Kirby, said, 'I met Frank Kelly at the Forty Foot this morning and he was telling me what you said to those fellows the other day.' Dear Reader, he told everyone: I think he still stops strangers in the street in case they might not have heard.

❧ ❧ ❧

Tom Donnelly, the President of the District Court, told me that when he was arranging the vacation sittings, he had telephoned the senior clerk in a Munster court area to say that he was sending down a Judge Kotsonouris to take the court on a particular day. Greeted by a surprised silence, the president explained that because of Ireland's membership of the European Union, he was obliged to accommodate foreign judges from time to time. For good measure, he (the least sexist of men) added, 'And what's even worse, she's a woman!'

When the official found his voice, he asked nervously – and naturally – if the judge spoke English.

'Well, I'll tell you,' said Tom, 'she makes a brave stab at it.'

❧ ❧ ❧

While I was still learning the ropes, I was assigned to Court No. 4 in Dublin's Bridewell. In that week there were three separate brothel cases. During one prosecution for allowing a premises to be used as a brothel, several of the items found there were produced as evidence that the premises had, in fact, been so used. Among them was a bunch of canes. The owner of the premises, who had pleaded not guilty, was being examined by his own counsel and was asked to give his explanation of the paraphernalia, which was already taking up a considerable amount of space in the courtroom. Asked if he recognised the canes, he admitted that he did.

'And when did you first see them?' queried the barrister.

With quiet certainty came the answer: 'They were holding up the pot plants when I purchased the premises some years ago.'

~ ~ ~

Some time in the 1980s, it was decided, for reasons which I have never wholly understood, that it was not legally correct for Peace Commissioners to grant applications for bail in garda stations as heretofore. If an accused was not going to be released on his own bail, he should be brought before a court. Thus night courts were introduced, which meant that a judge would be telephoned and asked to come down to the Bridewell courts. During winter when it was dark, a garda car would arrive to collect the relevant judge around ten o' clock.

One night, as we hurtled through the streets, a young officer told me that there was a crowd already gathered outside the court and that I was going to be escorted through the adjoining garda station and out through the enclosed yard, into the back entrance to the courthouse. I caught a glimpse of a lot of people milling around Chancery Street.

'Try to look like a person in custody,' the gárda whispered to me urgently as we got out of the car. We hurried through the station, across the yard and into the courtroom, which was almost empty. I reached the chamber safely.

I expected that there must have been some arrest which had aroused public anger to the extent of having people gather in protest at such a late hour. However, outside the barred windows of the chamber, the sound of many voices was unexpectedly cheerful, no threatening chorus, only chatter and children laughing. No dramatic cases emerged in court either, just a few routine bail matters. When I came out, Chancery Street was empty. Two gardaí had arrived from a different station to drop me home. Tentatively, I mentioned that there had been a crowd outside earlier when I had arrived.

'Oh, yes,' said the driver, 'I heard that. Apparently, there was a big fireworks display in the Phoenix Park and a rumour went around that the fellow they call the General had been arrested and was being brought to the Bridewell, so people left the entertainment in large numbers and rushed down. There was no truth in it.'

So my star performance as Woman in Custody was utterly wasted.

❧ ❧ ❧

There must have been something about night courts that stirred the ghost of Max Sennett. Another judge was picked up by a garda car to be driven home. On the far side of the Liffey there was some kind of disturbance going on, in which members of the force appeared to be outnumbered. The driver stopped and he and his colleague ran across to render assistance. A few minutes later, a third garda emerged from the melee holding a young fellow by the back of the collar. He rushed over to the patrol car, opened the back door and dumped the alleged miscreant on top of the judge, whom the garda had not noticed. He then rushed back to the action. The mistake was soon realised when the officer returned and the prisoner was relocated. However, it is a scene not difficult to imagine: the two back seat occupants gazing at each other 'in wild surmise, silent upon a peak in Darien.'

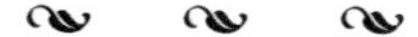

I had finished the list in the same court one Saturday morning when I was asked to hang on because they were bringing in a murder case from Dun Laoghaire. After a further delay, it was suggested that perhaps I would go out to Dun Laoghaire instead in the afternoon. At home there was a telephone call from Mr Brennan, the chief clerk in Dun Laoghaire, to suggest that I should meet him in Cabinteely Garda station and he would drive me since it appeared there might be some difficulty in getting to the court. I have no recollection of questioning these unusual arrangements, only the surprise when we arrived of seeing the mass of people crowded on the street in front of the small courthouse with the Garda station behind. I was probably one of the few people in the country who did not know that a man had been arrested for the recent murder of a nurse in the Phoenix Park.

That court and garda complex is gone now but the judge's chamber was in the front of the building. Mr Brennan, who was of a literary and philosophical bent, was scanning the crowds outside the window while we waited, making quiet comments on the scene. There was a lady in a wheelchair being pushed to the front, although there was nothing whatsoever to see.

'There's a couple greeting someone they obviously haven't seen for a long time. I wonder if they are saying, "Imagine if that unfortunate girl hadn't been killed, we'd never have run into each other like this!"'

The entrance to the gárda station was down a long narrow lane and the public door to the court a little up from that but, normally, prisoners were brought through an underground passage and directly into the dock of the court itself. For some reason, the gardaí decided to take this prisoner out of one door and in through the next. There was no way that anyone standing as far away as the road could see him in the gap, but through the barred windows I heard a sound that was neither human nor animal, a low but thunderous swelling of noise that was as inchoate as it was meaningless. It is a sound I hope never to hear again – the baying of the crowd.

Five minutes later, Malcolm McArthur was charged with two murders and remanded in custody to appear at the Bridewell court the following Thursday. There much the same scene was enacted and he was attacked in the yard, while being brought into court in garda custody.

Tom Donnelly as President of the District Court protested so strongly that from then on Mr McArthur's further appearances in the District Court were processed in the same way as all other prisoners, that is, by being brought up from the cells into the dock. It was a case that aroused a great deal of public interest and I got caught up a little in the backwash solely because of my peculiar name. A RTÉ reporter told me that his mother insisted that they had brought in a foreign judge to try the case, despite his telling her that he was in court and that I was as Irish as herself. (Mr McArthur was, of course, tried in the Central Criminal Court.)

The same year, there was another case in which the setting was ten times more dramatic and the accused had a name as exotic as my own. Mr Tromboli was wanted by the Australian authorities for serious offences and had been on the run for over ten years. He turned up in Ireland, was arrested, and Australia made an application for his extradition. He was also, apparently, a Mafia member and it was feared that they might want to kill him in case he decided to betray them by doing a deal. I have no idea whether or not there was a word of truth in this scenario but it was the story going around.

What was real and there to see was that our authorities were taking it very seriously. He was represented by a distinguished Senior Counsel and a Queen's Counsel reputed to be the leading British extradition lawyer. He was also being protected by armed gardaí and soldiers. It was a heavy scene. The proceedings began in an unused and unheated court in the Bridewell on a Saturday morning, filled with Australian state officials and detective officers, loads of people from the State Solicitor's office and the defendant's impressive legal team. He sat on a chair, looking ill: he was receiving treatment for cancer. It went into a second day and, rather than have all that palaver going on during a busy court week in the inner city, Tom Donnelly decided that the adjourned hearing would be taken in Dundrum court the following Tuesday.

The entire area around the courthouse was cordoned off. There were snipers on the roofs and I bumped into a garda with a machine gun checking the tiny lavatory. The hearing went on for most of the day. There were nineteen charges in all – including murder, attempted murder and drug dealing, as I recall – and I granted the extradition orders in sixteen of them. After the judgment was given, the prisoner was escorted out, and the armed convoy, police escort, prison vans and the elite of the legal fraternity departed. The circus was leaving town, so only the registrar and myself remained to draw up and sign the sixteen separate warrants.

Michael remarked that it showed how important we both were in the scheme of things; that it would be just too bad if the Mafia got the times mixed up and arrived late and so had to settle for us. There wasn't even a single garda within hailing distance. Darkness had fallen by the time we locked up the court and left.

Mairead Kane, with whom I had worked years before in a Dublin solicitor's office, wrote from Sydney: 'I would have fallen down, were I not in bed at the time, when I heard your name on the radio here this morning!'

If I were called Doyle or Kelly or Murphy, no one would have remembered my name; the cases were notorious, not the judge. Perhaps, the gentleman from Justice who had telephoned to offer me the job might have thought, 'we should have insisted on the Irish version . . .'

Chapter 5

Children and the Law

IT IS SAFE ENOUGH TO ASSUME that if one were to ask a judge what was the most upsetting type of case she or he had to deal with, the answer would be having to make a child care order. I remember often standing in my night clothes at two in the morning with a garda holding a Bible and swearing information to enable me to issue a place of safety or emergency care order so that a baby might be taken to Madonna House in the middle of the night because it was too dangerous to leave him in his home.

The power to commit children to a place of safety is in the Children's Act of 1908, which remained the foundation law governing children's rights for almost a hundred years. Not that the idea of children's rights was one which actively motivated the drafters – my impression is that its main purpose was to settle any problems the little nuisances might cause. (I may be forgiven – or not – for once more drawing attention to the fact that the only non-self-serving submissions made to the Judiciary Committee, designing our present legal system in 1923, were by women's groups and were exclusively concerned with children's rights.) Under the Act there are two main types of committal – one in an emergency where it is deemed vital that a child be removed from his home and put in a place of safety as a matter of urgency, and the other where children are committed because they have been neglected, out of control, orphaned or for a variety of other reasons. The memory of babies and toddlers being taken from their mothers is heart-scalding.

A former colleague, Judge Mary Martin, was waiting in the maternity department of a regional hospital during one Christmas week:

'There was a baby about to be born but it was not a joyful occasion. I was there to make an immediate care order as, sadly, it was far too dangerous to leave the child any length of time with the unfortunate mother. About two years later, I found myself in the same hospital, same circumstances, same mother.'

Among my own memories, at least three are still vivid. First, a beautiful dark-haired boy with huge brown eyes looking over the shoulder of the care worker. He was not yet three years old but this would be his eighteenth move. He was loved by his mother, who was damaged and vulnerable and could cope only intermittently with him. Next, an older boy, about ten, who adored his mother and wanted to be with her, but she kept rejecting him. The disappointment was unbearable and he had twice tried to kill himself; the child psychologist feared that the torment was about to happen again and that the child would succeed. The application was that he should be in care under a court order so that she could not take him out of the juvenile home and put him through it all over again. Third, a mother crying her eyes out in court and begging to have her children returned. They had been taken from her because of her drinking. The evidence was that, although she was making a great effort, she was not yet competent to look after them.

~ ~ ~

A woman in her seventies told me that the first – and only – time she had been in a District Court was when she was seven and she was with her two-year-old sister. Their mother had died, the father drank and they had been taken into care by the state. Her brother had gone to relatives. A garda had come to fetch them and they travelled by train to the court. She had a hazy recollection of standing in a big room and a man sitting above them in a high place. They were sent to an orphanage where they had to work very hard; eventually, she went into domestic service in a provincial town. She made a happy marriage and had loving children. At different times, both her father and her brother traced her whereabouts and called to see her, but the only reason they had sought her out was to cadge money for drink.

~ ~ ~

Dr Patricia Roche, Justice Johnson's daughter, told me in a letter: 'Every time my father came home having signed orders committing children to the care of orphanages, if they were girls, or to industrial schools in the case of boys, he would be upset and angry. He believed that in many cases children were neglected because the parents were too poor to care for them and that, if the government would only give to the parents the money which it was about to grant to the orphanage or the industrial school for their keep, the family would be able to stay together.'

Richard Johnson was later to write a powerful play on the same theme. Some years ago at a law conference in County Clare, it was striking to hear a judge from Chicago expressing much the same sentiment about her own court experience.

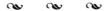

I knew a woman over a long time who had been the subject of a place of safety order when she was as child but, mercifully, appeared to have no memory of it and indeed nothing of her childhood apart from the orphanage where she was brought up. She went into domestic service with a family who lived nearby and stayed with them until her death, some fifty years later. The children grew up with her and around her, and so did their children.

At the stage when she felt she should be entitled to the old-age pension, she did not have a birth certificate. A search was instituted on her behalf which proved difficult because the convent had hardly any records of their charges. However a clue as to her native town led to the surprising and sad discovery that when Mary was six, in 1927, she had been found begging in the streets and Philip O'Donoghue, the District Justice, had made an order committing her to the orphanage until she was sixteen. She had been born in the workhouse of an unmarried mother. She obviously had no memory of the early years and, of course, the people who loved her told her a fairy story about her origins. She was pleased: 'Somehow I always knew that I came from decent people.'

❧ ❧ ❧

Dick Robinson, formerly regional manager of court services in the Munster area (and currently historian of the National Lifeboat Service), has been a generous source of court history as well as knowledge. I first met him when he was Chief Clerk in Clare and, among other memories, he told me of this experience.

> It was a different day in the rural courthouse; the normal pre-court banter was absent. The first business of the day was an application to commit two children to a place of safety. This was the story of a young woman to whom the world had dealt a devastating blow and she could not cope. Financially secure and with a fine house, she had no will to carry the weight of the world. There was nobody to whom she could turn, so the authorities came to assist her. The two children would have to be removed to a place of safety until the mother could cope again. They were blond children with beautiful skin, but their hair was matted and lice crawled around their heads. The justice on the day was tearful as he signed the order and the mother sat in silence. All had been explained to her and she knew that it had to

> be done. Then two young women gardaí came to take the children. Despite the children being filthy and covered with lice, they cuddled and consoled them. Then they turned to leave. The children waved and their disconsolate mother screamed. Even now, some forty years later, the scene and the scream come to the surface of the mind . . .

~ ~ ~

The following report appeared in the *Wicklow People* of 9 February 1924:

> There was a prosecution in Bray court of a boy called Mathew Lyons accused of stealing a wrist watch from a house in the town. A shopkeeper, who was also a church warden, gave evidence that the accused had come to his shop and begged for the price of a night's lodging which he refused. The boy then offered to sell him the watch for a shilling, saying he had found it on the road. The witness bought the watch for that price as it was a very wet night. Evidence was given that the family had only recently come to Bray from Arklow: there were eight children of which Matthew was the eldest. The husband, an ex-soldier, was in delicate health as was one of his daughters. The lad's solicitor asked the justice to give him a chance and not to send him to an industrial school. He would be 14 the following Monday. Mr. Little, district justice, said that as the woman had so many other children to attend to, including the delicate girl, it would

> be far better that she would not have to take care of the boy and the court would send him to Carriglea Industrial School.

The justice had no word of rebuke for the churchwarden who, on his own admission, knew that the child did not own the watch and yet seized the opportunity to buy it for a pittance. The self-righteousness and cold-hearted disposal of the family and its needs could have been written by Charles Dickens.

The following case is equally difficult to understand but it happened about twenty years ago. It was also the prosecution of a youth for theft. The boy was barely seventeen and he was before the court charged with breaking into a shop premises in the early hours and stealing a packet of biscuits. The prosecuting garda said in his evidence that the accused had run away from home after a row with his parents, and that he was diabetic. During the night, his insulin level had fallen dangerously low and he had no medication with him. He knew that he had quickly to find something to eat, hence the desperate breaking and entering. The garda added helpfully that the boy would probably have died otherwise, and that he had no previous convictions. What kind of a society hauls a person into court because he stole a few paltry biscuits in order to stay alive?

As a recently qualified solicitor, I had to supervise the handing back of a baby girl who had been fostered by an adoring family. She had been brought to Ireland by her parents to be abandoned on the steps of a church at the edge of a town outside Dublin. They knew so little about Ireland – only that it was at the end of a short boat crossing – that they chose the Protestant church on a weekday rather then the Catholic one in the middle of the town, where she might have been discovered much earlier. She was not found until some time the following day with a broken leg sustained from a stumble in the churchyard.

The gardaí subsequently traced the couple, who were extradited from Britain and tried in Ireland. I think the father was jailed for six months and the woman was given probation. Some years after these events, my firm was instructed by English solicitors to represent the mother, who was applying to the High Court to have her daughter returned to her. Although the application was strenuously opposed by the local authority, the order was that the child be returned to her natural mother. Hence the small group gathered in the lounge of a Dublin hotel. The lively toddler bounced about between her foster parents while the wife explained to our client what her favorite cereals were, her bedtimes, the things she disliked, while handing over the youngster's most loved soft toys. You could feel the husband desperately holding himself together; it became unbearable and he stood up and left, while his wife's voice continued steadily filling in the background. To my censorious eye, the mother did not appear to be paying any great attention. Her attitude was in strong contrast to the other woman's steely determination to stay calm and to try to soften what would shortly be a nightmarish experience for the small child.

❧ ❧ ❧

A juvenile was being prosecuted in a court in County Limerick when an argument developed between his father and the presiding justice; both men got very cross and the father stormed out. The case was continuing when the judge noted a reporter covering the proceedings in the body of the court.

'Who are you?' he called down.

The young man stood up and nervously identified himself as Michael O'Toole from the *Limerick Chronicle*.

'And what are you writing down?'

Michael gulped, took a deep breath and blurted out, 'I am writing that you are hearing this case in the absence of the father.'

There was a horrified silence while everyone waited for the seismic explosion. This time it was the turn of the justice to storm out but, after a decent interval, he came back and so did the father and the hearing resumed within the correct procedure.

The late Michael O'Toole was a first-class court reporter. He was passionately interested in the administration of the law and wrote a lively and incisive column about courts in the *Evening Herald*.

Chapter 6

Family Law

PERHAPS IT IS DIFFICULT TO REALISE that there was a time when there was no such branch of law as family law: it is even of more recent vintage than the law relating to children. We in Ireland were slower than many other jurisdictions in the development of either. Of course, there would have been the total certainty that the law had no business whatsoever meddling with family matters; indeed, one may still come across individuals who would be of that opinion. Admittedly, their numbers are dwindling and they tend to be men rather than women.

When the Judiciary Committee was planning the structure for the new courts of the Irish Free State in 1923, several bodies put forward ideas to Hugh Kennedy, the Attorney General, about how they thought their interests might best be reflected in the administration of justice. As I have already recalled, only the recommendations of women's groups were manifestly disinterested: they concerned children. The Children's Care Committee had gone to the trouble of researching the juvenile court system already established in Canada. However, no correspondents expressed any thoughts on laws relating to marriage, women's rights or family relationships.

In 1993, Olive Caulfield, then senior Court Clerk in the family law court of the Dublin Metropolitan District, with the permission of the Minister for Justice, gave a account of the development of family law in Ireland to a fascinated audience at the Merriman Summer School. It was based on her personal knowledge and experience, and I am indebted to her for making her notes available to me.

She spoke of how, before 1976, a single mother, wanting to obtain some financial support from the father of her child, could make the application only to an office – a kind of Nissen hut – in the yard of the Bridewell Gárda station. She did so in the presence and hearing of everyone crowded into that space who were also waiting to speak to the clerk. If the complaint was one of domestic violence, then the often graphic details were recited across the counter so that a common summons for assault, as it was known, could be drawn up. The subsequent proceedings were naturally heard in public. In time, the interest of politicians and the media in the subject of domestic violence, as well as the growing feminist movement, led to legislative efforts to remedy the situation. The coming into force of the Family Law (Protection of Spouses and Children) Act 1976 brought about radical change. A court could bar a violent spouse from the family home for up to twelve months, and the breach of such an order would be a criminal offence.

From then on, all proceedings were to be heard *in camera* and interviews with the court's staff were to be private. In Dublin, a purpose-built family court was opened, with consultation rooms and with probation and welfare involvement. The law was further developed in 1981 with the court being given powers to determine matters relating to children, such as custody and access, as well as applications for guardianship. The same year saw the introduction of orders granting Garda protection to spouses waiting to have barring applications heard.

A District Court clerk has statutory powers to issue proceedings. Originally, the remedies were confined to married couples. There was no divorce possible under the law at the time so these acts afforded the chance to have maintenance, custody and protection issues sorted out fairly quickly and without cost. There is civil free legal aid available for family law, but there is a very strong demand on these services. Naturally, where one side has legal representation, fairness demands that the other party not be put at a disadvantage.

In outlying courts, there was a particular time set aside for family law cases, and that was usually after lunch. One young couple had a row which went on for some time. The underlying cause had its origins in an event which should have been a great improvement in their lives. They had moved from a small flat in the inner city to a modern house with every convenience in the suburbs. The husband was self-employed and doing well in his own business as a craftsman and they had one child. However, the wife missed living near her mother. (This regularly cropped up in Dublin cases: girls were very attached to their mothers and a better house outside the city rarely seemed to compensate for the physical distance.) She became even more unhappy when she discovered that she was pregnant again. Rows became more frequent and one night the husband slapped her – once. All the facts were agreed. He instantly regretted it but it was too late: she wanted him barred from the house.

It was explained at great length that a court would not bar a spouse from the family home on the basis of this evidence alone, and it was adjourned so that the couple could talk things through with the court welfare officer. However, at the resumed hearing some weeks later, the woman's resolve had not shaken. She accepted that her husband would not be barred, but neither was she going to remain in the home.

It was a dark November evening in a small bleak building with a high ceiling – a former Petty Sessions court – her husband was standing at the far side. He screamed, 'But I love you', and the despairing wail seemed to rise up and hang in the gloomy air over the few people there while she walked out of the door without a backward glance.

❧ ❧ ❧

Once the family law legislation was passed, it seemed that prosecutions for domestic violence dwindled, even in cases of serious injury. It was as if the Garda authorities had decided that it was a family matter, rather than a criminal one.

In the very bad snow of 1982, I was driven to a court in County Meath by the gardaí to hear an application for a protection order from a woman with a black eye who had been brought by ambulance from, I believe, County Kildare. When I left, she was standing on the icy street with her two children and none of them was wearing a coat. I was new to the job so did not know there was another way, until I mentioned my adventure in the snow – we had rather a bad skid – to Tom Donnelly a few days later. He was enraged at the whole set-up. 'Why didn't the gardaí arrest the husband, charge him with assault and bring him before the next court in Kildare?'

There was an application for a protection order in a case where the husband threatened his wife, who was in bed at the time, with a lit cigarette lighter. He explained, without any great remorse, that he had done it to force her to join in some fun and games the fellows in the pub had been talking about that evening and he had felt deprived of the experience. I had an almost irresistible impulse to lean over the bench and murmur, 'I wouldn't bother if I were you; it's very overrated, you know.' Instead, I confided to him that were we in another court, I would be giving him the opportunity to have lots more discussions on the subject with the fellows up in Mountjoy.

Perhaps in the future, a social historian will examine the effect of protection legislation on married life in Ireland over the past thirty years. It put a great deal of power into women's hands and, of course, in the rough and tumble of marital rows, it was inevitable that it would be turned into a threat. One occasionally got the impression that it was being used as a kind of choke leash on a frisky dog. Doubtless, between the jigs and the reels, some kind of balance worked itself out.

I remember a case in Cork where it transpired that at least two further children were conceived and born during the course of a barring order which twice had been extended. On the other hand, a man before the criminal court on a charge of breaching a protection order, where the main evidence was that he had torn the lead out of the telephone, wearily admitted it. He had got tired of his wife constantly threatening to telephone the Gardaí if he as much as raised his voice in argument or protested about anything.

Many women thought that they had an automatic entitlement to a barring order merely by applying for it; others simply wanted a divorce because there was none at the time. One could sense the bafflement at the discovery that it was not as simple as that. Sometimes with retired people, the rows had their roots in the reluctance of the husband to go out and enjoy himself, while becoming cantankerous because his wife had taken up dancing. When I was a judge, most of the people had no jobs, so it was a question of trying to allocate very small sums of money, particularly in cases where the husband had acquired 'another family'. Nothing perhaps better illustrates how difficult it is to legislate for the human condition than a long afternoon in a family court.

~ ~ ~

Section 40 of the Civil Liability and Courts Act 2004 relaxed the *in camera* rule to allow for the reporting of family law cases in certain defined circumstances, principally by persons carrying out reports. The Courts Services engaged Dr. Carol Coulter to initiate a pilot project to carry out a study of family law proceedings. They then continued with the work and the report was published in a series. In Dr. Coulter's words, it was 'an attempt to give the flavour of what typically happens in a family law hearing'. It has certainly succeeded. In fact, several vignettes might serve as an the outline for a short story, telling of what remains when the excited hope of the wedding day has played itself out. Some couples are still arguing furiously before the judge over money, child custody, blame and possessions, while others, with their new arrangements well in place, are practical, organised and are already immersed in different lives. It is difficult to be certain which group is the sadder.

Chapter 7

Crime and Punishment

THERE SEEMS TO BE A WIDESPREAD perception that courts are primarily concerned with criminal trials, although these do not form the bulk of the proceedings in any court area. However, it is true that the more lively events in the District Court generally take place during the exercise of its criminal jurisdiction. While there are 'funny incidents' which catch the eye, there can be drama, fury and despair too. The atmosphere is less formal than in civil cases and doubtless is affected by the way the story emerges. There is quite a lot of verbal evidence which makes participants, not least the lawyers, spark off each other. It is clear that, of all proceedings, at every level of court, criminal trials are the most frequently reported in the press. Members of the public, who have no knowledge of or connection with the involved parties, express confident verdicts all their own. Everyone is Miss Marples, which is surely not surprising given the popularity of crime fiction.

Leaving aside the exception of the Special Criminal Court, all criminal prosecutions begin in the District

Court. Once a person has been arrested and charged, they must be brought before the next court in that area. Minor crimes are heard in the District Court, although every accused is entitled to trial by judge and jury, even if the charge is the theft of a chocolate bar. If an accused is bailed on someone else's surety, then that person is obliged to come to court and show that they are good for the sum that has been set.

Because of the bleak times in the 1980s, my memory is that the only person in a household earning any money was most likely to be the mother, and she would come in with her post office savings book. Her legs were swollen from cleaning hospital floors and she was probably bringing up the children of a drug-addicted daughter. Perhaps, in my own mind, I frequently wronged an accused young male, but I used to think that maybe the only time the son noticed his mother's existence was when he needed her to come down to court with her savings book. One of the best and most imaginative charitable deeds I have ever known was that some probation officers, at their own expense, used to organise a 'knees-up' kind of weekend at country hotels for those mothers.

I understand that the taking of depositions is almost obsolete now, but it was once quite a regular proceeding. The prosecution or the defence could ask that a witness whose statement was given in the book of evidence be examined on oath. The unfortunate individual must have felt he had stepped into a video recording of the trial in *Alice's Adventures in Wonderland*. The procedure seemed artificial and, to me, purposeless. Counsel would ask a simple question such as, 'Did you see a red car in the lane?' The answer should naturally be 'yes', because it is, in effect, his own statement being put to him, albeit in a labyrinthine fashion. The court registrar, who was the star turn in the procedure, had to write it all down in longhand, but would transcribe it thus: 'I saw a red car in the lane.' It was explained to the witness that he must confine his answer to a yes or no, although he was free to qualify it further after the registrar had written it down, and to keep his eye on the writer's hand. Invariably, the person tended to add something to flesh out the bareness, in an effort to be helpful, or to explain himself more clearly.

The unfortunate scribe, who resembled a monk writing his bit of the Book of Kells, might be still in the middle of the first sentence and, despairingly, would turn his eyes in a silent plea to the bench. The process was explained again. 'Please keep looking at the registrar and do not speak while his pencil is moving.' But after a short time, the witness would feel compelled to elaborate to the judge: 'You see, I was coming back from the shop: I had gone down to buy a bottle of milk.' And so it went on through the afternoon, because a whole afternoon was always wisely set aside in Court No. 5 for the taking of depositions.

After the deponent's statement was read back to him and he did not wish to alter it, it was signed by him and the judge and was included in the book of evidence. I have no idea what happened to it after that; whether, one day, in the Circuit Criminal Court the deposition was triumphantly flourished before some witness, like that great Thurber cartoon with the seal, and a lawyer bellowed, 'and what do you have to say to this?' Judge Hubert Wine took a deposition that went on for a year because of all the adjournments!

~ ~ ~

Once, in Dun Laoghaire, there was a small, elderly woman with a beautiful lined face and brown hair coiled around her head. She was charged with shoplifting, but she was curiously detached from the surroundings. Her escort was a young garda, who seemed fiercely protective of her. He glared around while he helped her into the witness box. He laid out the items which were the usual garish consumer fodder – a cheap, leatherette-covered cardboard hat box and a pair of tights in a bright wrapper. She had been arrested and accused of failing to pay for them in a local shop, which she did not deny.

The legal aid solicitor gently prompted her to tell her story, which she did in an abstracted way. She had come into the town that morning to shop for her daughter, but had met a woman friend whose birthday it was and who had invited her for a drink. She was on medication for her heart and for arthritis. The garda, whom it was difficult to believe was the prosecutor, rummaged in her bag to show the court the different pill bottles. Her daughter, who had been deserted by her husband, had suffered a bad breakdown and was a patient in Portrane Hospital. She had been at home for a few days but her mother could see that she was getting worse and that she needed to be back in hospital, so the mother had come to town to buy some treat with which to coax her poor child on to the train for the journey. The woman had gone to the shop and picked out the treats but, befuddled with medication and alcohol, did not remember to pay; at that point in her evidence, she half-fainted.

The prosecuting garda put his arms around the accused, lifted her to her feet and helped her out of the court in complete silence. They did not return. So much for her day in town and the forlorn hope that she might lovingly tempt her daughter back to the mental institution with the gaudy trifles for which she, in her semi-drugged state, had forgotten to pay. How small they had seemed laid out on the courtroom table, compared with the stoic hopelessness of that mother and daughter. Balzac said that the ordinariness of people's lives can be no measure of the courage which it takes to live them. Years later, I met the young solicitor and the first thing he asked me was if I remembered the case.

Tom Donnelly was hearing a prosecution for growing cannabis where a neighbour of the accused was giving evidence of seeing the plants in the adjoining garden on a date in April. Questioned by a sceptical lawyer on his certainty of the actual date, the witness looked at him in scorn. 'Wasn't it Good Friday?'

Disgusted at his questioner's continuing lack of understanding, the reluctant gardener exploded, 'Why else would I be in the garden only that the pubs were shut?'

A friend from Nenagh remembers a well-known character in the town, down-at heel, not very bright but self-confident enough to lift things off the shelves in shops and leave quickly with them under his arm. Consequently, he was frequently up before the bench. On one such occasion, in the days before legal aid, several charges were being run together. A succession of prosecuting gardaí gave evidence in turn, but were being ignored by the indifferent accused. Finally, the court asked him what he had to say to the evidence given so far. He had the absolute defence to these outrageous charges. With an air of weary disdain, he turned to put the judge right, 'Tis all lies, your Worship'.

A judicial colleague, taking sittings in the south-west, was told of an incident outside his court that morning. An officious mother was escorting her adult son for his court appearance on a driving offence and spied two gardaí struggling on the pavement with a prisoner who had attempted to escape. The woman upbraided the guardians of the law for what they were doing to 'the poor young lad and what had he done anyway?'

A garda, in the midst of his efforts, said that he had stolen a chalice from the local church, which changed her world view in a thrice.

'Let me at him,' she cried, aiming an accurate kick at the man's legs. 'Hanging's too good for the likes of him.'

'He got off on a technicality.' Why do we think that this excuses a badly prepared or presented case? The law is meant to protect us from tyranny, from the false accusation and the trumped-up charge. If it says I am guilty of drunken driving when I have consumed a defined amount of alcohol, within a defined time of driving a motor car, then it is up to the person who accuses me of the offence to prove that it was what I was doing. If he fails to make a connection between the time I was driving and the time the alcohol level was measured, then he has not proved his accusation. All this is written down; it is the law. It is neither advanced science nor legal devilry.

When a woman was charged with soliciting under the Dublin Police Acts, there had to be evidence by the gardaí not only that she was known to be a common prostitute, but also that she was soliciting to the annoyance of people passing by or living in the neighbourhood – which, after all, is the only thing that would make her behaviour offensive, in both senses of the word. It was surprising how few prosecutors gave evidence of a complaint having been made. For the most part it was academic because the women generally preferred to plead to the charge and pay the fine of two pounds.

Many people are scandalised because witnesses lie on oath, but those who tell lies without a qualm are not going to be put off by the prospect of doing so with their hand on the Bible or the Koran. Ironically, it is the witnesses who ask to affirm rather than swear who show that they are the ones taking the idea of religion seriously. In any case, the repetition of the oath so many times during a single day can hardly inspire awe. The offence of perjury is lying to the court. While it may also be a sin, it is a crime. If, instead, a judge was obliged to tell all witnesses individually, including the police, of their obligation to tell the truth, to inform them of the penalties for perjury and to ask if they understood, it might take a little longer, but it might also put the fear of God – and of punishment – into some liars, while removing a cause of scandal to the pure of heart.

One day in a suburban Dublin court, an accused was charged with attempting to obtain money with menaces. The substance of the charge was that a person had phoned a video store in the area claiming to have found one of their videos and enquired about the possibility of a reward. Several telephone calls later it became clear that he was looking for payment to return its own property to the company. A complaint was made to the local Garda station where a plan was drawn up to have two female workers in the store arrange to meet the man in another area, about five miles away. One of them would wear a 'wire' and would ask questions designed to prompt the answer that, without payment, the suspect would not return the video. The rendezvous was duly arranged at the corner of a busy street. The two young gardaí proceeded to the corner. One looked into the window of a bakery shop while his colleague stood at a bus stop, ostensibly immersed in a newspaper. In due course the sting fell out as planned: the forces of the law arrived like the U.S. Cavalry and the culprit was arrested with the necessary evidence captured on the tape one of the girls was wearing. It was clear that a great deal of resources, energy and time had been put into recovering the lost video whose value was given in the charge sheet as £16. And its title? *Stakeout*.

❧ ❧ ❧

There was a publican in County Tipperary who had been convicted of keeping his premises open outside the licensing hours and had lost his licence. He appealed the conviction. In preparation for the hearing, his loyal customers held a succession of moot courts in the pub so that the publican might become familiar with the proceedings. The appeal was successful.

❧ ❧ ❧

She was tall, beautiful and nineteen. The defendant, a stranger, had crossed to the side of the street where she was standing and had touched her in a most offensive way. He was rightly charged with indecent assault, which was admitted and, through his lawyer, he offered financial compensation. Asked for her reaction to this development, she said that what she wanted was an apology. He stood facing her and he said he was sorry. She regarded him in silence for a long minute, gave a cool nod in the direction of the Bench and walked slowly out of the court, leaving at least one person there breathless with admiration.

Chapter 8

The Rose Tattoo Case

It is indeed surprising to realise that the Rose Tattoo case happened over fifty years ago and that it has remained in the public memory, even if the details are somewhat vague. At the least, people remember it as some kind of scandal and related to a prurience which would now be judged outlandishly ridiculous, although some have more vivid memories. In November 2002, forty-five years later, Michael D. Higgins raised the matter in Dáil Éireann in a passionate plea that even at that late stage all the relevant State papers should be released. The report in the *Irish Law Times* of the judgment – strictly speaking a finding by District Justice Cathal O'Flynn – covers twelve pages and may well be the only report of District Court proceedings to appear in that weighty journal. Whatever about the legal fireworks or the tortuous verbal machinations of the prosecution, or the vociferous support of the Dublin and international litterati, the drama was all the more ironic because its raw material was a play.

An Tostal was conceived as part celebration, part marketing festival and it was under its auspices that the first Dublin International Theatre Festival was held. There was a veritable feast in prospect for any theatregoer: *Aida*, Grand Opera Society at Gaiety; *Swan Lake*, Royal Ballet at the Theatre Royal; *The Importance of Being Earnest* at the Olympia with Margaret Rutherford as Lady Bracknell; *Juno and the Paycock* at the Abbey with Eileen Crowe, Philip Flynn and Harry Brogan, to be followed by *The Playboy of the Western World* with Ray McAnally and Marie Keane; *The Old Lady Says 'No!'* at the Gate, with Micheal Mac Liammóir as Robert Emmet.

There was a Folk Dance Festival with teams from Israel, England, Sweden and West Germany, as well as a Feis Ceoil and the Theatre National Populaire coming to the Olympia with works by Balzac and Molière. The Pike Theatre would have two shows nightly: Tennessee Williams's *The Rose Tattoo,* which was the first English production of the play in Europe, at 7.30 and *Say it with Flowers*, the late night revue at 11.00.

Any city in the world would have been proud to have such a festival programme of great plays and well-known actors, but over the following weeks it was the production in the smallest of the playhouses which was destined to dominate the headlines and remain the abiding public memory of the first Dublin International Theatre Festival.

The Pike was a tiny theatre in a converted coach house down Herbert Lane, off Baggot Street. It had gained a reputation in the few years of its existence for bringing new work like *Waiting for Godot* to Irish audiences and for continental-type revues. *The Rose Tattoo* opened to a packed house and earned a splendid notice from Harold Hobson, the legendary critic from the *Sunday Times*. However, there had already been more than a hint of a disapproving underground swell from the likes of the League of Decency, and the file in the National Archives shows that a Dáil deputy had made a strong protest to the Minister for Justice who alerted the Attorney General's office.

Alan Simpson, the Pike's owner/manager, was a captain in the Army Corps of Engineers and a former stage director of the Gate Theatre. Shortly before curtain-up on the second night, an Inspector Ward arrived at the theatre to inform Simpson (reading to him from a document) that the play contained 'objectionable passages' and demanded that the performance be cancelled or Simpson would be arrested. Nevertheless, in the best tradition, the performance went on that night, and indeed every other night of the week. Con Lehane, Simpson's solicitor, demanded to be told, at least, what the objections were, but without success. A squad car with four detectives arrived the following evening but could not get access to the lane. The press had been alerted and there was a huge crowd milling around, including patrons who failed to get seats – the theatre had only a 70-seat capacity – and personages from literary, legal and stage circles. In the interval, the goat, a member of the cast, was being walked up and down for exercise. Brendan Behan, who, naturally, was among the moral supporters, sang 'The Peeler and the Goat'.

The startling headline in the next morning's *Irish Times* was 'Dublin Theatre Director Arrested', over a photograph of Carolyn Swift, Simpson's wife and the co-producer of the play, trying to gain access to her office while a detective, with her husband in his grasp, is shutting the door in her face. The play had gone on, although the gardaí had individually warned each member of the cast that they would be prosecuted.

Alan Simpson had been arrested on a warrant signed by District Justice Kenneth Reddin, himself a playwright. The charge was 'that on the 13th May 1957 at the Pike Theatre, Herbert Lane, within the Dublin Metropolitan District, the defendant did show for gain an indecent and profane performance', and two further counts in relation to other dates. Unlike books or films, there was no legislation governing stage performances, so Simpson was charged under common law, which made him liable, in theory at any rate, to be sentenced on conviction to life, or whatever term a particular court might decide. Interestingly, it emerged during the hearing that the book of the play was on sale in Dublin and had never been banned by the Censorship Board, which banned so much else.

Alan Simpson was lodged in a cell in the Bridewell Garda station overnight and appeared before District Justice Rochford, who had been given a copy of the play, which, according to the solicitor for the Attorney General, was 'generally lewd, indecent, offensive and tends to corrupt the mind and destroy the love of decency, morality and good order'. As might be expected, the court was crowded; the *Irish Times* noted that some of the press representatives present – four times the usual number – could not find seats. The father of the accused, a Church of Ireland priest, was in court. Kate Binchy remembers him in clerical black, white dog collar and big hat. 'He was very tall, had snow white hair and was a most reassuring presence.' The justice pressed for the matter to be disposed of that day, 'in the absence of evidence that the defendant was guilty of any offence and in view of the hardship that could be caused….' There was a judicial colleague who was available to hear the matter the same day. The prosecution had no intention of facilitating this move and, unsuccessfully, opposed bail. Although Simpson remained away from the Pike on legal advice, the play finished its scheduled run.

The Irish Times, which reported assiduously on the affair, noted on 27 May:

> The Rose Tattoo ends its run, though not transferring to the Gate as had been intended – however, honour has been satisfied. It has been an eventful week in the life of the Pike Theatre. Its name has featured in the headlines of the press of many countries and it has been given the close attention of detectives and of thieves, who stole £30.

The enterprising burglars must have blessed the opportunity afforded by the chaotic situation.

The action had, by then, moved to the District Court where it proved as equally dramatic and, from a lawyer's viewpoint, absorbing. For any judge of that court, past or present, it can be said to be full of the 'Wow factor'. The preliminary investigation of the charges was opened on 4 July before District Justice Cathal O'Flynn. The received wisdom on *The Rose Tattoo* has long been that the prosecution arose because the script required a condom to fall on the stage during the course of the action. Not only was contraception then banned by law, but any literature that was considered, however obliquely, to advocate it was regularly banned by the Censorship Board. Not that the words 'condom' or 'contraceptive' were used very much during the long drawn-out proceedings. For example, Detective Garda Martin's evidence was:

> . . . that if a certain portion of the stage direction in the book had been carried into the play, the play would be objectionable, but it was not carried into the play.

Alan Simpson was aware that this particular scene might prove contentious, so a small, nondescript package had been substituted for the condom. However the gardaí, having failed in their evidence to substantiate any objectionable behaviour in that regard, moved on to speculate about the motives and morals of the different characters. Reading what they said is to sense how art informs our perception. These decent, serious men, for whom the theatre was a rare experience, had become caught up in the action and pondered the lives of Serafina, Alvaro and Rosa as if they were real, and not the fictitious creations of a playwright. The four gardaí, who had attended performances over three evenings, were the principal witnesses and all the first day was taken up with the evidence of Detective Garda Martin. There was a close cross-examination of the second witness, Sergeant Kenny, which appears to have exposed the fallacies of the conclusions he had drawn, not just about the stage action and the words that were said, but about the moral motives of the individuals. When the barrister for the defence pressed the witness to say where his instructions had come from, counsel for the State claimed that this was privileged information. The justice did not agree, but the prosecution asked him to state a case on the point to the High Court.

It meant that another year was added to Simpson's trial. Three judges heard the case over five days, and by a majority decision held that the witnesses were protected by privilege. The dissenting judgment was that of the President of the court, Cahir Davitt, who made the sensible observation that the defence was not really affected by the withholding of the information, and that the public interest would not have suffered by the disclosure of the communications with the gardaí. However, the decision was appealed to the Supreme Court, which held that the justice had no right to state a case in the middle of holding a preliminary investigation, which, in fairness, had also been his opinion. So neither side gained any advantage by the expensive exercise. The interval had, however, given Cathal O'Flynn the opportunity to read up on the law as well as on life, literature and the play itself, and he was well prepared when the case back into his court on 4 June 1958.

I vaguely remember O'Flynn as a large, jowly man with an air of self-importance, perhaps reinforced by his nickname of Nanky Poo, from *The Mikado*. There were two further days of evidence and cross-examination, and the proceedings were fully reported in the press. The matter of instructions was raised again, but the justice refused to allow it to be pursued, even though it was in a kind of limbo because of the Supreme Court judgment. (No one in court had a copy of it when he enquired.) He felt that he should follow the majority opinion of the High Court, and disallow the question.

Why it was a matter of such importance to the defence is somewhat puzzling, but it was a question of principle to the State. The Minister for Justice sent firm instructions to the Attorney General that disclosure was not to be conceded. It may be that he was fearful of a precedent being set in other trials. Justice O'Flynn delivered his decision on 9 June 1958. The most lowly of judges would have to be a saint not to derive considerable judicial pleasure from the opportunity to prepare and read out a lengthy judgment in a sensational case to a packed court, and with learned counsel hanging on every word.

It is not surprising then to note that Justice O'Flynn made a veritable feast of it. It took an hour and a half to read and is peppered with references to leading English and American cases, the development of the common law, the Irish Constitution and the amendments to that of the United States, the office of the Lord Chamberlain in Britain and the rise of theatre clubs. There follows an analysis of obscenity, prurient interest and lustful thought. The justice seems to have read the play, although one doubts if he and Tennessee Williams would have been on the same wave length. For someone who had neither seen nor read the play, Cathal O'Flynn makes it sound like *East Lynne*, a gothic drama with a moral purpose. He finds it to be:

> . . . the sad story of a humble woman who misses the intimacy of her dead husband and lapses once from the path of virtue. How could this be a producer exploiting a filthy business and showing a complete disregard of the primary requirements of decency?

Maybe he is showing off with irrelevant references to the great playwrights Euripides, Aeschylus, Sophocles and Shakespeare. He quotes the English judgments which insist that a work is not obscene because it is distasteful, undesirable or unsuitable for the young. As he builds up his arguments – and they make little pretence to be anything else but his arguments – he plunges into several recent American decisions and quotes whole chunks of diverse dicta which seem a bit garbled. To a skimming reader, none of them appears to prove very much except that a particular judge uttered them and that they happened to catch O'Flynn's eye as he read this mass of material. He cannot see how the gardaí – who are the only persons reporting what was actually seen and heard on the stage – gave evidence which supported the prosecution's allegations. Then he comes to the climax:

> You, Alan Simpson, are in a position here today that is noteworthy for two reasons: 1) You are the first person as far as I am aware to stand accused in the dock of this Courthouse on the charges of showing a performance of a play

> alleged to be indecent and obscene and profane, and 2) you are also the first citizen in this country in my experience of many thousands of criminal cases to stand in the dock of this Courthouse in a preliminary investigation and to find your case brought to the High Court and then, by your appeal, to the Supreme Court.

Having stated his opinion that no prima facie case on which a jury might reasonably convict had been made, he went further and said they ought not to. He refused informations, which meant that he found that Alan Simpson had no case to answer and therefore he discharged him.

The finding marked the end of the judicial process. The State could have had another shot at it by virtue of Section 62 of the Courts of Justice Act 1936, which gave power to the Attorney General effectively to overrule the District Court decision and direct that the accused be sent forward for trial. However, the prosecution made no further application. (The Supreme Court in 1984 found the section to be unconstitutional, although a more recent act has altered the position yet again.) More interestingly, the State made no move to introduce legislation to censor stage performances, then or since.

After it was all over, Alan Simpson said to Kate Binchy with remarkable prescience: 'We did not have a Lord Chamberlain here before *The Rose Tattoo* and we shall never have one now.'

There is no doubt that the theatre-going public were the biggest losers: the Pike struggled on bravely for a short while and then closed for lack of funds.

In the middle of all the brouhaha in the press, there was a short news item to the effect that an unemployed Dáil deputy, Jack Murphy, had gone on hunger strike in protest at the level of unemployment and the removal of food subsidies. Bread and circuses, indeed.

Chapter 9

Some Judges and Justices

WAS IT THAT THEY HAD MORE leisure time which allowed the judges of the District Court to devote it to writing plays, novels, historical research and to long hours of fieldwork in the topography and monuments of their district? The number of those in the early District Court who had a plethora of talents is striking, and they all pursued their academic and literary interests in tandem with their judicial careers. There can be no question of a slight gift on a par with the cliché of Sunday painting. All the fruits of their labours were of a professional standard.

Kenneth Reddin was a solicitor who had taken part in the Easter Rising and was interned in England. Under a pseudonym, Kenneth Starr, he wrote two novels. In *Somewhere to the Sea*, the hero is a solicitor who serves as a Dáil Court judge, and a second, *On Another Shore*, was made into a film. Reddin also had two plays produced in the Abbey. He was one of the few justices who wore the rather continental-looking judicial robes which had been specifically designed for the District Court. In his *Evening Press* column of 16 June 1994, Michael O'Toole described a passage of arms between Reddin and another playwright whose name is still famous, which must have given both of them considerable pleasure.

Brendan Behan was in court to offer himself as surety for a defendant and Reddin asked him with heavy joviality, 'Do I take it you are offering yourself as a hostage for this young man, Mr. Behan?'

Right on cue came the reply, 'Yes, your Worship, I am going to make sure that he doesn't abscond to another shore.'

Louis Walsh practised as a solicitor in the north and had also been interned, but in Ballykinlar Camp, near Belfast. Shortly after his release in 1921, his memoir of the camp, *On My Keeping and in Theirs*, was published. For a prison diary, it is strangely gentle and very funny, as was almost all Walsh's writing. A play he had written called *The Pope in Killybuck*, a farce on sectarianism, was performed in the camp on Easter Sunday 1921, as it had been performed in the same venue some years before by the soldiers of Carson's Ulster Division stationed there during the Great War. Walsh served on the Judiciary Committee and took an active interest in the formation of the new constitutional courts. More than ten years on, he expressed his bitter disappointment about the development of the Circuit Court. He saw it as being dominated by barristers when costs could have been kept low if solicitors had taken the initiative to appear on behalf of their clients, instead of being discouraged 'by the curl of a lip or the slight raising of a gowned shoulder'.

Louis Walsh was appointed to County Donegal where he was a vivid presence and an excellent judge. (As a student in UCD, he had beaten James Joyce to win the prize for oratory at the Literary and Historical Society.) The late Dr Patrick Henchy of the National Library of Ireland told the story of an application in court for maintenance of a child in a seduction case. The solicitor for the defendant suggested a sum of £20, adding, rather unwisely as it turned out, that this was the usual sum in nearby Lahey in the county. The mean calculation drove the usually genial Walsh into such a rage that he stamped his fist on the bench and bellowed, 'By Christ, we'll raise the price of Lahey – two hundred pounds!'

Liam Price was a barrister who had been educated at a public school in England and had served in the British Army, both in Ireland and France during the Great War. He was among the first appointments to the District Court and spent almost his entire judicial career in County Wicklow, which was blessed to have him because he tramped the length and breadth of it in the company of its natives, of archaeologists, scholars and academics, as well as anyone else he could rope in who might have information about a locality. Naturally, local court sittings also provided him with a captive and constantly changing pool of possible informants. A noted antiquarian, Price became the outstanding authority on the topography and monuments of his bailiwick. He examined rent rolls, leases, maps and gravestones, and talked to everyone he met about their own neighbourhood, its history, geography and folklore. The judge was elected a member of the Royal Irish Academy and was President of the Royal Society of Antiquaries of Ireland. The results of his research were meticulously recorded in a series of notebooks, with photographs and detailed sketches. His work was first published by the Dublin Institute for Advanced Studies but, as recently as 2002, Dúchas, the Heritage Service, brought out the Price notebooks in three very handsome volumes, *Place Names of County Wicklow*, edited by Christiaan Corlett and Mairead Weaver.

In 1939, over 5,500 acres in the Liffey Valley were flooded to create a reservoir to provide a hydro-electric scheme for Dublin. The homes, holy wells, bridges, ring forts and burial places of the indigenous population were obliterated in a veritable deluge of water. Their history, and indeed geography, would be lost forever. Dr Corlett, in his remarkable book, *Beneath the Poulaphuca Reservoir*, has published a survey carried out by a brave band of individuals who were determined, without any state help, to preserve in words, drawings and photographs the lives of these people, before the world they had always known would disappear for ever.

> During the summer months of 1939, small teams of people from various backgrounds, co-ordinated by Liam Price, volunteered their time and skills in an attempt to record as much information as possible about the landscape to be flooded. This is the Poulaphuca Survey: a moment in time of a forgotten Irish landscape.

It was another lasting service which Justice Price gave to the area to which he had been appointed. When he died in 1967, an obituary noted that 'his side interests took precedence over his formal work, so that in the minds of his contemporaries, he appeared to be a scholar of note whose hobby was the law'. If he could have read it, would Liam Price have been more hurt by the reference to his 'side interests' than by the implication that he saw his judicial function as a 'hobby'?

James Crotty was appointed the justice in Cork in 1924. In 1960, he published his *Practice and Procedure in the District Court* as a successor to O'Connor's *Justice of the Peace*, long the bible of summary jurisdiction, but the last edition had been in 1915, so this energetic man was bringing matters up to date. In contrast to the apparent success of other talents in finding publishers for their work, poor Dr Crotty (as he was) laboured for seven years to get his manuscript published, all the time assiduously keeping his text revised since 'changes were made by statute and by rule of court and as the law has been glossed . . . and clarified by new cases', according to the foreword by Judge

Cearbhall Ó Dalaigh. The index of cases cited in the text fills twenty pages. The author in his preface remembers a Bandon solicitor saying to him 'there is a power o'law in the District Court', referring to the maze of legal technicalities that go to make up its practice, 'a kind of *damnosa hereditas* which it enjoys as legal successor to the old Petty Sessions Court.'

Crotty's interesting theory was that the complex rules were intended to curb the arbitrary exercise of summary jurisdiction which had, in part, limited the citizen's ancient common law right to be tried by his peers. His book is a model of its kind, each procedure clearly set out, and the relevant cases, which he uses to illustrate the law, are up to date. For example, in the section on the procedure in Case Stated, he cites *Attorney General* v. *Simpson*, which was heard only the previous year and was still unreported. After all the hard work, it is to be hoped that Crotty's book had the success predicted by Ó Dalaigh.

Another one of the early appointees, Liam Coyne, was the justice in Mayo. In 1920, he had been imprisoned by a Crimes Court for carrying papers relating to the Dáil Courts. He lived in Castlebar and is remembered by both Professor Tom Mitchell and Judge John Garavan as an imposing figure who was accorded great public respect. He and his wife were observant Roman Catholics, and were leading figures in establishing the Marian Shrine at Knock as a recognised place of pilgrimage, and for which he received a papal honour.

He also wrote *The Law Courts in Eire*, a short book of about a hundred pages, dedicated to the personnel of the Dáil Courts. It urged the de-anglicisation of the legal system, the widespread use of Irish, reform of the law and codification. It is quite clear that Coyne was a competent and well-read scholar who had given a great deal of thought to how the legal system should be constructed differently, and that he was steeped in the idealism of early Sinn Féin. Admittedly, serving judges are, quite properly, discouraged from making critical comments on the law. However, for a modern reader, the immediate reaction might be some surprise at his remark, when speaking of disturbances during the Civil War, that 'the new Courts were never interfered with, beyond public threats that anyone attending them would be punished by death'. Perhaps such stoicism is understandable in a man who had already been punished for his association with courts in the past.

In contrast to the image of this eminently respected figure of the local justice, committed Christian and learned writer – Yeats's 'smiling, public man' – the Attorney General's papers in the National Archives reveal an unremitting effort to paint him more like the figure of some disreputable judge in a cowboy film. Both the Minister and the Secretary at the Department of Justice had Coyne firmly in their sights for most of the 1940s. In 1943, the Secretary wrote admonishing him about his book and his references to the Constitution. He was reminded of his judicial oath and was asked to consider whether he 'should be allowed to continue in office as a Justice of the District Court'.

It appears that Coyne's book upset people other than the Minister. The Secretary of the Incorporated Law Society wrote to the Department, taking grave exception about the sentiments expressed in the book regarding the way the Society dealt with complaints. There was correspondence with the Supreme Court Office to set up the Advisory Committee provided for by Section 49 of the Courts of Justice Act 1936 to enquire into the conduct of a district justice. A meeting had been arranged for 19 October when it was discovered that a Waterford solicitor named Quinlan was bringing a libel action against Coyne because of his book. The department was informed that 'the Chief Justice and the President of the High Court think it is inadvisable that the Advisory Committee should meet until the action is determined'. The libel action was successful and damages of £750 awarded against Coyne and his publishers.

There were other complaints which had nothing to do with the book. The local gardaí were furious with what they saw as the justice's leniency towards certain defendants, and there are thirty-six pages of closely typed foolscap from Chief Superintendent Butler listing their grievances against the justice between 1942 and 1945, meticulously compiled, including one that Coyne did not return the greeting of a garda in the street. The main plank of their complaint, reiterated again and again, was his alleged friendship with a Dr Flannery in the Hollymount area of Castlebar. The accusation is non-specific, but the medical practitioner was believed to be in control of some kind of a rowdy gang, against whom it was impossible to get a conviction in Coyne's court. Many of the grievances seemed to be concerned with dance licences. Even the Opposition joined in, with Deputy Richard Mulcahy asking in a parliamentary question in July 1945 if the Minister was aware of local dissatisfaction regarding the manner of the proceedings at Hollymount District Court.

The Minister was becoming increasingly frustrated in his efforts. Once a justice was assigned to an area, he could not be transferred without his consent. The Advisory Committee was proving difficult to set up. The Chief Justice, Timothy O'Sullivan, was ill and, in any case, was not showing great enthusiasm for the task. The Minister, Gerard Boland, enlisted the help of the Attorney General to draft a letter to O'Sullivan to suggest ways in which a lengthy investigation might be circumvented and, when that failed, began working on the idea of establishing a tribunal as a matter of urgent public importance. At the same time, he was fearful that the Chief Justice might recover in time to object. The matter dragged on without a conclusion. It is difficult to understand why no mediator could be found to speak privately to the justice and explore the issues, or that it was beyond the wit of the Attorney General to frame some charges against Dr Flannery and Co. which could be brought in the Circuit Court to test the evidence.

That all was not well in the particular locality is borne out by a newspaper cutting from the *Mayo News* of 14 July 1945. Even given the occasional self-importance of the provincial press, it surely must be on par with the *Skibbereen Eagle* and the Russian Czar:

> Berlin may have been reduced to a heap of smouldering ruins; Hamburg may have completely disappeared from the face of the earth; Dresden may be no more and Tokyo may be threatened but Hollymount lives on.

The file ends abruptly but perhaps some of the protagonists left the scene. However, Liam Coyne was still the justice in Mayo when he died in 1953, and his term in office had just been extended for the second year. The next time the authorities had a perceived turbulent justice on their hands, they dealt with him in a much more straightforward fashion.

When the commission to wind up the Dáil Courts was established in 1923, Michael Lennon, who had been called to the Bar three years previously, served as court registrar to the Chief Commissioner. Lennon had taken part in the Easter Rising and been imprisoned in England. In 1937, he was appointed a justice and he has the distinction, thus far at any rate, of being the only judge of the District Court to have been effectively sacked.

He seems to have been something of a loose cannon. During a case under the Offences against the State Act 1939, which came before him in Dublin early in 1957, he remarked, 'This Proclamation does not end with the words "God save the King"', adding that they were used in proclamations when he himself was prosecuted – meaning, of course, during the Troubles. It appears to have been interpreted as more offensive because he had given his words an interrogative inflection rather than stating an obvious fact. He also made reference to the term 'Oglaigh na h-Éireann' as it was in the Defence Acts, but the IRA also so styled itself. It is probable that the general unease about the current use of emergency legislation and the continuing subversive threat made the authorities feel they should react.

The Minister for Justice requested the Chief Justice to nominate a judge of the High Court to hold an enquiry into Lennon's conduct, and Mr Justice Teevan was duly nominated. His report was completed within a month (in contrast to the case of Justice Coyne above) and he did not find that the justice had been guilty of misconduct. When requested to provide an addendum, Teevan wrote:

> While the conduct of the District Justice was misconduct in the sense explained in my report in that it was objectionable, merits disapproval and justified objection to it, it was not misconduct justifying a motion for removal from office. If I might add an impression, without certitude of its accuracy (and consequently, I cannot include it as a finding), I would say District Justice Lennon has a propensity for introducing ideas or questions in startlingly extravagant or explosive language which may often result in shock or obscurity, or both.

In the meantime, there had been a change of government and the new administration, in spite of Judge Teevan's exoneration, called upon Lennon to resign, which he did immediately, thus saving it the undoubted dilemma of having the Houses of the Oireachtas debate a motion for his dismissal.

Lennon's nationalist background was such that there can no question of someone hankering after the days of Empire, any more than he had any covert sympathy for 'the lads'. In fact, his observations were to do with history and the law, which had changed because of Irish sovereignty and they were comments on fact. He appears to have been a judge who said things for effect, or to be difficult, or perhaps even out of occasional boredom – not unlike others, who might come to mind from time to time. Nevertheless, it is surprising that he would be unaware that his musings were inappropriate and were open to the interpretation that he was questioning this very controversial legislation. Within the year, the same legislation was challenged in the first case to be brought by an individual to the European Court of Human Rights, *Lawless* v. *Ireland*, 1960 and, by coincidence, Gerard Lawless had been one of the accused in the case that caused the trouble for the judge.

The *Irish Independent* published a blistering editorial on 27 May condemning the government action. It stressed that Mr Justice Teevan's report had concluded that Lennon's conduct did not merit removal from office. 'What is of far graver import, the Minister and the Government have struck a blow at the independence of the Justices.' Some of his colleagues spoke out in court in a tribute to Lennon. His nephew, Dr Michael Lennon, remembers him with affection and would probably not quarrel with Judge Teevan's assessment. He thinks that his uncle, who was very interested in Irish history and spent most of the days of his retirement in the National Library, was pretty sanguine about the affair and that he certainly did not lose his pension.

~ ~ ~

Richard Johnson, who would have been appointed around the same time as Kenneth Reddin, was born in Rathkeale and served his judicial career in Kerry. He wrote a powerful play on a theme that has only in recent times come to the fore of the public conscience. *The Evidence I Shall Give* was produced in the Abbey Theatre in 1961. The entire action takes place in a rural District Court and, while there are well-observed comic interludes, the central theme is the heartless treatment of girls in an orphanage. Deference in religious matters was then much stronger, so the sense of a *coup de foudre* was palpable in the theatre during the relentless cross-examination of a nun forced by a solicitor to confront her own cruelty. It was an extraordinary play for the time and even more extraordinary that it was written by a sitting judge. He told me that a woman had come to him with her story and said, 'you must write about this'.

Richard Johnson had the appearance of a crusty, short-tempered individual with a fierce directness, but the woman must have known instinctively that he was the right person to approach. It is difficult, however, to imagine him being invited up to the local convent for a cup of tea to celebrate the play's success! In April 2010, the Abbey players gave a reading of the play as part of the series

Dark Corner to mark the publication of the Ryan Report, and some months later it was performed in the very appropriate setting of the old Green Street courthouse by the Zyber Theatre Company.

Garry Kilgallen, as a junior official in the Bank of Ireland in Tralee during the late 1950s, recalls being surprised to learn that the man in the shabby greatcoat, topped off with a long trailing woollen muffler, who drove a battered van, was the local District Justice. He was clearly his own man, unpretentious, unassuming and definitely unconventional. Garry, who became a member of the drama group, so ably directed with great flair by the judge, says he was loved and respected by all in the group. He now realises how privileged he was to have known and 'trod the boards' with the author of such a remarkably prescient play: 'Anyone who remembers the conventional and confessional Ireland of fifty years ago has to be filled with admiration for someone who had the moral courage to challenge any facet of the enormous power then wielded by the Catholic Church. *The Evidence I Shall Give* was an amazingly prophetic work and one can now see why it had a short run when first produced in 1961. The mystery is that it ever reached the public stage at all at that time. It is a fitting memorial to an extraordinary gentleman, District Justice Richard W.F. Johnson.'

Chapter 10

More Judges and Justices

THE FIRST TIME I WAS IN A District Court as an apprentice solicitor it was to accompany a barrister to a road traffic case in Balbriggan. There was a long list and our case was the last to be heard. While we sat there, I was mesmerised by the extraordinary variety of matters which featured and by the personality of the judge. He was sharp, kindly, impatient in turn, but cross where he thought someone had been unfairly treated. He seemed to be totally concentrated and immersed in each case. I later learned that he was Donnchadh Ua Donnchadha and would hear older colleagues remember 'Dinny', as they all called him, with admiration and affection. Not only judges. When he transferred from Meath to Dublin, Frank Roe, then junior counsel, later to be the President of the Circuit Court, wrote him a long letter full of praise for his qualities as a judge:

> You will be sadly missed from all your courts. You were one of those judges for whom there

> was great respect, but at the same time very high regard and personal devotion.

He retired in 1977 and died suddenly less than three years later. Bob Ó hUadhaigh, who practically prided himself on his lack of sentiment, wrote a moving tribute to his friend:

> He was shy beyond comprehension to the on-looker and covered it up with a pretence of irritability. His sense of humour was always bubbling a hair's breadth below the surface. The tenderness of his manner in dealing with the down-and-out was an example to all.

The only time I saw him was that day in Balbriggan, so I was fortunate that Justice Donnchadha was the memorable part of my first experience of the District Court.

As we drove back to the city that evening, it was clear my barrister had been equally impressed. 'I'd love to be a country justice one day,' he said. 'It would be very satisfying work, driving around from court to court and becoming a local character, much more exciting than being a circuit or high court judge.'

Wistfully, I agreed. It was as remote a chance for me as being invited to take the leading role in Covent Garden, but it certainly was a possibility for the young man, who was talented and likeable and making a name at the Bar. Strangely, then, for all his promise, he did not get his wish. His name was Liam Hamilton and he only became a Chief Justice.

~ ~ ~

I did not know Michael McGrath as a judge but as a neighbour. When I called to tell him of my appointment, he was already very ill, but he sat in the kitchen in his pyjamas and dressing gown and talked to me for over two hours about being a judge. He died a few months later. Tom Donnelly said in a public tribute that he always told students that if they wanted to see the District Court at its best to go and sit for a while in Judge McGrath's courtroom. When I went around the country to take sittings, court staff, caretakers and solicitors regularly asked me if I had known him and invariably everyone added, 'Judge McGrath was a lovely man'.

He was only thirty-two and practising in his native Nenagh when he was appointed a temporary justice. Around this time, another justice, Donagh MacDonagh, son of the executed 1916 leader, Thomas MacDonagh, had achieved considerable fame with his verse play, *Happy as Larry*, and was being interviewed late one Sunday evening on the BBC Third Programme.

The interviewer asked, 'I understand that you are a stipendary magistrate in Ireland. How do you manage to find the time to write with your other work?'

The playwright said that it was not that his 'other work' was time-consuming but that it was badly organised. If courts were better arranged, he could do it in half the time.

An interested listener to this exchange also happened to be the senior official in charge of courts at the Department of Justice. Within days, the process of tightening up court areas and sittings was underway and the need for extra judges drastically reduced. As a result, at the end of six months, Michael and two other temporaries were returned to civilian life and it was to be another year before a vacancy occurred and he was appointed permanently. The sudden hiatus came about because of a mandarin who had a passion for the Third Programme!

Undoubtedly, the best-known judge in the Dublin Metropolitan District was Robert Ó hUadhaigh: he was right out of central casting. A tall, handsome man, who held himself straight as a die in impeccably tailored suits, he spoke in a deep growl, saying exactly what he thought. Court No. 6 in the Bridewell was his domain, which meant that for over twenty years he only heard criminal cases. He loved his work and he loved his wife, Marie (she told me they had been in love since their teens), and I don't believe he had any other interests, certainly at the time I knew him. He hated having to retire. The word legendary is overused, but the stories about him are legion – and they are all true.

He had an extraordinary ability to recognise someone at a glance. One day he asked a woman in his court, 'Don't I know you?'

The defendant admitted a previous acquaintance which had been in Donegal.

'But that was not the name you had then.'

'No,' she said. 'I got married.'

It was more than thirty years since he had sat in Donegal. Some years after his retirement, he and Gregory Murphy hailed a taxi one evening. The car began to move away and then suddenly stopped. The driver turned around in his seat and snarled aggressively at Bob, 'I recognise you; you're that judge who gave me six months in the "Joy".'

Gregory felt quite nervous but Bob replied immediately, 'I did indeed and that's because you were a fusilier.'

'What do you mean?' said the very cross man.

'You took your belt to your wife: any man who does that deserves to be sent to prison.'

The driver muttered in a subdued voice, 'I never laid a hand on her again.'

The former judge commented equably, 'Well, there you are then.' He had been unruffled throughout the exchange.

~ ~ ~

Tomás MacGiolla was the Lord Mayor of Dublin when my book on the Dáil Courts was published. He and his wife, May, graciously allowed it to be launched in the Oak Room in the Mansion House and attended in person. Maeve Binchy was talking to Ms MacGiolla when Bob Ó hUadhaigh joined them. He looked at her keenly and said, 'I know you.'

Maeve murmured, 'She's the Lady Mayoress, Judge.'

'Yes, I know that,' he said, impatiently, 'but I know her from someplace else and I cannot remember how.'

Whereupon the lady replied, 'Perhaps it was from the time you gave me a month's jail for a protest march.'

Having 'placed' his hostess, he and she proceeded to have a relaxed and amiable conversation.

~ ~ ~

When Judge Michael Moriarty was a junior counsel, he listened to a young barrister earnestly lecturing Bob on his judicial duty to give due weight to any reasonable doubt that might exist in his mind about the guilt of the accused. The exposition of the principle went on at some length with considerable lucidity. Justice Ó hUadhaigh replied that he was impressed with the argument which was a valid one.

He confessed that he did indeed have a doubt and, just as counsel turned to nod triumphantly towards his instructing solicitor, snapped, 'but it isn't a reasonable doubt: Guilty.'

Another aspect of Justice Ó hUadhaigh's career (he preferred the title of 'Justice') which might surprise his critics was that he was the judge with more defendants on probation than any other.

~ ~ ~

Tom Donnelly was one of those men who seem to have been born to be judges, yet he had been a classics master and was in early middle age when he was called to the Bar. His nickname was 'The White Tornado', partly because of his shock of silver hair and partly because of the impression of a whirlwind in his swift walk and in his articulate and direct judgments. He was equally feared, respected and loved: I have seen the faces of solicitors contort in their efforts to emphasise how fair he was, no matter how cross. One of them said, 'he'll wipe the floor with you if you put your case badly, but if he glimpses the slightest hint of complacency in your opponent's face, he'll turn and give him the same!'

As President of the District Court, he accompanied me to the Supreme Court the day I was sworn in and then spoke to me in his chamber for several hours about offences, fines, evidence, proofs and so much else. All of it was totally new to me then, but I still remember a little of it. Having read some newspaper report, he might send you a short note to point out that a statutory fine cannot be increased even if it happens to be the sixth conviction for the same offence. Here is Ms Justice Catherine McGuinness's memory of him:

> I was instructed in a case before Judge Tom Donnelly, where a woman who earned her living as a prostitute was suing in a civil action for assault at a garda station. Far from appearing in a meek role, she looked very smart and self-assured in a fur coat. She had given her occupation as unemployed. On being pressed as to what other work she did, she said she helped with the invalid pilgrims in Lourdes every year (which was true). At the end of the hearing Tom Donnelly said that there were totally different accounts given by the plaintiff and by the defendants; there was, however, one piece of independent evidence. The woman's face had been unmarked when she was brought to the station and was bruised when she left, and she had had her injuries treated in a nearby hospital. He awarded damages. At the time, it was very unusual for a court to find for

a prostitute against the gardaí. I learnt subsequently that the decision was appealed and was overturned by the Circuit Court.

Although women had been judges in the Dáil Éireann Courts, the first woman judge to be appointed in Ireland was Eileen Kennedy. In his book *The Irish Judiciary*, Paul C. Bartholomew credits her appointment to a public statement by Seán Lemass when he was Taoiseach, that there should be more women in civic life. She had been a trained nurse who then qualified as a solicitor and was coroner for County Monaghan. On the suggestion of a Supreme Court judge, she wrote to the Minister for Justice expressing an interest and she was appointed to the District Court shortly afterwards. That was in 1964 when I was a law student and I well remember the ferment of excitement and the sense of novelty. She first sat in Court No. 2. Morgan Place, and it was difficult to get through the crowd coming to stare. I am ashamed to say that, as female law students, our first thoughts were not on the shattering of the glass ceiling, but whether she would wear a hat. In those days and for several years after, women were obliged to keep their heads covered in court. This pioneering judge was bareheaded. Most of her career was in the Children's Court and, in 1970, she chaired a far-reaching examination of the reformatory and industrial schools system – the Kennedy Report.

Other women judges trickled in over the next twenty years until it became a steady stream. Mary Martin, however, would have been the first pregnant judge. When she was expecting her fourth child, she applied for maternity leave. There was something of a stir in the dovecotes of Justice because there were no precedents. However, after due and weighty consideration, Mary Martin was told that the legislation did not apply since she was not an employee within the meaning of the statute, but an office-holder. She also heard that a minister had said that they would never again make the mistake of appointing a woman of child-bearing age to the Bench. Happily they have – and moreover, a more liberal interpretation of the Act has given judicial mothers the same rights as their sisters.

❧ ❧ ❧

There have been several unfortunate judicial appointments since the foundation of the state, but for understandable reasons, the perception is that the District Court has been unduly favoured in this respect. Here are a few examples, more than likely true, which serve to strengthen that perception.

Many years ago my father was asked by a political friend if there was anyone he might care to recommend for the District Court bench. For someone who had little time for lawyers, he surprisingly had a name – that of an older barrister, who had returned from practice abroad and was finding things a bit difficult. A mild, courteous man of dapper appearance, he may well have been ex-

perienced in colonial law, but knew little of the summary jurisdiction of the Dublin Metropolitan area.

When I was an apprentice, my master would become furious at any mention of his name. Apparently, the Justice had taken exception to some independent witness in a road traffic case and bound him over to keep the peace. The man was a senior civil servant who had come forward to do his civic duty and he had to go to all the expense and trouble to have the ruling overturned in the High Court.

On another occasion he fined a passenger £10 for spitting on a bus. The court registrar whispered that the statutory fine was a fiver. The judge snorted, 'I don't care what the statutory fine is. Spitting is a filthy habit and I consider £10 is more appropriate.'

A solicitor from a midland town was doing very badly, mainly through his fondness for drink; his friends were concerned and decided that the best thing for him would be to leave practice altogether and take up alternative employment. They made enquiries and found that there would shortly be a vacancy for a rate collector in the locality. Representations were made on his behalf and it was arranged for him to meet the constituency Dáil deputy at Leinster House. The solicitor was tidied up generally and put on the morning train to Dublin. The kind friends were waiting on the platform when he returned that evening. Their faces fell when he told them that, unfortunately, the rate collector's job had already been given to someone else.

'It's not so bad,' he said; 'they are going to make me a district justice instead.'

I love that story; a legal friend told it to me shortly after I became a judge. It may have been a not-so-subtle warning not to get notions!

❧ ❧ ❧

There was a barrister with an even worse drinking problem: it had been a long time since he was entirely sober. The drinking did not stop with his appointment to the bench and he was inclined to doze off after lunch. The unfortunate registrar was obliged to find excuses to wake him up, from time to time. A restaurateur was before the court for breach of food safety regulations, and considerable evidence of the remedial work that had been done in the meantime was given on his behalf. The solicitor made a strong plea for mitigation of the fine: there was silence, broken only by the soft snores coming from the seat of justice. The clerk, his back turned tactfully to the body of the court, eventually succeeded in rousing the occupant who was now ready to give his finding. 'Defendant is fined £50, disqualified from driving for one year, licence to be endorsed,' before falling back to sleep again. It was left to the poor solicitor to explain to her client how he succeeded in losing his driving licence through having a dirty restaurant.

❧ ❧ ❧

Dick Robinson remembers a dramatic incident in a country court involving an older colleague, whose experience went back to the Dáil Courts, as described below.

The court clerk was a serious man who took an informed interest in the minutiae of legislation. He had noticed a potential problem in the licensing quagmire and it needed resolving. Though knowing what he believed to be an answer to the legal question, he would always do the justice the courtesy of asking. 'That might very well be so' was the guidance received.

There was no meeting of minds between the two on liquor, irrespective of the laws that govern it. The clerk abhorred it and had no toleration. The justice wallowed in it.

The following week the clerk called, 'All rise, please'. The judge, endeavouring to maintain a stable relationship with the perpendicular having come to court from an all-night session, fell prostrate on the steps to his bench. The clerk, following, stepped over the protruding legs and went to his bench. He placed the Minute Book on the (empty) court bench, turned to his bundle of papers and proceeded to call the first case. With a great furore, solicitors and gardaí lifted the justice to his room. There was a garbled direction to adjourn the court.

'Why didn't you pick him up?' the clerk was asked.

'Because I didn't knock him down,' was the reply.

At present, all judges, except those of the Supreme Court, are appointed after recommendations by a commission, which comprises the various court presidents and lay people. Lawyers must first apply to be considered, so, at least, there is some transparency in the system. There is no question that for many years judicial appointments were viewed as a kind of tombola into which politicians or their activists might occasionally dip for a trophy or a reward. If the District Court seems to have attracted the more glaring examples, it is because there were more positions available. It may be a truism (but that's because it is true); the wonder is not that there were bad ones, but that so many were good and that some shone. Who shall judge the judges? Perhaps, in the first instance, it is the people who appear before them. That assessment cannot rest on whether a person won or lost his case, as it so frequently does. It surely must be if, on calm reflection, a litigant believes that he was given the opportunity to state his case and was listened to. As for those charged with a crime, they are in a perfect position to judge if the verdict was fair, because they are the only ones who know with absolute certainty.

Chapter 11

Dressed for the Occasion

THERE IS SOMETHING ABOUT the dress code in court that seems to excite general interest and might almost be used as testing the waters for the temper of the presiding judge. Perhaps it has its origins in the strange costume which barristers – and by extension judges – wear. There is the wig; distinctive, of course, because no person's hair could ever have grown like that. Striped trousers, waistcoat and 'bands' which are short rectangle pieces of white linen on elastic string which goes under the shirt collar and are worn instead of a necktie. (When Liam Hamilton was young at the Bar, he forgot to remove his bands when he went to a nearby pub for a hurried lunch. Within two days, he had received a rebuke from the Bar Council.) A black gown goes on over all that; it is made of a kind of thick cotton (stuff) in the case of junior counsel, but seniors wear silk; hence the expression 'taking silk'. A junior's gown has a scrap of cloth hanging from one shoulder. This signifies the beggar's pouch worn by medieval lawyers who could not ask for a fee for their services, so a grateful client was expected to slip in the appropriate coins in a tactful manner. Shakespeare knew all about it:

> Time hath, my lord, a wallet at his back, wherein
> he puts alms for oblivion – *Troilus and Cressida*

And barristers still cannot sue for fees owed to them.

What to wear in court is a question which frequently arouses controversy or even more rules. Well into the 1960s a woman had to cover her head. There were a few solicitors who still wore a plain gown. Hugh Kennedy, the Attorney General, shortly to be the first Chief Justice, gave a lot of thought to court dress when he was planning our present system, and that designed for the justices of the District Court was considerably more elaborate than the outfit worn by barristers today. Indeed, it was quite dashing, with a French-style tricorn hat! There still exists a photograph of Kenneth Reddin in one. Not many justices wore it and even they did not do so for long. When Louis Walsh first appeared in his new robes, he spotted the look of astonishment on a solicitor's face. 'Well, Mr McFadden,' he asked, 'do you not recognise the court?' In the early years of independence, the Irish Bar decided that wigs and gowns would be worn in the new courts when they were established, and Michael Lennon had an interesting piece in the *Irish Independent* of 8 April 1923 tracing the origin of wearing a wig in court back to the Norman Conquest.

When Judge Frank O'Donnell of the Circuit Court was the president of the Law Society, a few discreet representations were made to him about the informal dress some solicitors wore to court and he consulted Tom Donnelly, the President of the District Court, on the matter. As usual, Tom's reply was circulated to the judges. Frank agrees with me that the letter deserves to be reproduced in full:

> When I was young at the Bar, I remember a self-important Circuit judge was indulging in that ridiculous 'I can't see you' routine to a solicitor wearing a violent red pullover. We all disapproved of the solicitor's garb, but we were unanimous that the judge was a word that I won't ask my secretary to type. (It was a jury trial and the solicitor, having ignored the judge, won, I'm glad to say.) No! Particularly in this country, I could damage someone's career by commenting in open court on his or her dress, or undress. I have recently told your students in Blackhall Place that in court they are on stage; that so long as they are in court they are under critical observation, not merely by their own clients, but by other people's clients; that, like actors they must dress the part and act the part; that, in the main, they will be taken at their own valuation and that it pays to give the impression that they are engaged on important business even in so death-defying a trick as obtaining a licensing exemption. That being so, and I firmly believe it to be so, anyone appearing in jeans or without a tie lets the whole side down. All practitioners suffer because their profession is devalued in the eyes of the public. I

> myself have always regarded this 'respect for the court' approach as looking through the wrong end of the telescope. I am so armed in my own self-conceit that how people dress is a matter for them: they let themselves down, they don't let me. Me, I don't care a damn. From the foregoing, you will gather that I am firmly of the opinion that the father of the local bar, or a senior member, should take the 'offending' junior aside and intimate tactfully that 'it would be in the interest of the entire profession if . . .' – because it is in the interests of the entire profession.

Nevertheless, in some discerning eyes, the poor solicitors cannot win. When rent restriction was set aside, having been found to be unconstitutional by the Supreme Court, there existed for a short while a court to determine rents affected by the fall out. It was the nicest court I ever sat in. There were no contentious proceedings as such because it was to fix rents on property where the tenants had been in occupation for a long time. Most of them were older women, and some of them said they had not been down in Dublin for years. They were, without exception, of limited means, but they were all beautifully turned out in well-tailored coats, with hats or blouses of a toning colour and, to a woman, they wore gloves. They provided a mine of information on prices in the 1950s. A lady spoke of how one could be taken out to an evening at the cinema and a meal afterwards for less than a pound, and how a good suit of clothes for her husband could be got for three guineas – 'and he was much better dressed than any of those gentlemen there,' she said, her eyes sweeping dismissively over the row of solicitors in their bespoke suits from Dublin's leading tailor.

Early one beautiful sunny morning in Dun Laoghaire, my eyes were drawn to a man standing at the back of the courtroom, directly in my sight. He was of medium height, with strong muscles and he was tanned all over. I observed this because he was wearing only the very briefest of bathing trunks – what the French call *le slip* – and flip-flops. I asked, in a mild enough way, if the gentleman standing at the back of the court would kindly go home and put on some clothes. He turned around as if to see to whom I was referring, but there was just a blank wall behind him. He happened to be standing between two gardaí – although he was not in custody – so I asked if one of them would escort him to the door. Whereupon the two gardaí turned their heads in bewilderment and also found themselves looking at the wall. I called down, 'he's beside you, garda,' sounding even more than usual like a pantomime dame. The officer of the law looked at the man, then at me as if I was not quite the full shilling, and after a pause, but rather reluctantly, they walked out together. I got the distinct impression, which persists to this day, that not only the near-naturist and the gardaí thought I was being decidedly unreasonable, but that everyone else in the court thought so too.

Perhaps I was unreasonable because, around the same time, my friend and colleague, Jarlath Ruane, dealt with a full naturist in his habitual, unruffled manner, according to a report in the *Irish Press* of 31 August 1986:

> A man who appeared stark naked before a District Justice yesterday had been taken from Mountjoy Prison where he had been held on remand. Just before his case was called, Mr Coleman, totally naked came up the stairs leading from the cells. Before his appearance, the woman clerk had been replaced by a male colleague and a Garda officer stood at the entrance to the court to prevent people getting in. Mr. Coleman was totally naked. Asked by Justice Ruane why he had no clothes on, he said that he had been in handcuffs. The accused had arrived naked in the prison van. Clothing had been offered to him which he had refused, also a blanket. When Justice Ruane remanded him for a medical and psychiatric report, he shouted, 'Thank you. Justice has been done'. The Department of Justice said that he had been examined by a doctor and was presumed fit to plead. He had refused clothing and a blanket.

There is no doubt that some judges take the question of dress a bit more seriously than others. When my daughter was working in a Dublin solicitor's office, she was instructed to go to court and move for the adjournment of a case which had come up unexpectedly. After waiting most of the morning, and her case had still not been called, she was approached by a somewhat embarrassed registrar who said, 'Anna, the judge will not hear you in court because you are wearing jeans.' Anna went to the judge's chamber and apologised, explaining that it had been an emergency and that it was not her day to be in court. However, she was still puzzled that evening.

'Mum, I was at the very back among all the benches, wearing my long red jacket; even standing, I would have been invisible from the waist down. How could Judge Ballagh have possibly known what was covering my legs?'

It is not just clothes which offend. An elegant, instructing solicitor was seated opposite her counsel during a case at hearing in the High Court, when the judge's crier came up to her. 'The Judge has asked if you would remove your bracelets; he finds them distracting.' (If it was the sound of jangling, His Lordship should have been in Court No. 7 Dolphin House every other day trying to contend with the noise of the metal beer barrels being rolled along the pavement and into the cellars of the hotel next door.)

Under the headline, 'Judge gives a dressing-down', the *Irish Times* of 19 July 2006 had the following short report:

> Judge Aeneas McCarthy told a Polish interpreter at Galway District Court yesterday that she was inappropriately dressed for appearing before his court in a professional capacity. The young woman, who was wearing tight, low jeans and a skimpy top, which left her midriff exposed, had been assigned to the court in an official capac-

> ity to interpret for Polish defendants who came before the court. 'At the risk of sounding prudish, I think you are inappropriately dressed for this court bearing in mind that you are here in a professional capacity,' the judge admonished the young woman. She made no reply.

I think nothing illustrates Tom Donnelly's principle more than this incident. It is difficult to see how the interpreter did not consider that her compatriots, already in a stressful situation, were deserving of the assurance of professionalism on the part of someone who was representing their words to the court.

In his book *Judges*, David Pannick relates the story of Mr Justice Byles, who sat on the Bench in the second half of the nineteenth century. He is reported to have said that he always found 'difficulty' in appreciating the arguments of counsel whose legs were encased in light-coloured trousers. Pannick also has two other accounts of judges with a strong sense of the deference due to them. In 1926, a County Court judge fined a man who had inadvertently failed to remove his hat, and in 1972 a Scottish judge fined a man £10 for contempt for shaking his head silently when the prosecutor was summing up: 'It is not for you to shake your head at what you hear in this court.' The man won his appeal against the imposition of the fine.

That last story reminds me of the late Sean Delap, speaking at his retirement dinner, recalling two elderly gentlemen who regularly attended the weekly court in north County Dublin. They listened attentively to the proceedings and he noticed that, if they agreed with his finding, they tended to emphatic nods, but at other times, he judged by the frowns and pursed lips, that his sentencing had fallen short of expectations. He found he had to stop himself glancing involuntarily at the pair to assess how he was doing. A fiercely independent-minded man, whom I liked a lot, Sean Delap was considered a very fair judge, although he was inclined to fly off the handle on occasions. Lawyers were a bit wary of him, which is why I find the story below of Mel Christle S.C. to be particularly charming.

> I had been an amateur boxer when younger. Judge Delap was sitting in Balbriggan when I appeared before him in a case. There was a short interval between the end of his 11.00 a.m. list and the midday one, and when he rose, he asked me to have a word with him in chambers. Somewhat mystified, I followed him in where he talked about his interest in boxing, that he had also boxed and that he was still quite fit. To demonstrate, this short balding man in his sixties crossed to the wall and with little effort proceeded to stand on his hands and continued to speak to me from an upside-down position. Then he said it was time to hear the next list and strolled back into his court without any sign of exertion.

Chapter 12

The Tales of Others

For several years I have asked people if they had been in a District Court on any kind of business and had been struck by a case at hearing, or something a witness said or the rude behaviour of a judge. I have talked to those who work in courts, and also read through court reports in old newspapers; in other words, below are some scraps from a magpie's hoard. However, for the most authentic of stories from the District Court, vividly written and all of them told by a professionally observant eye-witness, the reader will find them in Nell McCafferty's *In the Eyes of the Law*.

Our neighbour in County Limerick, Major Deakin, used to play golf in Lahinch in the 1960s with Gordon Hurley, the legendary Clare justice, who told him this experience. Apparently, he had a soft spot for an old rascal who was frequently in front of him on public order-type charges and more often than not would himself surreptitiously pay the fine. Following a spate of convictions one day, he was trying to think of an appropriate fine to impose, when the defendant murmured helpfully, 'Now don't you go being too hard on yourself, your Worship.'

Peter Ward of Nenagh told of his first visit to a court: 'When I was a young apprentice at Dunnes Stores in Dublin, I was instructed one morning to get down to the District Court in a hurry and bring the Certificate of Incorporation which was needed in connection with an application to be made there. There was a case being heard when I arrived. A man had admitted to taking and carrying away a bail of chicken wire from outside a well-known hardware business in Capel Street. He was a thin, pale, low-sized chap who looked as if he could hardly have managed to carry a substantial parcel, let alone the heavy wire bail, which was the exhibit in court. It was obvious from the expression on the judge's face that he was experiencing the same mixture of incredulity and commiseration as myself. He murmured words to the effect that the offence must surely have been out of character. "I don't know so much about that, Justice," said the prosecuting gárda stoically, "but he has twenty-six previous convictions for similar offences."'

In Rathkeale District Court, the Justice said an assault where the accused grabbed another man by the coat, called him a spy and threatened to break a second man's false teeth was 'not in the £50 class'. He imposed a fine of £3. (*Limerick Leader*, 19 September 1964).

~ ~ ~

That kissing in public was not an indecent offence was the decision of acting Justice O'Sullivan at Ballinlough, County Roscommon, when Patrick Fleming, Cloonfad, was summoned by Garda Hynes for embracing and kissing a girl outside a dance hall at 11.45 p.m. The case was the first of its kind under the Criminal Law Amendment Act 1935 (*Roscommon Champion*, 30 November 1935).

~ ~ ~

In 1982, I was assigned to the court in Rathfarnham for about eighteen months. The courthouse was the old Petty Sessions one in the main street. It was woefully inadequate, being little more than one room. When family law matters were being heard *in camera*, everyone else had to go outside and stand in the street. We thought it was wonderful when we heard we were getting a bigger place, but it turned out to be a kind of parish hall. It frequently was locked when the public and the court arrived after the weekend, and then there would be a frantic search to discover where the keys were. Siobhán Hayes was the court registrar and this is her memory of the story she told me when I arrived on a particular Monday morning.

'I did have the keys, but unfortunately I had managed to lock my car with both court and car keys still inside. Defendants, gardaí and witnesses were milling around on the footpath, but help was at hand. Within ten minutes or so, we were all safely inside the courthouse and the administration of justice was under way. Later in the day, I was telephoned by a city newspaper – no doubt having been contacted by an informant – to ask if it were true that some youngster who was making a court appearance that day on motor offences had broken into the courthouse to open the doors from the inside. It was with a clear conscience that I able to deny the story. It was, of course, into my car he had "broken" to rescue the situation.'

In the short-lived Rent Court, it was necessary to decide on a fair rent for houses where the rent had previously been controlled. The valuers for the landlord and those for the tenant gave evidence in turn to suggest what each judged to be an appropriate amount. The tenants were entitled to credit for the improvements they had made. There was a small terraced house in the vicinity of St Patrick's Cathedral in Dublin where a great deal of work had been done by a son who lived with his mother. There was no doubt that, in DIY talent, his price was above rubies. The elderly tenant sat between her son and daughter. Having fixed the rent, I remarked how lucky she was and that I should love to adopt him. It was obvious that she had not heard my comment and asked her daughter what I had said. On being told, her hand shot out instinctively to grasp his arm. She did not smile.

Below is a letter my friend Gerard Fanning wrote in 2003, the year before his death.

> One bleak November afternoon a young man appeared at my office accompanied by his rather timid-looking girlfriend. He had been summoned under the Road Traffic Acts for leaving the scene of an accident, known in the vernacular as 'hit-and-run'. Other than the damage to his car, there was no way he could have been implicated. After all, on the night in question, he had gone to the girlfriend's house from where they had left for the cinema, picked up a curry and chips on their way home and embarked on a passionate interlude only to be interrupted by the arrival of the gardaí the following morning, alleging that the damaged car outside the door had been involved in an accident. He was dumbfounded: his car had obviously been stolen, crashed into some other vehicle and coincidentally been returned to the original spot. Perhaps it was even a friend who had done it. He was an earnest, adamant young man whose account remained rock solid. The young woman confirmed that he had never left her side. I was persuaded this was one case for which there was a convincing explanation. I asked what the film had been and with one voice they answered *On Golden Pond*, which was creating quite an interest at the time. I wanted to be sure of all the facts because the case would be coming before Judge Sean Delap. A kindly man in many ways, he had a particular hatred of hit-and-run drivers, especially if they fought a case where they turned out

> to be guilty. Just as an added precaution, I made enquiries about the movie and discovered that it had opened in Dublin two days after the alleged accident. I met them outside the court on the day of the hearing as arranged, and ensured that it was my wrath they had to endure and not that of Judge Delap. I felt I had earned my fee in saving that young man from an almost certain prison sentence: I also thought it wise to secure payment before I laid into him.'

It is a shame that the gentleman about whom this piece appeared in the *Clare Champion* of 1 October 1976 did not write a memoir of all he had witnessed:

> The retirement of Dinny O'Loughlin of Kilvoydane, Corofin has brought to an end a link with every Government since the State was founded and even the Government before that period, as he was appointed clerk of the Sinn Féin Courts in 1920. He held the unique distinction that he was court clerk for fifty-six years and held office under Sinn Féin, Cumann na Gael, Fianna Fáil and Coalition Governments. He was first appointed by Austin Stack [Minister for Home Affairs under the First Dáil] and later by Kevin O'Higgins as clerk for Ballyvaughan and Corofin courts and reappointed until 1968 when Michael Moran, Minister for Justice, added those of Milton Malbay and Ennistymon. He was imprisoned during the War of Independence in Ennis, Belfast and Wormwood Scrubs in

> London. Having been 'inside' as well as 'outside' he knew the long arm of the law from shoulder blade to fingertip.

There was a particularly soft-hearted judge, now dead, who sat only for a short time in the Bridewell court because he found it all too upsetting. The story is told that there were two women before him on shoplifting charges, for whom their solicitor was making a powerful plea. They were unfortunate, deserted wives, each with large families, and it was a desperate struggle to feed and clothe them. The defendants were not paying a great deal of attention, trying to keep their numerous children in order and looking around the courtroom. The judge was very sorry for them and ordered £50 to be given for clothes to be bought for each family. The solicitor was to accompany them to a store to make sure the purchases were bought.

When they were outside, one of the women peeled off a fifty note from a roll and asked, 'Who do I pay this to?'

It was explained with some difficulty that the court was giving her the money.

'What? Fifty pounds, for robbin'?'

When the shopping expedition was organised, it was said that as soon as the party arrived in the large store, the women were instantly surrounded by the staff because their activities were so well known.

It is not difficult to be made a fool of but it is better, surely, to be made a fool of than to trust no one. It is not surprising that the court poor box might sometimes benefit the unworthy poor (if that is what they are), such as the woman living in a tent on Bride Street with a clatter of children and no gas cylinder and who breaks your heart with her story, and then to be told afterwards that she had got the price of a cylinder the previous day from Judge Hussey in Court No. 4. Sometimes you had to gauge carefully the amount you might authorise so as to provide the money necessary for the immediate purpose, but insufficient to finance a further occasion of sin.

There was a young lad from Westmeath who had come up to Dublin the day before. He had got so hopelessly drunk that he was not able to supply the gardaí in Store Street with his name and address until the following morning, and his parents had no idea where he was. I explained that the court would give him the few pounds for his fare, but he was to go straight to Busáras and get the afternoon bus home. His odd reaction was to look blearily at the clock on the wall and then ask me in a tone of utter bewilderment, 'Is it tomorrow already?'

A man who gave gardaí seven addresses and had three different women claiming to be his wife was before the District Court. He had been arrested as James Walsh of Rialto for an alleged drink-driving offence. He gave a name and address in Ballyfermot which gardaí discovered to be false. Then while he was held at Kilmainham Garda station, three different women with three different addresses called and claimed to be his wife. The mystery was finally solved yesterday when Garda Ciaran Goulding told Kilmainham Court that he was satisfied that the man was Anthony Thomas of 142 Cherry Orchard Avenue, Ballyfermot. The garda asked for a remand in custody for further charges concerning his driving (*Irish Press*, 4 February 1994).

A neighbour of mine in Castleconnell, Brendan Edwards, who is a retired Garda Sergeant, was speaking to me of Judge McGrath whom he admired greatly:

> During the course of a prosecution in the District Court, I was being cross-examined by the defendant's solicitor. He was a good friend of mine but for some reason he got het up at a particular point and began shouting at me, 'Answer the question, Sergeant, answer the question,' while not really giving me time to comply. I appealed to the judge that I was quite willing to answer, but that it was difficult to do so while I was being shouted at. Judge McGrath, a gentle but authoritative man, restored calm on all sides and then requested the solicitor to put the question again. Whereupon the poor man hesitated, looked at me in consternation and confessed, 'I have forgotten the question!'

Richard Johnson, a legendary figure, was among the first appointments to the District Court Bench and served in Kerry for over forty years. Robert Pierce, the well-known solicitor from the same county, told me that his favourite story about Dick Johnson was that he had found himself in a pub in Tralee one night with two solicitors after hours. There was a raid but the wily judge slipped out the back door in time to avoid an embarrassing situation. The two solicitors were summonsed in due course in the Irish versions of their names. Judge Johnson fined them ten shillings each, saying that one shilling was for being in the pub and nine shillings for having been caught!

I first met Alice Leahy when I was anxious about a woman called Pauline who regularly appeared on charges of drunkenness, public order, solicitation and the like. Far from cooperating with any effort towards rehabilitation, she was inclined to hector me in cut-glass tones about my right – or indeed, ability – to make a judgment at all. One day, in despair, I asked the prosecuting garda if there was anyone who knew her and her circumstances. The following day Alice arrived down to see me and we have been friends since. This is her vivid memory of the reality of the Dublin District Court as she knew it:

> When I first went to work in the Simon shelter I could not but notice a kind of hierarchy in that those who were there the longest knew the most about everything, particularly the courts, and it

seemed more important to accompany a resident to court than to collect fruit or visit them in hospital. So it was with trepidation that I accompanied a seasoned articulate worker to court who seemed au fait with the jargon. I took in all my surroundings, the dampness of the building, the coughs and creaking doors and many of the public, poorly dressed, and the harrowed look on the faces of the mothers. The judge was always male, betraying little of his feelings, and beating regularly on the bench with his gavel for silence. Some of the accused were familiar with the surroundings and seemed not too unhappy with their lot. Life stories were laid bare and opened up for discussion; solicitors, seeming to speak with passion, made their case, successfully or not. Some prisoners availed of the opportunity to meet relatives and have a cigarette, while others went back down to the cells. If we were advocates on behalf of the residents, the word was never used. I realised that the judge had heard it all before and generally knew the accused. There was almost mutual respect and camaraderie between the gardaí, the solicitors and some of the regulars, like 'Lily the Pink'. The reality was that we outsiders were surplus to the drama taking place in that tight circle. My last visit with Pauline to the District Court was in 1982. There was now a female judge and a male solicitor trying to see if anything could be done to make her life safer and healthier. Pauline died several years later in sad circumstances.

Shortly after Michael O'Reilly's appointment to the District Court, he was packing his car to take the sittings in a country area. He wondered aloud to his wife whether he should take a gun in case there might be the chance to get some shooting. His small son asked fearfully: 'Do you have to shoot them too, Daddy?'

Seamus Given, a Kerryman who practices as a solicitor in Dublin, had this experience in his native county in the autumn of 2008:

> Recently, I attended a District Court in Kerry. It was early on a very busy morning and, as usual, the crush was a bit chaotic with people trying to catch the attention of their lawyers, or lawyers that of other lawyers or gardaí, and a crowd around the registrar pushing to have their business dealt with before anyone else's. There was one man, however, who seemed to be attracting the most attention. He was wearing an identification card around his neck and standing at the back of the court dealing with the queries of numerous litigants, gardaí, lawyers and reporters. I was intrigued to know who he was and asked a nearby garda. 'Oh,' he answered, 'he's the most important man in the court – the interpreter.' Sure enough, when the judge came in to take his seat, the first thing he said was, 'Is the interpreter in court?'

The above puts me in mind of my favourite Bob Ó hUadhaigh story. A Norwegian ship made an official visit to Dublin. One of the crew was having a convivial night out and got into trouble for being drunk and disorderly. He was arrested and appeared in Bob's court the following morning. The garda explained that the defendant was repentant and had apologised. It should have been the end of the matter, but the judge was not prepared to let it go at that. He requested that a consular official from the Norwegian Embassy should attend, and the case was put back for an hour or so. At the resumed hearing, Justice Ó hUadhaigh said to the consul, 'I want you to explain something very clearly to this young fellow. Years ago, we had trouble here in the city from other sailors who came from his part of the world. They did a great deal of damage, stayed for a considerable time and caused a lot of upset to the people of Dublin. I want him to understand that this kind of behaviour cannot be allowed to happen again.' The startled official was obliged to enlighten his compatriot on the Viking invasion of a thousand years before, still a sensitive issue in Court No. 6 of the Bridewell!

On one occasion, in the adjacent No. 4 Court, I had counsel plead some element of Poynings' Law in defence of his client who had been charged with disorderly conduct. Poynings' Law was passed in 1494 and its purpose was to make the Irish Parliament subject to the say-so of the King of England on any laws it might pass. I have no idea why it was thought that it would still have a bearing on a minor charge in a court of summary jurisdiction some 500 years later. It particularly intrigued me that the young barrister making the application was American!

There was a judge in the Metropolitan District Court in the nineteen forties called Matthew Hannon. He was a byword for indecision. By all accounts, he was a very nice man and inspired affection as well as exasperation among his colleagues. Gordon Henderson was a newly qualified solicitor when he first appeared before him:

> Justice Hannon of the Dublin District Court was a deeply religious man who took his judicial duty seriously, frequently to the point of high anxiety. When he found it difficult to come to a decision, he had the habit of rubbing his hand back and forth over his face, at the same time pondering aloud about his dilemma. In a simple civil case seeking payment for a debt of 17 shillings and 6 pence (about 1 euro today), he wondered if he had the jurisdiction to make the award to the plaintiff. Since there seemed no prospect of finality, I, on behalf of the plaintiff, suggested that if he had that much doubt, perhaps he would strike out the case. Whereupon, the rubbing of his face became more agitated and he groaned, 'Ah, but do I have the jurisdiction to strike it out?'

Chapter 13

Conclusion

On 21 April 1899 Bridget Reilly was fined two shillings and sixpence with a shilling costs at the Petty Sessions at Rathcoole for keeping an unmuzzled dog. She paid the fine two weeks later. Daniel Cummins of Dorset Street in Dublin was also fined a half-crown at Rathcoole on 28 July for cycling on the footpath. Thomas Duffy on 26 December was convicted and fined at Lucan for being drunk in charge of a horse. I know this because a Garda Sergeant once gave me an old notebook he found in the office at Kilmainham Court. It is the clerk's day book for the area of Lucan, Blanchardstown and Rathcoole for the year 1899. Sadly, the vast majority of offences over the three districts was drunkenness, and the remainder of the other charges for the most part seem to concern either unmuzzled or unlicensed dogs. The lists, even given that these were rural districts in 1899, were quite short, an average of five cases a session.

The basis of the jurisdiction of the Petty Sessions was established in the reign of Edward III when certain persons were assigned to keep the peace in each county, which developed into the hearing and determining of complaints. The procedures became formalised, and justices of the peace were appointed by statute or by the Lord Chancellor, not unlike the early development of the Dáil Éireann Courts. However, there was a difference. Under Section 26 of the Local Government (Ireland) Act 1898, it was stipulated that 'the chairman for the council for the district, shall, unless a woman or personally disqualified by any act … be a justice of the peace for the county.' There was no such disqualification under the Dáil Courts regime; several women served as judges, in both parish and district courts.

Under the District Justices (Temporary Provisions) Act 1923, the twenty-seven men who had been appointed the previous year were confirmed by name as temporary justices. Their districts covered wider areas than the Petty Sessions, as had also the Dáil District Courts. In the preface to the *Guide to the New Rules and Practice of the District Court* by Edward Burne, Kevin O'Higgins, Minister for Justice, wrote:

> The District Court is perhaps the most novel and striking of the Saorstát's new judicial system. There was nothing in the old order of things that can fairly be compared to this Court. Sitting at frequent intervals in every town or large village, presided over by a qualified lawyer, and vested with jurisdiction to deal not only with criminal cases, but with civil cases, in contract up to a limit of £25, and in tort, of £10. The setting up

> of the Court represents a real and serious effort to put legal remedies within easy reach of all the people and to make every citizen familiar with the spectacle of the impartial and dignified administration of justice.

It was not only a wider geographical area which the new court covered, but it also had a wider jurisdiction. Although, up to recently, court districts remained much as they were in 1924, the jurisdiction has changed beyond recognition. The District Court now hears civil cases to a limit of €6,350 and the term of imprisonment it can impose is up to two years. Naturally, the technological advancements have also surfaced in courtrooms, from electric light to central heating, from microphones to video links, although the essentials of the interior are the same: the bench, the witness stand, the dock, the rows of seats. The changes outlined by the Chief Justice in 2009, already cited, were accompanied by an evolving ethos of social responsibility. There is little reflection of the latter in the press reports of proceedings in the early years; persons found guilty were given prison sentences, often quite short ones. Although the Probation of Offenders Act had been passed as far back as 1907, there were little practical resources provided for its implementation, especially in rural areas. The modern professional probation service, as we know it, was not fully in place until after 1970.

The late Myles Shevlin, a solicitor whom I admired, once said to me in court, while suggesting some particular solution, 'I know the District Court was not intended to be a social service, but it is a role that it has been pushed into, one way or another.' It is part of the evolution of general problem-solving in civic life, which explains, among other developments, community service, the Small Claims Court, the Drugs Court and now restorative justice. The latter concept was much favoured in Brehon law and was the bedrock of the earlier Dáil Courts. In the latter case it was not because of any conscious hearkening back to ancient precepts, but the only way a cottage industry system of justice could impose its judgments, so a man had to walk five miles across a mountain in bare feet carrying the harness he had stolen on his shoulders.

The sanctions capable of being imposed in a modern state are somewhat different, and mercifully free from the element of public humiliation that most of us would find distasteful (unless exclusively reserved for one's own particular enemy!) The Courts Service Annual Report for 2009 shows that the total of offences disposed of by the District Court in the year was 521,058, of which – *o tempora, o mores* – about two-thirds were road traffic offences. In every category of offence, except theft, community service and probation orders outnumber prison sentences. Some other random facts: in the family courts, barring orders were granted in 1,106 cases (but 1,660 applications were withdrawn and struck out), and there were 941 childcare orders. The total number of licences granted was 78,747.

Kevin O'Higgins would be astonished at the expansion of the District Court and, no doubt, there will be further extraordinary changes in another fifty years. The essentials of a court will not. O'Higgins, who was very much a politician, was taking credit for 'putting legal remedies within easy reach of all the people', but it is no more than the duty of any state to do so, first by its laws and then by establishing courts so that they can be enforced. What no state can do is to guarantee that every citizen who takes his grievance to court will get the result desired. People are so often convinced of the rightness of their cause that they cannot imagine any other outcome. If they do not succeed, they contemplate a round of appeals as far as they can take it.

No advances in technology or sociology are likely to change our perception that the justice of our cause should be acknowledged in open court in the presence of our opponent. It remains to be seen if the high hopes for arbitration, mediation, restorative justice and other well-planned projects will work over time to change our ideas on what the word 'justice' really means. Courts have been around for a very long time, in whatever form, although the judge most frequently referred to as if he were the epitome of judicial wisdom is surely the most cynical and lazy individual imaginable. Perhaps any rethinking on the structure of courts might begin with considering why we think that Solomon's judgment was wise and not egregiously and cruelly shallow?

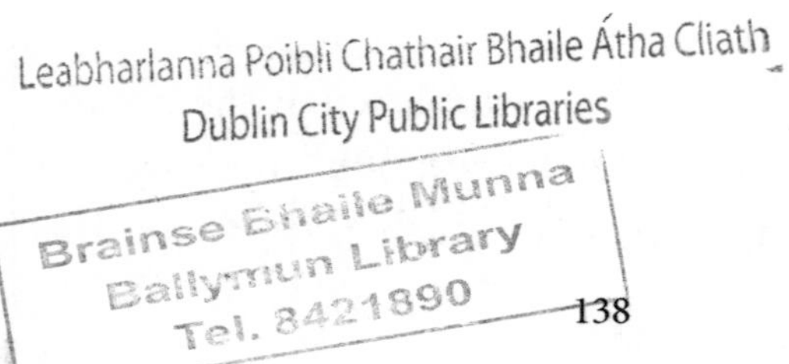

Index